INTERNATIONAL PERSPECTIVES ON EMERGING TRENDS AND INTEGRATING RESEARCH-BASED LEARNING ACROSS THE CURRICULUM

INNOVATIONS IN HIGHER EDUCATION TEACHING AND LEARNING

Senior Series Editor: Patrick Blessinger, St John's University and Higher Education Teaching and Learning Association, USA

Associate Series Editor: Enakshi Sengupta, Higher Education Teaching and Learning Association, USA

Published Volumes:

Volume 21	Civil Society and Social Responsibility in Higher Education: International Perspectives on Curriculum and Teaching Development – Edited by Enakshi Sengupta, Patrick Blessinger and Craig Mahoney
Volume 22	Introduction to Sustainable Development Leadership and Strategies In Higher Education – Edited by Enakshi Sengupta, Patrick Blessinger and Taisir Subhi Yamin
Volume 23	University–Community Partnerships for Promoting Social Responsibility in Higher Education – Edited by Enakshi Sengupta, Patrick Blessinger and Craig Mahoney
Volume 24	Leadership Strategies for Promoting Social Responsibility in Higher Education – Edited by Enakshi Sengupta, Patrick Blessinger and Craig Mahoney
Volume 25	Integrating Community Service into Curriculum: International Perspectives on Humanizing Education – Edited by Enakshi Sengupta, Patrick Blessinger and Mandla Makhanya
Volume 26	International Perspectives on Improving Student Engagement: Advances in Library Practices in Higher Education – Edited by Enakshi Sengupta, Patrick Blessinger and Milton D. Cox
Volume 27	Improving Classroom Engagement and International Development Programs: International Perspectives on Humanizing Higher Education – Edited by Enakshi Sengupta, Patrick Blessinger and Mandla Makhanya
Volume 28	Cultural Competence in Higher Education – Edited by Tiffany Puckett, and Nancy Lind
Volume 29	Designing Effective Library Learning Spaces in Higher Education – Edited by Enakshi Sengupta, Patrick Blessinger and Mandla S. Makhanya
Volume 30	Developing and Supporting Multiculturalism and Leadership Development – Edited by Enakshi Sengupta, Patrick Blessinger and Mandla S. Makhanya
Volume 31	Faculty and Student Research in Practicing Academic Freedom – Edited by Enakshi Sengupta and Patrick Blessinger
Volume 32	International Perspectives on Policies, Practices & Pedagogies for Promoting Social Responsibility in Higher Education – Edited by Enakshi Sengupta, Patrick Blessinger and Craig Mahoney
Volume 33	International Perspectives on the Role of Technology in Humanizing Higher Education – Edited by Enakshi Sengupta, Patrick Blessinger and Mandla S. Makhanya
Volume 34	Teaching and Learning Practices for Academic Freedom – Edited by Enakshi Sengupta, and Patrick Blessinger
Volume 35	Humanizing Higher Education through Innovative Approaches for Teaching and Learning – Edited by Enakshi Sengupta, Patrick Blessinger and Mandla S. Makhanya

INNOVATIONS IN HIGHER EDUCATION TEACHING AND LEARNING   VOLUME 36

INTERNATIONAL PERSPECTIVES ON EMERGING TRENDS AND INTEGRATING RESEARCH-BASED LEARNING ACROSS THE CURRICULUM

EDITED BY

ENAKSHI SENGUPTA

Centre for Advanced Research in Higher Education, New York, USA
International HETL Association, New York, USA

PATRICK BLESSINGER

St. John's University, New York, USA
International HETL Association, New York, USA

Created in partnership with the
International Higher Education Teaching and Learning Association

https://www.hetl.org/

United Kingdom – North America – Japan
India – Malaysia – China

Emerald Publishing Limited
Howard House, Wagon Lane, Bingley BD16 1WA, UK

First edition 2021

Copyright © 2021 Emerald Publishing Limited

Reprints and permissions service
Contact: permissions@emeraldinsight.com

No part of this book may be reproduced, stored in a retrieval system, transmitted in any form or by any means electronic, mechanical, photocopying, recording or otherwise without either the prior written permission of the publisher or a licence permitting restricted copying issued in the UK by The Copyright Licensing Agency and in the USA by The Copyright Clearance Center. Any opinions expressed in the chapters are those of the authors. Whilst Emerald makes every effort to ensure the quality and accuracy of its content, Emerald makes no representation implied or otherwise, as to the chapters' suitability and application and disclaims any warranties, express or implied, to their use.

British Library Cataloguing in Publication Data
A catalogue record for this book is available from the British Library

ISBN: 978-1-80043-477-6 (Print)
ISBN: 978-1-80043-476-9 (Online)
ISBN: 978-1-80043-478-3 (Epub)

ISSN: 2055-3641 (Series)

Printed and bound by CPI Group (UK) Ltd, Croydon, CR0 4YY

ISOQAR certified
Management System,
awarded to Emerald
for adherence to
Environmental
standard
ISO 14001:2004.

Certificate Number 1985
ISO 14001

INVESTOR IN PEOPLE

CONTENTS

List of Contributors — vii

Series Editors' Introduction — ix

PART I
FUTURE OF RESEARCH – AN INTERNATIONAL PERSPECTIVE

Chapter 1   Introduction to International Perspectives on Emerging Trends and Integrating Research-Based Learning Across the Curriculum
Enakshi Sengupta and Patrick Blessinger — 3

Chapter 2   The Future of Scientific Research in Turkish Higher Education
Ahmet Su and Engin Karadağ — 13

Chapter 3   University Partnerships for Developing Research at the University of Prishtina, Kosovo
Arlinda Beka — 33

Chapter 4   Integrated Approaches for Supporting Academic Research: Models that Reveal the Future While Promoting Success
Russell Carpenter, Jonathan Gore, Shirley O'Brien, Jennifer Fairchild and Matthew Winslow — 47

Chapter 5   University Policies and Arrangements to Support the Publication of Academic Journals in Chile, Colombia, and Venezuela
Jorge Enrique Delgado — 69

PART II
EMERGING TRENDS IN RESEARCH

Chapter 6   Humanizing a Teacher Education Program in a Small Liberal Arts University
Edith Ries, Ellina Chernobilsky and Joanne Jasmine — 87

Chapter 7 Navigating Tricky Terrain: Early Career Academics Charting a Research Trajectory in the Neoliberal University
Mohamed Alansari, Jennifer Tatebe and Carol Mutch   *101*

Chapter 8 Infusing Twenty-First-Century Research Activities into Traditional Classrooms
Ryan Menath   *119*

About the Authors   *135*

Name Index   *141*

Subject Index   *147*

LIST OF CONTRIBUTORS

Mohamed Alansari	University of Auckland, Auckland, New Zealand
Arlinda Beka	University of Prishtina, Prishtina, Kosovo
Patrick Blessinger	International Higher Education Teaching and Learning Association, New York, USA
Russell Carpenter	Noel Studio for Academic Creativity & Eastern Kentucky University, Kentucky, USA
Ellina Chernobilsky	Caldwell University. New Jersey, USA
Jorge Enrique Delgado	University of Pittsburgh, Pittsburgh, USA
Jennifer Fairchild	Eastern Kentucky University, Kentucky, USA
Jonathan Gore	Eastern Kentucky University, Kentucky, USA
Joanne Jasmine	Caldwell University. New Jersey, USA
Engin Karadağ	Akdeniz University, Turkey
Ryan Menath	US Air Force Academy, Colorado, USA
Carol Mutch	University of Auckland, Auckland, New Zealand
Shirley O'Brien	Eastern Kentucky University, Kentucky, USA
Edith Ries	Caldwell University. New Jersey, USA
Enakshi Sengupta	International Higher Education Teaching and Learning Association, New York, USA
Ahmet Su	Mount Royal University, Canada
Jennifer Tatebe	University of Auckland, Auckland, New Zealand
Matthew Winslow	Eastern Kentucky University, Kentucky, USA

SERIES EDITORS' INTRODUCTION

The purpose of this series is to publish current research and scholarship on innovative teaching and learning practices in higher education. The series is developed around the premise that teaching and learning are more effective when instructors and students are actively and meaningfully engaged in the teaching–learning process.

The main objectives of this series are to:

(1) present how innovative teaching and learning practices are being used in higher education institutions around the world across a wide variety of disciplines and countries,
(2) present the latest models, theories, concepts, paradigms, and frameworks that educators should consider when adopting, implementing, assessing, and evaluating innovative teaching and learning practices, and
(3) consider the implications of theory and practice on policy, strategy, and leadership.

This series will appeal to anyone in higher education who is involved in the teaching and learning process from any discipline, institutional type, or nationality. The volumes in this series will focus on a variety of authentic case studies and other empirical research that illustrates how educators from around the world are using innovative approaches to create more effective and meaningful learning environments.

Innovation teaching and learning is an approach, strategy, method, practice, or means that has been shown to improve, enhance, or transform the teaching–learning environment. Innovation involves doing things differently or in a novel way in order to improve outcomes. In short, Innovation is positive change. With respect to teaching and learning, innovation is the implementation of new or improved educational practices that result in improved educational and learning outcomes. This innovation can be any positive change related to teaching, curriculum, assessment, technology, or other tools, programs, policies, or processes that leads to improved educational and learning outcomes. Innovation can occur in institutional development, program development, professional development, or learning development.

The volumes in this series will not only highlight the benefits and theoretical frameworks of such innovations through authentic case studies and other empirical research but also look at the challenges and contexts associated with implementing and assessing innovative teaching and learning practices. The volumes represent all disciplines from a wide range of national, cultural, and organizational contexts. The volumes in this series will explore a wide variety of teaching and learning topics such as active learning, integrative learning, transformative learning, inquiry-based learning, problem-based learning, meaningful learning, blended learning, creative learning, experiential learning, lifelong and lifewide learning, global learning, learning assessment and analytics, student research, faculty and student learning communities, as well as other topics.

This series brings together distinguished scholars and educational practitioners from around the world to disseminate the latest knowledge on innovative teaching and learning scholarship and practices. The authors offer a range of disciplinary perspectives from different cultural contexts. This series provides a unique and valuable resource for instructors, administrators, and anyone interested in improving and transforming teaching and learning.

Patrick Blessinger
Founder, Executive Director, and Chief Research Scientist,
International HETL Association

Enakshi Sengupta
Associate Editor, International HETL Association

PART I

FUTURE OF RESEARCH - AN INTERNATIONAL PERSPECTIVE

CHAPTER 1

INTRODUCTION TO INTERNATIONAL PERSPECTIVES ON EMERGING TRENDS AND INTEGRATING RESEARCH-BASED LEARNING ACROSS THE CURRICULUM

Enakshi Sengupta and Patrick Blessinger

ABSTRACT

Research in higher education provides the foundation for the future of education and hence attracts the attention of policymakers who debate the merits and demerits of it in various contexts. Research in higher education is expected to anticipate emerging trends, problems faced by educationists, and to develop concepts that would be reliable to generate the curriculum needed for knowledge-based nations. Universities that are conscious of the future and want to contribute to coping with this rapidly changing world have been engaged in meaningful research agendas. Education now has to deal with issues like globalization, climate change, refugee crisis, new models for education systems, steering the entire system toward internationalization, and manage the institution with a scarcity of resources. These challenges call for extensive research and in-depth analysis of the problems so that a possible solution can be worked out by academics in identifying thematic areas of work and emerging fields of education. Research-based universities occupy a prime position in the 21st-century global knowledge economy.

These institutions have multiple roles to play besides teaching–learning and academic achievement of their students. This book demonstrates how research is being viewed in different countries having completely diverse socio-cultural backgrounds. The authors have explored the university's contribution toward the advancement of global science and scholarship in countries like Turkey, Kosovo, Latin America, and the United States. Authors have also explored new information and processes that are contributing to emerging trends that are significant in understanding the human condition through multiple academic and societal roles. These authors discuss issues related to culture, technology, and society, which are the foundation of intellectual and scientific trends.

Keywords: Emerging trends; research agenda; globalization; academics; scholarship; intellectual trends; societal roles; universities; policymakers; teaching–learning

INTRODUCTION

A well-developed system of education rests on the pillars of quality learning and engagement in research. These pillars are considered essential in the emerging knowledge economy. The contribution of education toward the progress of a nation and its economic development is undeniable. Both developed and developing countries are putting equal emphasis on qualitative and quantitative expansion of higher education (Ved, 2007). Higher education research is much needed not only for the economic growth of the nation but to promote its cultural diversity, its trade, and providing opportunities for individuals. Discussions and debates of the future of education center around technology, competitive markets, internationalization, and open resources. In the recent past, a paradigm shift has been noticed in the realms of higher education; it has changed from a national focus to a global focus, from being controlled solely by the state to a more market orientation, from one-time degree to lifelong education and has become increasingly learner-centered (Venkatasubramanian, 2002).

The weakness and flaws in the social forecast and the impending gloom in the economic scenario are not unknown to us; education is capable of providing a solution to deal with such issues in the future. Research-based higher education intertwined with policies and practices of an institution has the desired practical relevance to shaping the conditions for the future (Teichler & Sadlak, 2000). A research-driven institution that involves the students and the faculty toward generating new knowledge might be useful in solving some of the pressing needs that the world demands. Research is time-consuming and resource-intensive; it is not expected to provide immediate solutions and hence research readiness and constant engagement in this area need careful strategic planning and support of the leadership of the institution.

The reality of 21st-century education has been the massification of enrollments, privatization of public universities, and the on-going debate between public versus private good in higher education (Altbach, 2011). Research-based universities have become an integral part of global higher education and are expected to play a vital role in developing the social environment (Altbach, Reisberg, & Rumbley, 2010; Organisation for Economic Cooperation and Development, 2008). The implications of massifications cannot be underestimated as it encompasses larger financial implications, challenges faced in infrastructure, quality control and every year churning out more graduates than the economy or the market can sustain.

It is thus understood that universities will be facing several constraints to fund quality research and will have to find innovative ways to support and sustain their research agenda. The relentless pursuit to adapt to the ever-expanding knowledge-based economy and cross border global mobility of education has impacted the development of the research-based university and the future trends in higher education (Marginson & van der Wende, 2009). Advancement in higher education has been growing and the salience for research in economic development has led to universities occupying a pivotal role in the economic progress of a country. Such demands are felt by both faculty and student alike.

RESEARCH-BASED UNIVERSITIES – A HISTORICAL BACKGROUND

If we travel back in history, we will find that research was not a key function of the universities centuries ago; they were mainly engaged in imparting knowledge on law, medicine and theology, and preservation of history. The contemporary research-based university developed in the 19th century and began with Humboldt's reformed university (Fallon, 1980), which stressed research as a key to national development and application of work in the form of research. While science-based subjects like physics and chemistry started emerging, so did social science with economics and sociology as emergent areas of study. The university was financed by the Prussia government and the staff comprised of civil servants. The Humboldtian University was based on Lernfreiheit (freedom to learn) and placed values on academic freedom and freedom of expression. The model was adapted later by both the United States and Japan in the 19th and 20th century who viewed university education and research conducted by academics as a great contributor to the development of the nation.

With the Land Grants Act in the last half of the 19th century, American universities started emphasizing the need to engage in meaningful research (Geiger, 2004), focusing on agriculture and science to support the rising industrialization. Service to society and the general welfare of people was a key area that every department was expected to address. Gradually the world started accepting this American model by the mid-20th century and a significant amount of resource was being earmarked to support research-based activities (Geiger, 2004). Research-based universities became the gold standard and were considered imperative for the advancement of higher education.

EMERGING TRENDS

Research in social science needs detailed and advanced planning as it involves several processes from drafting a proposal to the acquisition of funds and finally, a report analyzing the data – which may take several years to complete. Researchers have to anticipate problems that are futuristic in nature, engage in debates, and start working on emerging trends in higher education, at least five years in advance so that the issues are at the forefront and are ready for action (Teichler, 1996).

An array of social, economic, and technological forces is driving the much-required changes in society and institutions required to address those changes. Duderstadt (1999) has listed some of these changes as emerging trends in higher education, although the context of his writing has been the United States such changes are global in nature.

Age of knowledge – Post-industrialization countries are now relying on knowledge-based economies. Agrarian and labor-intensive nations are investing in capacity building with the advancement of information technology to help shape their future. Countries have realized that they can no longer depend on their depleting natural resources such as oil or iron ore and hence social institutions such as universities need to create a highly educated population who will shape their knowledge-intensive society.

Diversity – The mobility of people has become more pronounced in today's world. Tolerance and sensitivity along with an inclusive culture, is a reality that every educational institution needs to cater to. Segregation and non-assimilation of the minority population is no longer an option. Social pluralism and multi-cultural education have become a key responsibility of universities. Students need to be exposed to diverse racial and ethnic backgrounds, learn to respect, and become aware of the diversity of the world and integrate it as a part of their learning.

Globalization and internationalization of education – With the world shrinking and global mobility being the future, universities are now setting up campuses in other parts of the world and inviting international students to enroll in their programs. In this global economy, nations are increasingly interdependent and a worldwide communication market has grown that facilitates the growth of knowledge professionals, research, and other educational services. Universities are helping to foster ties among students from different nations that will result in a truly global economy. Universities are expected to display a truly international character reflected among its students, international faculty, and integrative curriculum. It is the responsibility of the university to enable students to appreciate human culture and traditions and help them work and thrive in a multi-cultural environment.

Research agenda – Society is seeking a bigger contribution from universities and engaging in research is one of them, which will help society alleviate from its current problems. Education needs to prepare students to combat issues in healthcare, infrastructure development, food crisis, and environmental disaster. Solutions are needed as natural resources are dwindling and the Earth is stressed. Traditional academic institutions are giving way to a knowledge-intensive organization with the growth of telecommunication, service-oriented industries, and information services.

Rise in competition – Higher education is widely considered to be a public or common good and is meant to serve civic and economic purposes as designed by policymakers. Yet institutions are competing for students, faculty, and resources. Universities are portraying themselves as the ticket to future success and the prestige associated with their degrees. Their exist clamor and clutter in such a market, each trying to distinguish itself and prove themselves to be better than the others through rankings, etc. Very few universities now enjoy the heavy subsidy offered by patrons or governments. Repositioning themselves as the front runners have led universities to plan for an aggressive strategy that is more futuristic in nature.

Insecurity and apprehension – University's support and commitment toward academics, job security, and equal treatment for all have eroded considerably in the recent past. There has been a sense of loss of scholarly community, a decline in public support of research that has led to stress and tension among academics. The concept of education as a public or common good has been challenged by some stakeholders. Nations have altered their budget and many of them spend less of their budget in education compared to their defense budget. Financial aid, scholarships, and grants have reduced considerably with protest against frequent fees hike.

CONCLUSION

Universities are evolving to serve a new age. Academics have been engaged in responding to the challenges faced by higher education in future. In this period of uncertainty, the traditional definition is giving way to consider a reflective process that will allow the universities to be more responsive and transform to create new institutional forms, global learning network, interdisciplinary research, and result-oriented outcome for students. Technology has unleashed greater market potential and that needs to be harnessed for enhancement of students. Future is still uncertain, and academics are not certain which model will work in the future. Will it be enough to teach skills to cater to market employability or does the preservation of cultural heritage has a place in today's curriculum? These are uncertain circumstances that prompt frequent interventions, case studies, and research preparedness. Some of these attempts and approaches are discussed in this book which will help serve the academic world and provide directional guidance to others who are still trying to adopt a definite approach toward progress and betterment of society.

CHAPTER OVERVIEWS

The Future of Scientific Research in Turkish Higher Education, by Ahmet Su and Engin Karadağ, describes that scientific research and delivering education at undergraduate and graduate levels are the main responsibilities of higher education institutions. Considering these points, the authors aimed to provide insights on an array of topics pertaining to scientific research and tertiary education in Turkey and the future of Turkish higher education. The authors focused on research-based education, lifelong learning, research and higher education institutions, research grants and funding in Turkey, performance management in higher education, international collaborations, future of hands-on approaches, and lastly the issue of brain drain in Turkey. In the endeavor to present these issues in detail, the authors employed sector analysis method. Throughout the chapter, they aimed to provide detailed and comparative evaluations making use of both national and international literature.

University Partnerships for Developing Research at the University of Prishtina, Kosovo, by Arlinda Beka, writes about university partnerships that have been promoted and implemented a good deal in Europe since the approval of the Bologna Declaration of June 19, 1999 (Bologna Declaration, 1999). Over the past two decades, the University of Prishtina has developed many bilateral and multilateral initiatives to strengthen cooperation and partnership among universities from different countries and regions (University of Prishtina, 2004, p. 2). The University of Prishtina embraced the Bologna Declaration in 2001, and since then has established several partnerships aimed at strengthening its capacities and improving the quality assurance of its higher education (Brunnhofer, 2010, p. 107). In the recent years, the University of Prishtina has given priority to the area of research, aiming to increase the quality and quantity of research conducted by its faculty. The quality and relevance of the international partnerships of the University of Prishtina is the main focus of this paper, including the current state of research among the faculty. The author used a qualitative method for conducting this research. It shows the institutional and individual benefits of those partnerships. Finally, it presents the impact of cooperation on developing research and improving the quality of education in Kosovo.

Integrated Approaches for Supporting Academic Research: Models that Reveal the Future while Promoting Success, by Russell Carpenter, Jonathan Gore, Shirley O'Brien, Jennifer Fairchild, and Matthew Winslow, explores research models and practices that are changing rapidly. While evidence of such changes includes cross-campus collaborations and multi-authored scholarship, faculty development opportunities also signal what is to come. In this case study, authors representing diverse disciplines examine what faculty development programs reveal about the future of academic research. The authors offer an analysis of faculty support programs across the country as a foundation, then provide an examination of initiatives in place at their four-year regional comprehensive institution in the United States. The authors then report on the outcomes of these programs for research productivity, with a focus on opportunities that were available to all faculty across the university. Finally, the authors offer perspective on the future of academic research based on findings from examining these programs. The authors suggest that the future of research will focus on (1) collaborative design(s) of research-related support, (2) support structures and programs that encourage and facilitate cross-campus and interdisciplinary research collaborations and sharing, (3) incentive for integrating areas of research with teaching and service, and relatedly (4) programs that encourage faculty to span academic research with industry or community partnerships and collaborations, especially ones that can generate revenue or produce future research, development, or funding streams.

University Policies and Arrangements to Support the Publication of Academic Journals in Chile, Colombia, and Venezuela, by Jorge Enrique Delgado, is about peer-reviewed indexable journals that have expanded in recent decades as a result, in part, of the value given to research productivity (measured through citations). Latin American journals have grown prompted by the open access (OA) movement, the emergence of regional repositories/indexes, and policies linking institutional rankings and faculty salaries/promotions to indexed publications. This study's aim was to map the ways Chilean, Colombian, and Venezuelan universities support journal publication. This qualitative study uses Margison and Rhoades' (2002) Glonacal Agency Heuristic to describe factors that shape higher education (i.e., global, national, and local dimensions), adding university as unit of analysis. Semi-structured in-depth interviews from a previous study, current institutional documents, and websites of 12 major universities from Chile, Venezuela, and Colombia conformed the data of the study. Besides the most prestigious global indexes (Web of Science and Scopus) three regional repositories/indexes, Latindex, SciELO, and RedALyC, have played an important role as countries link faculty salaries/promotions and university ranking systems to publications included in one or more of these services. Latindex collaborates with national science and technology agencies, SciELO has country chapters based at universities (Colombia and Venezuela), and RedALyC works with individual institutions and journals. At the national level, Chile has mechanisms to provide funding for the publication and/or upgrade of journals and incentives to institutions for publications in indexed journals. Colombia's journal evaluation system Publindex links articles in indexed journals to salary increases in public universities, standard that is also used by private institutions to grant monetary incentives to faculty for publications. Venezuela used to have a funding and publication incentive system that was discontinued in the last decade. Latin American journals are mainly published by universities. Institutions in this study have implemented strategies to support journals such as institutional repositories, discontinuation of print journals, technology support for OA publication, and funding mechanisms.

Humanizing a Teacher Education Program in a Small Liberal Arts University, by Edith Ries, Ellina Chernobilsky, and Joanne Jasmine, is about educational training programs, which at times, are criticized for inadequately addressing issues that occur in the field (Brydon-Miller, Greenwood, & Maguire, 2003). This omission in relevancy might possibly be attributed to the fact that teacher education faculty no longer engage with K-12 students on a daily basis. The authors have decided to fill that relevancy void through their graduate student action research projects. Action research projects, undertaken by graduate students within the program, not only foster reflection upon the needs of the students within their K-12 classrooms, but also inform the authors, as education faculty, as they prepare their undergraduate students for the world of teaching. In this chapter, the authors outline action research as a framework of inquiry. The authors argue that engaging students in the individualized action research projects has benefits for multiple stakeholders ranging from the learners in K-12 classrooms to students in pre-service teacher education programs. Using four case studies, they illustrate how the action research process works and the ways it fosters inclusivity in classrooms at numerous levels. The authors discuss the benefits and challenges to their approach and conclude by discussing the lessons that can be learned from their experiences in humanistic education.

Navigating Tricky Terrain: Early Career Academics Charting a Research Trajectory in the Neo-Liberal University, by Mohamed Alansari, Jennifer Tatebe, and Carol Mutch, seeks to respond to the existing literature on early career researchers, using an auto-ethnographic approach to further unravel the crossroads of identity formation, research politics, and successful promotion through the eyes of early career researchers. Combining autobiography and ethnography, the authors systematically analyze their own experiences to make sense of wider social and political practices. Ellis, Adams, and Bochner (2011) remind the authors that autoethnography is not to be dismissed as a form of self-therapy but is to be presented in a rigorous manner as other research forms by carefully justifying the data sources and techniques, analyzing the data and crafting the findings. The author's sources were both found texts (e.g., university policies) and created texts (our journal entries and personal communications). Using analytic techniques such as highlighting critical incidents or epiphanies, the authors structured coherent narratives to illuminate the complexity and uncertainty of the lives of early career academics. This chapter's focus on early career researcher experiences makes poignant commentary on neoliberalism's impact on and within higher education. The chapter concludes with the authors' reflections on the dilemmas of academic and research choices made within the limitations of institutional structures, processes, and systems that shape career trajectories.

Infusing 21st-Century Research Activities into Traditional Classrooms, by Ryan Menath, writes about modern society searching for information primarily though handheld internet devices. Universities, on the other hand, traditionally rely on printed textbooks. If the main purpose of higher education is to graduate a civically minded and high functioning member of society, then there is a disconnect between society and the undergraduate when it comes to the ability to research and find information quickly. In other words, the university-societal pact is broken when it comes to digital research. Thankfully, it can be restored. The following chapter highlights the author's technique to eliminate required textbooks and nightly assigned readings. Instead of daily pages for students to read, each assignment is based on the ability to answer historical questions through whatever research methods most interest the student. Using questions, discussion, and debate, the semester revolves around student research throughout the multimedia domain, including social media and online academic databases. In the process, students learn to differentiate between sources, judge online biases, and discover their preferred method of scholarly research. The case studies show that the elimination of assigned textbooks and the re-imagining of research projects that include publicly consumable projects are a unique and engaging way to integrate 21st-century digital research methods into the traditional institution of higher learning. In doing so, college classrooms can once again begin to mend the fractured university-societal pact.

REFERENCES

Altbach, P. G. (2011). Rankings season is here. *International Higher Education, 62*, 2–5.
Altbach, P. G., Reisberg, L., & Rumbley, L. E. (2010). *Trends in global higher education: Tracking an academic revolution*. Rotterdam: Sense Publishers.
Bologna Declaration. (1999). Retrieved from https://web.archive.org/web/20080211212119/http://www.bologna-bergen2005.no/Docs/00-Main_doc/990719BOLOGNA_DECLARATION.PDF
Brunnhofer, M. (Ed.). (2010). *Higher education in South Eastern Europe. University economy partnerships for enhancing knowledge transfer*. WUS Austria. Retrieved from https://www.wusaustria.org/files/docs/manual5_endps.pdf
Brydon-Miller, M., Greenwood, D., & Maguire, P. (2003). Why action research? *Action Research, 1*(1), 9–28. http://journals.sagepub.com/doi/pdf/10.1177/14767503030011002
Duderstadt, J. J. (1999). The future of higher education new roles for the 21st-century university. Issues in Science and Technology Online. Retrieved from http://milproj.dc.umich.edu/publications/newroles/download/newroles.pdf
Ellis, C., Adams, T. E., & Bochner, A. P. (2011). Autoethnography: An overview. *Historical Social Research, 36*(4), 273–290. doi:10.12759/hsr.36.2011.4.273-290
Fallon, D. (1980). *The German university: A heroic ideal in conflict with the modern world*. Boulder: Colorado Associated University Press.
Geiger, R. L. (2004). *To advance knowledge: The growth of American research universities, 1900–1940*. New Brunswick, NJ: Transaction.
Marginson, S., & van der Wende, M. (2009). Europeanisation, international rankings, and faculty mobility: Three cases in higher education globalisation. In Organisation for Economic Cooperation and Development (Ed.), *Higher Education to 2030, Volume 2: Globalisation* (pp. 109–141). Paris: OECD.
Margison, S., & Rhoades, G. (2002). Beyond national states, markets and systems of higher education: A glonacal agency heuristic. *Higher Education, 43*, 281–309. https://doi.org/10.1023/A:1014699605875
Organisation for Economic Cooperation and Development. (2008). *Higher Education to 2030, Volume 1: Demography*. Paris: Author.
Teichler, U. (1996). Comparative higher education: Potentials and limits. *Higher Education, 32*, 431–465.
Teichler, U., & Sadlak, J. (Eds.). (2000). *Higher education research: Its relationship to policy and practice*. Oxford: Pergamon/IAU Press.
University of Prishtina. (2004, July 5). Retrieved 2018, from https://www.uni-pr.edu/inc/doc/statuti1.pdf
Ved, P. (2007, August 4). Trends in growth and financing of higher education in India. *Economic and Political Weekly, 42*(31), 3249–3258.
Venkatasubramanian, K. (2002, February 19). Financing of higher education. *The Hindu*.

CHAPTER 2

THE FUTURE OF SCIENTIFIC RESEARCH IN TURKISH HIGHER EDUCATION

Ahmet Su and Engin Karadağ

ABSTRACT

Scientific research and delivering education at undergraduate and graduate levels are the main responsibilities of higher education institutions. Considering these points, we aimed to provide insights into an array of topics pertaining to scientific research and tertiary education in Turkey and the future of Turkish higher education. We focused on research-based education, lifelong learning, research and higher education institutions, research grants and funding in Turkey, performance management in higher education, international collaborations, future of hands-on approaches, and lastly the issue of brain drain in Turkey. In the endeavor to present these issues in detail, we employed sector analysis method. Throughout the chapter, we aimed to provide detailed and comparative evaluations making use of both national and international literature.

Keywords: Turkish higher education; sector analysis; research; funding and grants; brain drain

INTRODUCTION

Turkish higher education is comprised of public universities and non-profit foundation universities, both of which have four-year faculties, two-year colleges, and graduate schools under their administrative bodies. The universities are responsible for providing tertiary education and keeping up with the technological and scientific developments. In this process, research and education have crucial roles. Considering this fact, focusing on research and tertiary education with a comparative approach will be an important contribution to the international literature.

In this chapter, we aimed to provide insights into an array of topics which are important for the future of research in Turkey. Among these topics, research-based education, lifelong learning, and hands-on approaches are crucial in educating the higher education students. Further, a brief history of higher education institutions and detailed analysis of research funding in Turkey were covered in order to present the current situation together with a perspective for the future of research. Lastly, brain drain was presented with a detailed analysis to evaluate the current situation and implications for the future of research and development in Turkey.

In our effort to cover these issues, we employed sector analysis method to present a picture of the higher education sector in Turkey, provide evaluations and implications for future, and make national and international comparisons of the issues and institutions. Sector analysis studies collect data and analyze how the system under review functions including internal dynamics and external factors. Critical analysis of the system guides researchers to inquire about what the stakeholders must do in order to address the major issues, challenges, and opportunities. Sector analysis is the first step taken toward development. This method focuses on collecting data and critical analysis of internal and external factors (Chang, 2008). Similar steps like data collection, synthesizing, processing, and analysis of the data, identifying critical issues, providing stakeholders and policymakers comprehensive and valid body of knowledge are seen in sector analysis studies (Sebatane et al., 2000). Policymakers benefit from the findings of sector analysis studies to improve the system. We present our analysis of the sector in the following parts of the chapter.

RESEARCH-BASED EDUCATION

The relationship between education and research has been documented extensively (Brew & Jewell, 2012; Lambert, 2009), and bringing teaching and inquiry together is recommended and is stated as a productive method in learning environments (Darling-Hammond, Flook, Cook-Harvey, Barron, & Osher, 2019). As the nature of higher education and research has changed, teaching and research should be drawn together more firmly (Brew, 2012). Inquiry and research have been the focus of academic endeavor for a long time, and John Dewey stressed the importance of "learning by doing" in educational environments in the 1930s (Spronken-Smith & Walker, 2010). In the 21st century, inquiry and knowledge have become increasingly important for workplaces. For this reason, modern universities are expected to engage students with research and inquiry meaningfully.

Such practices have an impact on students' learning experiences and help students improve key competencies (Kuh, 2008). Research is defined as "an inquiry or investigation or a research-based activity of a student which makes an originally new scholarly or innovative contribution to that field" (Beckman & Hensel, 2009; Brew, 2010). This approach integrates research-based activities into the curriculum of the program and paves the way for students to take part in or conduct research studies with academics in their departments. Besides, sometimes students take part in research internship activities which aims to give university students real research experience for a period of time. Research-based activities integrated into curriculum include both traditional activities and research-based or inquiry-based activities. In these practices, the whole course or subject aims to give students experiences of different aspects of research (Brew & Jewell, 2012). Problem-based learning aims to solve daily life problems through research-based investigations. In problem-based approach, the students assume responsibility in the learning process and work with their peers in collaboration to strengthen their investigation, research, and problem-solving skills (Bilgin, Karakuyu, & Ay, 2015).

Inquiry-based learning and problem-based learning are used interchangeably with research-based learning very often (Healey, 2005). The terms used for learning through inquiry also includes "enquiry-based learning," "guided-inquiry," "problem-based learning," "undergraduate research," and "research-based teaching." Despite this diversity in terminology, there is a commonality of opinion about what constitutes inquiry-based learning (Spronken-Smith & Walker, 2010). In this learning approach, students learn through direct research experiences (Healey, 2005). However, there are still ongoing discussions on the nature of inquiry-based or research-based learning (Spronken-Smith & Walker, 2010). The core components of an inquiry-based learning approach that many researchers (Justice et al., 2007; Kahn & O'Rourke, 2004; Spronken-Smith & Walker, 2010) are in agreement are:

- Learning is structured around inquiry; students focus on questions, problems, and research.
- Students take responsibility for their own learning through a self-directed learning perspective.
- Learners are active in the process and learn by doing.
- Student-centered teaching is adopted and the teacher acts as a guide and facilitator.
- Constructing knowledge and a new perception are the foundations of learning.

Healey (2005) and Jenkins and Healey (2005) developed a matrix which shows the link between curriculum, research, and education. This matrix (Fig. 1) was amended and improved in a later study (Healey & Jenkins, 2009). The most traditional university teaching is indicated in the bottom left (research-led) side of the matrix. In this approach, the focus is on understanding research findings; little interest is given to research processes. He maintains that higher education should focus more on approaches and methods in line with the top half of the matrix, which is research-tutored and research-based education. These approaches

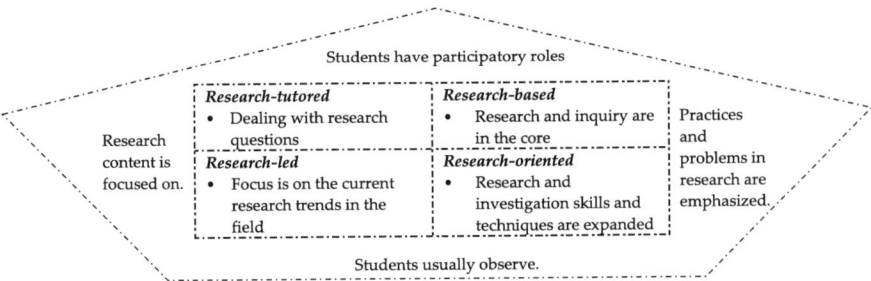

Fig. 1. The nature of undergraduate research and inquiry. Adapted from Healey and Jenkins (2009).

encourage students to take part in research activities actively, thus providing the most benefit for student learning.

In conclusion, research-based education is of vital importance in modern higher education. However, Turkish universities tend to opt for traditional teaching methods which prioritize theoretical teaching through the teacher's perspective rather than practice and research-based teaching in most of the faculties and departments (Gökçe, 2009; Üstüner, 2004). Inquiry and research are the key components that help the higher education students develop skills for their future work. Another key factor for higher education students is lifelong learning which helps not only students but other professionals and individuals to update their skills and knowledge throughout their lives. The following part discusses the issue in detail.

LIFELONG LEARNING

Lifelong learning policy, which was introduced into Turkish context through Bologna process[1] in 2001, is defined as non-stop learning in an individual's life and is essential for catching up with the rapidly changing social life, information and technology (Bryce, 2004; Onursal-Beşgül, 2017; Uzunboylu & Hürsen, 2011; Wächter, 2004; Wang, 2008). The fundamental principle of lifelong learning is to continue learning purposefully and consciously through one's life. Lifelong learning is based on being motivated and actively encouraged to learn throughout life. This approach to learning embraces social and individual development of all kinds and in all settings (Demirel, 2011). Lifelong learning may also be defined as "all learning activity undertaken throughout life, with the aim of improving knowledge, skills and competences within a personal, civic, social and/ or employment-related perspective." Moreover, Turkish Ministry of National Education makes a similar description for lifelong learning expressing that activities in which an individual takes part in to develop his/her skills, interests, and abilities (Köksal & Çöğmen, 2013). Beycioglu and Konan (2008) indicate that lifelong learning has a long history and was brought under light in 1970 and 1990. Lastly, in the 2000s, it was adopted as an educational policy of the European Union (EU).

According to *European Report on Quality Indicators of Lifelong Learning* (European Commission, 2002), the principle aims of lifelong learning are:

- To build an inclusive society where all the individuals have equal opportunity to access quality learning.
- To ensure that people's knowledge and skills match the changing demands of jobs and occupations, workplace organization, and working methods.
- To encourage and equip people to participate in all spheres of modern public life, especially in social and political life at all levels of the community, including at European level.

Lifelong learning consists of three main bodies at which learning activities are realized, which are formal, informal, and non-formal education (Eneroth, 2008). In order for the lifelong learning process to reach its aim, learners should have the following features: planning their own learning, self-assessment of learning, becoming active learners, peer-learning and teacher-oriented learning skills, being able to integrate various learning strategies in different situations (Kiley & Cannon, 2000). The competencies for lifelong learning listed by Otten and Ohana (2009) are as follows:

- Effective communication skills in both mother tongue and foreign languages
- Mathematical and basic competencies in technology and science
- Digital competencies
- Learning how to learn
- Social and civic competence
- Entrepreneurship skills
- Cultural awareness and expression

Parkinson (1999) summarizes activities supporting lifelong learning with Fig. 2 presented below:

In order to encourage and establish a culture of lifelong learning, both government and institutions and organizations must assume responsibility. Universities should not only focus on the current needs of students but also consider their needs in the future in terms of lifelong learning and future trends in their field of operation. For this reason, as institutions whose primary function is to teach and conduct research, universities must extend these functions to help students take their own learning responsibility and provide them opportunities to learn outside the classroom (Parkinson, 1999). The Bologna Process emphasizes that lifelong learning is a fundamental part of higher education activities (Kazu & Demiralp, 2016). Besides, accountability, competency, and adaptation to learner-consumer demands have been emphasized in recent times in institutional and organizational structures of universities. Lifelong learning is not just about reproductive activities in learning but also includes productive activities. The productive aspects of learning are related to current tasks and job specifications. However, productive learning emphasizes the generative forms of ongoing change, active citizenship, knowledge creation, and participation in innovation. Lifelong

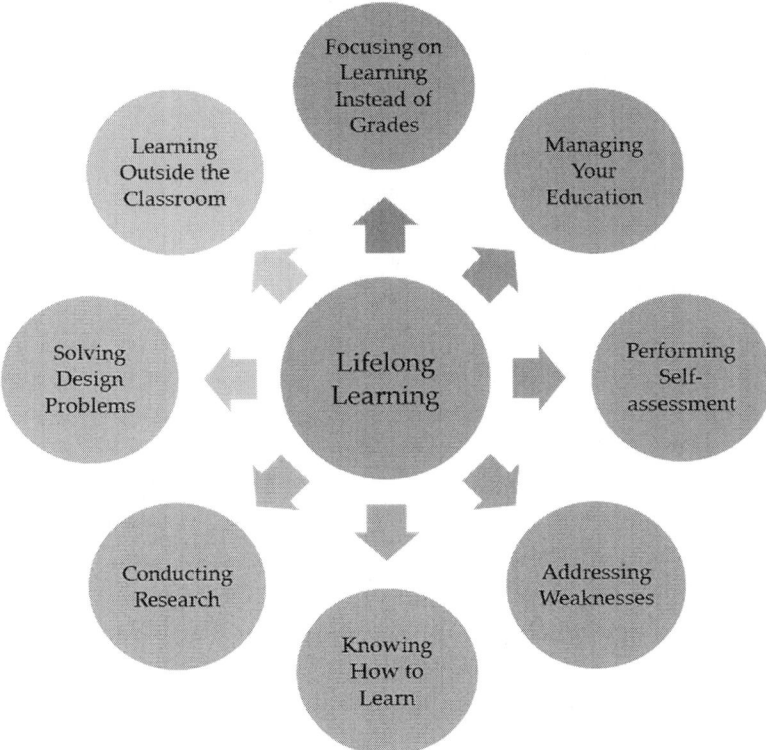

Fig. 2. Activities supporting lifelong learning.

learning is not limited to professional development or vocational training, it affects all aspects and periods of life (Allert, Richter, & Nejdl, 2004; Howell, Williams, & Lindsay, 2003; Online Education for Lifelong Learning, 2007).

In summary, research-based education ensures a solid foundation for the education at the tertiary level. Together with research-based education, teaching students lifelong learning culture will encourage them to keep up-to-date throughout their lives. This is the most important achievement and outcome for their professional lives and future research as well.

FUTURE OF HANDS-ON APPROACHES

Hands-on activities have a critical place in modern education with its various advantages. Hands-on learning can be more useful and efficient in schools. Additionally, peer interaction, collaboration, and peer learning are more obvious in hands-on activities (Ekmekci & Gulacar, 2015; Gerstner & Bogner, 2010). These teaching approaches, which are also referred to as constructivism, inquiry-based, discovery, or hands-on approaches are different than traditional learning approaches. In hands-on understanding, students are active in the classroom, and have first-hand experience in their learning adventures. In hands-on activities, students explore concepts and topics by observing, measuring, classifying, comparing, predicting, and inferring (McCarthy, 2005). Besides, some researchers express that hands-on instruction, as a student-centered approach, also enhances student motivation by improving the feeling of competence and achievement. To present a general perspective of the issue, hands-on learning can be viewed as an instruction method which concentrates on student-centered teaching combined with hands-on activities in which students take part actively (Gerstner & Bogner, 2010).

With the recent developments in technology, studies reveal that combination of hands-on practices with technology-based activities might also be effective. The literature presents findings supporting the integration of computer-based activities and hands-on activities (Ekmekci & Gulacar, 2015). Students may achieve cognitive, emotional, and social learning goals with these activities (Schaal & Bogner, 2005). Besides, in hands-on learning, as students shape the process and participate actively, they relate these learnings with their previous learnings, which also contributes to reinforcing new learnings and remind previous learnings (Bulunuz, 2012; McCarthy, 2005). Moreover, the students should be encouraged to ask creative and productive questions, make a plan to answer this question, carry out the plan and gather data; make inferences about the question, answer and the way of solving, and present their findings (McCarthy, 2005). To sum up, the literature supports the effectiveness of hands-on practices together with related approaches. It was found that students achieved goals with hands-on practices; similar results were reached through student-centered and constructivist methods (Ekmekci & Gulacar, 2015; Schaal & Bogner, 2005; Scruggs & Mastropieri, 2007).

As the research-based education, lifelong learning, and hands-on approaches are the pillars of effective education and research today and in the future, the first part aimed to present a comparative literature review and the picture in Turkey. A brief description and funding of research elaborates the issue into further detail. The following part gives a short description of the development of Turkish universities, and institutions that support scientific endeavors as well as funding of research in Turkey, which are vital points for research today and in the future in Turkey.

A BRIEF HISTORY OF HIGHER EDUCATION INSTITUTIONS AND FUNDING OF RESEARCH IN TURKEY

The foundations of the first Turkish higher education institution, Istanbul University, date back to the 1800s. With the foundation of modern Turkish Republic, higher education institutions went through a modernization and westernization process. In this process, new universities were founded and organized in more westernized structures. Istanbul, Istanbul Technical, and Ankara Universities were the first higher education institutions (Baskan, 2001; Namal, 2012). Turkish higher education institutions are managed by a central council and they can be categorized into four different groups according to the years they were established (Su & Karadağ, 2018):

1. 1933–1946: University Reform Period
2. 1946–1982: Period of New Higher Education Institutions around Turkey
3. 1983–1995: First Expansion Period
4. 1995–present: Second Expansion Period

In the first years of the Republican Period, there were a number of difficulties and shortcomings in terms of research and education facilities. In the following periods, with intensive efforts, universities were improved and went through institutionalization processes. Access to higher education was limited until the 1990s. After that period, access to higher education was improved by increasing the capacities of the universities and opening new departments and programs. With the changing conditions in recent years, universities are attempting to adapt to market conditions, gaining or creating an entrepreneurial character, eliminating the gap between theory and practice, and establishing intensive connections with industry (Kurul-Tural, 2007). This transformation is viewed as a shift toward academic capitalism by Kurul-Tural (2007), which is a term defined as "market and market-like behaviors on the part of universities and faculty" by Slaughter and Leslie (1997).

On the other hand, the Scientific and Technological Research Council of Turkey (TUBITAK) was founded in 1963, which has been one of the most important supporters of scientific studies since its foundation. The institution has administrative and financial autonomy, and the abbreviation of the institution is TUBITAK (Turk. Const. art. 278, 1963). The aim of the institution is to:

- Increase and perpetuate Turkey's competitiveness and prosperity.
- Develop science and technology policies in line with national priorities.
- Contribute to the establishment of the infrastructure and tools to realize them,
- Encourage, support, coordinate, and carry out research and development activities in cooperation with all segments of society and relevant institutions.
- Make science and technology leadership in the development of culture.

There are many government and private organizations which support scientific studies in Turkey depending on the area of study. However, compared to the Western countries, the economic resources allocated for research in Turkey are quite limited. According to Akbulut (2006), TUBITAK's grants and supports relieved financial problems for studies; however, the supports were still limited and did not change the reality that Turkey was behind the developed countries. TUBITAK provides funds and grants for various scientific activities such as publishing initiatives, international projects, and scholarships during graduate education and post-doctoral studies. Council of Higher Education in Turkey (YOK) also supported graduate education at different times (Atila, Ozeken, & Sozbilir, 2015).

In developed countries, foundations and associations play an important role in supporting scientific research. In particular, in the EU, research funds offer great opportunities through various programs. The biggest supporters in Turkey are TUBITAK and the Turkish Academy of Sciences (TUBA) (Akbulut, 2006).

Organizations, institutions, and foundations which support scientific studies as follows:

- TUBITAK (Scientific and Technological Research Council of Turkey)
- TUBA (Turkish Academy of Sciences)
- Scientific Research Funds (the funds provided by the related departments of universities)
- Research Institutes at the Universities (health sciences, etc.)
- State Planning Department
- Professional organizations (job associations, Expert chambers of a certain profession)
- International organizations (EU Funds, etc.)

Although there are a number of organizations and institutions supporting scientific research in Turkey, there is a vast literature expressing that the funds and grants are not enough and less than many developed countries (Arabacı, 2011; Güzel, 2009). Considering the fact that money spent on education, research and development is an investment in a country's future, Turkey's future seems to be similar to its current situation as the studies and statistics conducted by various institutions like World Bank, OECD, and EUROSTAT reveal that Turkey has not increased funds and spending over the years (Güngör & Göksu, 2014; Ünal & Seçilmiş, 2013). Besides, the welfare level of a society and its improvement depends on the development potential of the country, its ability to use and disseminate knowledge (CESIS, 2007). The development of new products and the investments in R&D are the main factors leading to the economic growth of countries (Güzel, 2009). But, as stated above, Turkey's funds, expenditures, and investments in R&D are low when compared to developed countries like Japan, the United States, Germany, etc. Similarly, although university–industry cooperation is an important issue for achieving regional development (Işık & Kılınç, 2011); think tanks are important for the generation of new ideas (Karabulut, 2010), and innovativeness for economic development and productiveness (Açıkgöz-Ersoy & Muter-Şengül, 2008), it is possible to say that Turkey is still far behind the desired place in these areas. But the goals for the future are promising, and initial steps have already been taken.

PERFORMANCE MEASUREMENT IN HIGHER EDUCATION

Performance measurement in public organizations has a long history dating back to the 1980s (Radnor & Barnes, 2007). Various precautions were taken to solve the problem of poor performance in the public sector such as forming audit commissions. The commissions aimed to create frameworks similar to the private sector and enhance management. To solve this problem, competition through compulsory tendering and the imposition of quasi-competition through internal markets were introduced. These reforms aimed to make public organizations more strategic and create "corporate vision" and "a shared culture" (Adcroft & Willis, 2005). Measuring organizational performance aims to understand the relationship between monetary inputs and outcomes. But the performance of the members of the organizations is influenced by both social events, market conditions, and the actions of management (Brignall & Modell, 2000). In Turkey, although there are publication and course load expectations from academics by the market conditions and the management, the performance measurement processes do not work well. Eren and Birinci (2013) allege in their study that Turkish universities do not keep up with the changes, developments, and competitive conditions about higher education and apply strategic management adequately.

Generally, performance measurement is started with the presumption that the results will turn out positive and bring tangible benefits. Salmi and Hauptman (2006) put forward that well-designed, competitive funds can increase the performance of universities greatly. However, the fundamental prerequisite to operate these funds is transparency and fair play through clear criteria. According to Meyer (1994), only if it can "tell an organisation where it stands in its effort to achieve goals," performance measurement will be useful. However, it is less useful in directing the organization on what to do differently. On the other hand, researchers still have quite a few reasons to put forward that good performance measurement and objective settings are beneficial (Adcroft & Willis, 2005). The biggest hurdle in performance measurement is the complexity of all organizations. Educational organizations are complex and include visible and invisible relationships; tangible and intangible elements and performance is affected by a number of multifaceted internal and external factors. Though the findings are controversial, experiences of measurement systems outside the public sector indicated that gains were not traded off by the struggles within organizations, and thus were not beneficial to customers outside the organization, either. In terms of performance measurement, Meyer (1994) summarizes as follows:

> The long held view of what gets measured gets done has spurred managers to react to intensifying competition by piling more and more measures on their operations in a bid to encourage employees to work harder. As a result, team members end up spending too much time collecting data and monitoring their activities and not enough time managing.

Performance reporting and measurement mostly focus on monetary issues such as expenditures, donations, and ratios of operating expenses. Success for nonprofits should be measured by how effectively and efficiently they meet the needs of their constituencies (Brignall & Modell, 2000; Speckbacher, 2003). Like other non-profit organizations, public higher education institutions in Turkey generally lack financial sides of performance measurement like profitability. These institutions are unable to determine measures of performance because they mostly have goals that are amorphous and offer services that are intangible (Kaplan, 2001). On the other hand, some studies reveal that not having performance measurement systems may result in failing to determine whether the organization is succeeding or not. Besides, a clear strategy is necessary for measuring performance as various problems may be faced if the strategy is not straightforward. Performance measurement and strategy should aim to determine the outcomes and output the organizations intend to reach (Kloot & Martin, 2000). At the start of performance measurement, there has to be a clear statement of the strategy. Performance measures focus on improvements instead of the strategy. But, the strategy statement can still be misunderstood or misinterpreted. Organizational goals often hide the disagreement on what the organization aims to achieve at the end. By measuring the strategy, organizations reduce and even eliminate ambiguity and confusion about objectives and methods. They gain coherence and focus on the pursuit of their mission (Kaplan, 2001).

INTERNATIONAL COLLABORATIONS AND PROJECTS

Collaborations contribute to organizations in various ways. Graduate students and research subjects are two examples of important but hidden actors in collaborative relationships. More local and international events are necessary for helping groups to meet and encourage collaborations (Garousi, Eskandar, & Herkiloğlu, 2017). Beddoes, Jesiek, and Borrego (2010) put forward that multinational collaborations are mostly the result of researchers partnering with colleagues at institutions where they formerly worked or studied. In international relationships, different collaborative initiatives may pave the way for various collaborations. Participating in or organizing a project may help researchers build institutional and interpersonal links. Such collaborations and networks shape how education becomes international (Beddoes et al., 2010). On the other side, with the help of collaborative software tools like Dropbox (for sharing and working on the same files and documents), Microsoft Office online (for sharing documents and working on the same file), Zoom and Skype (for online meetings), the Internet has created new ways for institutions and researchers to work in geographically scattered teams. Financial advantages of these changes make collaborations easier and more attractive. Besides, with technological development, more and more organizations undertake multinational projects, and universities have started opening courses to teach students to organize and take part in such projects at which the participants are in different parts of the world. These courses present a variety of assignments, ranging from e-mail correspondence to more complex global interactions (Harteis, Gruber, & Hertramph, 2010; Swigger, Alpaslan, Brazile, & Monticino, 2004).

The theoretical foundations focus on internationalization of organizations. The primary aims of internationalization can be expressed as follows (Kireçci et al., 2016):

- Development of research, investigation, and training for the benefit of students, stakeholders, international partners, and the staff.
- Integration and collaboration of undergraduate and graduate students, educational opportunities and support for partners and stakeholders.
- Providing equivalency for transnational education opportunities.

- Collaborating and creating partnerships with prestigious and high-quality higher education institutions for department accreditation, research purposes, and student and faculty exchange.

Organizing international projects means dealing with differences in educational settings like course objectives, lesson durations, the curriculum, and grading schemes. Other educational issues are motivating students, providing scaffolding, using collaborative technology, focusing on learning process, and end-product of the project (Cajander, Daniels, Kultur, Dag, & Laxer, 2012). The effect of cultural differences in international collaborations is investigated in various studies and it is revealed that cultural differences may affect the individuals' approach to tasks in projects, and in some cases, the multicultural environment contributes to the performance of the whole group positively. Cultural factors included attitudes about organizational hierarchy, organizational harmony, trade-offs between future and current needs (Swigger et al., 2004).

In international projects, collaborative technologies have an important place with the advance of various choices. The outcomes, advantages, and disadvantages of international collaborations on different projects over internet have been documented extensively in the literature. In their study, Chidanandan, Russell-Dag, Laxer, and Ayfer (2010) have compiled student feedback, drawn some conclusions, and come up with recommendations as follows:

- Taking part in a project at which an exchange of strengths between groups is possible and/or probable.
- Make plans about meeting times, time changes, academic calendars, and project deliverables.
- Synchronize the workload in a balanced way, inform the students/researchers about this.
- Development of communication among team members takes time, and it is important to clarify the expectations of contributors and students.
- Students may have varying paces. Follow students' and project members' work and be clear and warn them about their progresses and expectations from them.

Joint projects have become popular because of their importance as a strategic alternative in global competition. It is difficult to manage international projects as they have complex structures and involve parties which have different strategies and objectives (Ozorhon, Arditi, Dikmen, & Birgonul, 2007). According to Ozorhon et al. (2007), there are a number of factors that affect the performance of international projects. The summarized and adapted form of factors can be listed as follows:

- Performance of project management: Strategic control, operational control, organizational control.
- Partner performance: Sharing risks, sharing resources, decreasing costs, transferring technology from the partner, promoting internationalization, creating long-term relationships.

- Project-related factors: Relations with other project participants, competence of project participants, completeness of project definition, availability of resources, impact of external/environmental factors, performance of the project management.

Collaboration in research activities can be defined as "working together for producing new scientific knowledge" (Katz & Martin, 1997) and most research is conducted as a collaborative effort as two or more people can do better and produce more than working independently (Kyvik & Reymert, 2017). New collaborations on research activities help scientists produce knowledge as a team and strengthen trust to create shared perspectives, support political unity, increase understanding between project teams and countries, support innovation and sustainable development, and promote the exchange and dissemination of organized and tacit knowledge. Besides, international collaboration of academics has become easier because of decrease in costs of travel and communication, and technological developments (Gossart & Özman, 2009).

This internationalization stems from purposeful efforts as a variety of national and supranational practices and policies were developed to increase international collaborations in research. In this respect, supporting researchers who publish in international journals is one of the priorities of both the **TUBITAK** and the **TUBA**, which is also a result of increased international collaborations. These institutions aim to foster and improve scientific studies and collaborations; in line with this, they facilitate mutual cooperation with 16 countries and with international and regional institutions and partners. As a result of these policies and practices, publishing performance of Turkish academics showed an impressive growth recently. Also, these policies resulted in denser international networks with international partners (Gossart & Özman, 2009).

BRAIN DRAIN IN TURKEY AND POSSIBLE OUTCOMES

Brain drain can be defined as the moving and settlement of the highly educated, specialized, skilled, talented people with superior intelligence and capacity abroad (Kurtulmuş, 1992). In brain drain; well-educated, intellectual, and qualified labor force goes to another country for research or work at a point of their career when they are most productive, and does not come back. Brain drain causes the country's scarce resources, the human capital, to leave the country. The migration of human capital affects the country's adaptation to innovation and modern technology as well as economic performance and growth adversely. The escape of human capital from developing countries to developed countries increases international inequalities. The first wave of brain drain began with the migration of doctors and engineers in Turkey in the 1960s. Especially for the past few years, it is seen that skilled professionals and university graduates have gone to the European countries and other developed countries (Bakırtaş & Kandemir, 2010).

Another point in brain drain is student non-return, which has critical consequences and implications as well. The difference between student non-return and skilled people's migration is, in the former case, mostly graduate education is received in the foreign country. Therefore, there is a huge difference in terms of knowledgebase and practices between the host and home country, which causes emigrants' to be more productive and earn more in the host country than the home country as her/his skill set and work experience are geared to the host country (Güngör & Tansel, 2008). The case of those who received their highest degrees in their home countries can be viewed as brain drain in the traditional sense. They invest in their human capital in the home country and go abroad to work or improve their academic studies. A few studies in the literature provide perspectives about the student non-return and reveal that this case may be a more critical phenomenon than the brain drain in the traditional sense (Güngör & Tansel, 2014).

For many decades, the migration of highly educated and skilled has been a matter of consideration for policymakers and academics. In the early 1970s, studies on the migration of highly skilled and educated individuals and brain drain – from developing countries to the developed ones, especially to the United States – brought this topic under focus in terms of a dichotomy of loss of sending countries and gain of the host countries (Fortney, 1970). The literature on skilled migration concentrated on the negative sides of the earlier studies. For this reason, "brain drain" implied that a diversion, depletion, and drain of skills and knowledge which was built and structured from developing countries to the developed countries at a very little cost if any. In the 1960s and 1970s, the literature focused on the adverse effects of brain drain and student non-return. However, later the brain drain literature changed its direction with the idea that this process can be advantageous for the home countries. A number of researchers put forward that brain drain at an optimal amount can contribute to the economic development of the home countries (Güngör & Tansel, 2014). The issue of brain drain received interest from the Turkish media as well; it is often seen as a critical socioeconomic problem as it leads to loss of skilled and educated individuals. In the 2001 economic crisis, it received greater attention. Many Turkish engineers, scholars, and artists live in developed countries in Europe and America. The success of these Turkish immigrants attracts the interest of Turkish media, and sometimes it is depicted as "fetish of the successful Turk abroad" (Köser-Akçapar, 2006). On the other hand, brain drain is a problem not only in Turkey but also in all developing countries (Cansız, 2006). Industrial and developed countries such as Canada, Germany, and the United Kingdom are worried about losing their skilled individuals, but the field literature mostly focuses on the effects of brain drain on developing countries. By depriving developing countries of human capital, one of their scarcest resources, brain drain is usually seen as a drag on economic development. On the other hand, in various countries including Turkey, the rates of migration of skilled workers are stated to be around 35%–45% which is a controversial issue. In some studies, lower rates such as 5%–20% are also reported (Docquier, Lohest, & Marfouk, 2007).

There are two aspects of how brain drain affects the growth of sending countries negatively. On the one side, the human capital is reduced with the migration of skilled individuals. On the other side, skilled and educated individuals neglect educational activities while looking for future prospects or educational activities

Table 1. Pull and Push Factors of Skilled Immigration.

Pull Factors	Push Factors
High income	Low income
Better opportunities of promotion in professional life	Lack of opportunities for promotion in the profession
Better workplaces (flexible business hours, comfortable environment, etc.)	Low or no job opportunities in the area of expertise
Opportunity to find a job in the area of expertise	Lack of opportunities to further develop the field
	Failure to allocate sufficient resources to scientific studies, insufficient support for ideas and inventions
Possibility to improve further in the area of expertise	Being away from the major science centers in the field
Systematic and orderly life	Lack of financial support and funding to start a business
More satisfying social and cultural life	Unsatisfactory social and cultural life
Proximity to major science and innovation centers	Bureaucratic barriers, poor functioning of institutions
Spouse's job, preferring to stay abroad	Political pressures, unrest
Better education for children abroad	Lack of social security, concern about the future, poor management of education system
The project or work undertaken continues/hasn't ended	Economic instability, uncertainty

in their home countries. However, when the migrants are the individuals with low levels of education and/or human capital, the effect of this migration is positive on the home country. Besides, as a different perspective to the issue, migration and brain drain literature highlight some beneficial points of brain drain putting forward the re-migration process of skilled and educated individuals. The migration may not be a once-and-for-all decision. Migrants with human capital may go back to their home countries and help the dissemination of knowledge, experiences, and skills (Brzozowski, 2007; Güngör & Tansel, 2014).

There are a number of factors which include economical, educational, social, and political reasons for migration of skilled individuals. These factors are classified as "pull factors" which attract skilled migration to host countries and "push factors" which cause skilled individuals to migrate from their home countries. These factors may vary among individuals, fields, and according to countries migrated. The list of these factors is presented below based on the brain drain literature in Turkey (Bakırtaş & Kandemir, 2010; Cansız, 2006; Güngör & Tansel, 2014; Tansel & Güngör, 2004) (Table 1).

CONCLUSION

In this sector analysis study, the approaches and practices pertaining to higher education, scientific studies, research grants and funds, international collaborations, and brain drain in Turkey were covered. The comprehensive review of the literature reveals that although Turkey has policies and strategies to encourage research-based education and hands-on approaches, the institutions and academics still have shortcomings, which affect the quality of education as well as the future of research. In terms of lifelong learning, Turkey has been working on policies and practices and showed progress.

Turkish higher education system is developing to contribute to the future of research in Turkey. There are various organizations supporting projects and studies financially, the most prominent of those are TUBITAK, TUBA, and Council of Higher Education. However, the funding and research grants are limited and less than many developed countries. The funding and grants need to be increased.

Lastly, an issue that Turkey has been dealing with for a long time is brain drain. This issue has many underlying reasons as stated in the previous part. Many educated young professionals and academics leave Turkey to work in developed countries, which affect the development of Turkish academia in terms of the quality of education and research as well as the future of research. Besides, brain drain has implications for the economic development of Turkey as well. Some of the underlying reasons for the brain drain are political issues, scarce job opportunities, and low quality of education. In order to stop or slow down brain drain, Turkey has to adopt long-term policies which have a clear and straightforward roadmap.

NOTE

1. The Bologna process was launched by the European Union to create a European Higher Education Area. The process aimed to create shared practices, promote mobility of students, adopt clear and comparable higher education degrees, promote quality assurance networks and encourage lifelong learning, improve European Union dimension in higher education, etc. (Çekerol & Öztürk, 2012; Onursal-Beşgül, 2017).

REFERENCES

Açıkgöz-Ersoy, B., & Muter-Şengül, C. (2008). Yenilikçiliğe Yönelik Devlet Uygulamaları ve AB Karşılaştırması. *Yönetim ve Ekonomi, 15*(1), 59–74.

Adcroft, A., & Willis, R. (2005). The (un)intended outcome of performance measurement in the public sector. *International Journal of Public Sector Management, 18*(5), 386–400.

Akbulut, H. (2006). Bilimsel araştırma desteği. In O. Yilmaz (Ed.), *Sağlık Bilimlerinde Süreli Yayıncılık* (pp. 27–28). Ankara: TÜBİTAK.

Allert, H., Richter, C., & Nejdl, W. (2004). Lifelong learning and second-order learning objects. *British Journal of Educational Technology, 35*(6), 701–715. https://doi.org/10.1111/j.1467-8535.2004.00428.x

Arabacı, İ. B. (2011). Türkiye'de ve OECD Ülkelerinde Eğitim Harcamaları. *Elektronik Sosyal Bilimler Dergisi, 35*(35), 100–112. Retrieved from http://dergipark.ulakbim.gov.tr/esosder/article/view/5000068374

Atila, M. E., Ozeken, O. F., & Sozbilir, M. (2015). Academic staff's views about international scholarships and support programs. *Journal of Higher Education and Science, 5*(1), 68. https://doi.org/10.5961/jhes.2015.110

Bakırtaş, T., & Kandemir, O. (2010). Gelişmekte olan ülkeler ve beyin göçü: Türkiye örneği. *Kastamonu Eğitim Dergisi, 18*(3), 961–974.

Baskan, G. A. (2001). Development of the higher education ın turkey. *Gazi Eğitim Fakültesi Dergisi, 21*(1), 21–32. https://doi.org/10.17152/gefd.18858

Beckman, M., & Hensel, N. (2009). Making explicit the implicit: Defining undergraduate research. *CUR Quarterly, 29*(4), 40–44. Retrieved from https://www.mcgill.ca/senate/files/senate/beckman__hensel_making_explicit.pdf

Beddoes, K. D., Jesiek, B. K., & Borrego, M. (2010). Identifying opportunities for collaborations in international engineering education research on problem- and project-based learning. *Interdisciplinary Journal of Problem-Based Learning*, *4*(2), 9–19. https://doi.org/10.7771/1541-5015.1142

Beycioglu, K., & Konan, N. (2008). Lifelong learning and education policies of the European Union. *Electronic Journal of Social Sciences*, *7*(24), 369–382.

Bilgin, I., Karakuyu, Y., & Ay, Y. (2015). The effects of project based learning on undergraduate students' achievement and self-efficacy beliefs towards science teaching. *Eurasia Journal of Mathematics, Science and Technology Education*, *11*(3), 469–477. https://doi.org/10.12973/eurasia.2014.1015a

Brew, A. (2010). An Australian perspective on undergraduate research. *Council on Undergraduate Research Quarterly*, *31*(1), 37–42.

Brew, A. (2012). Teaching and research: New relationships and their implications for inquiry-based teaching and learning in higher education. *Higher Education Research and Development*, *31*(1), 101–114. https://doi.org/10.1080/07294360.2012.642844

Brew, A., & Jewell, E. (2012). Enhancing quality learning through experiences of research-based learning: Implications for academic development. *International Journal for Academic Development*, *17*(1), 47–58. https://doi.org/10.1080/1360144X.2011.586461

Brignall, S., & Modell, S. (2000). An institutional perspective on performance measurement and management in the "new public sector". *Management Accounting Research*, *11*(3), 281–306. https://doi.org/10.1006/mare.2000.0136

Bryce, J. (2004). Different ways that secondary schools orient to lifelong learning. *Educational Studies*, *30*(1), 53–64. https://doi.org/10.1080/0305569032000159732

Brzozowski, J. (2007). Brain waste, educational investments and growth in transitional countries. *SSRN Electronic Journal*. Retrieved from http://papers.ssrn.com/sol3/papers.cfm?abstract_id=991785

Bulunuz, M. (2012). Motivational qualities of hands-on science activities for Turkish preservice kindergarten teachers. *Eurasia Journal of Mathematics, Science and Technology Education*, *8*(2), 73–82. https://doi.org/10.12973/eurasia.2012.821a

Cajander, A., Daniels, M., Kultur, C., Dag, L. R., & Laxer, C. (2012). Managing international student collaborations: An experience report. Paper presented at the Proceedings - Frontiers in Education Conference (FIE), Seattle, WA, October 3–6. https://doi.org/10.1109/FIE.2012.6462413

Cansız, A. (2006). Son Yıllarda Beyin Göçünün Türk Yüksek Öğretimi Üzerindeki Etkileri. TMMOB Elektrik-Elektronik Bilgisayar Mühendislikleri Eğitimi 3. Ulusal Sempozyumu, 2006, İstanbul.

Çekerol, K., & Öztürk, Ö. (2012). Bologna process and Anadolu University open education system. *Procedia - Social and Behavioral Sciences*, *64*, 275–283. https://doi.org/10.1016/j.sbspro.2012.11.032

CESIS. (2007). Entrepreneurship, knowledge and economic growth. In *Foundations and Trends in Entrepreneurship*. Retrieved from https://www.diva-portal.org/smash/get/diva2:487467/FULLTEXT01.pdf

Chang, G.-C. (2008). Strategic planning in education: Some concepts and methods. In *Direction in educational planning: Symposium to honour the work of Françoise Caillods*. UNESCO: International Institute for Educational Planning.

Chidanandan, A., Russell-Dag, L., Laxer, C., & Ayfer, R. (2010). *In their words: Student feedback on an international project collaboration*. Paper presented at the SIGCSE'10 - Proceedings of the 41st ACM Technical Symposium on Computer Science Education, Milwaukee, WI, pp. 534–538. https://doi.org/10.1145/1734263.1734441

Darling-Hammond, L., Flook, L., Cook-Harvey, C., Barron, B., & Osher, D. (2019). Implications for educational practice of the science of learning and development. *Applied Developmental Science*, *24*(2), 97–140. https://doi.org/10.1080/10888691.2018.1537791

Demirel, M. (2011). Lifelong learning and its reflections on Turkish elementary education curricula. *Uluslararası Eğitim Programları ve Öğretim Çalışmaları Dergisi*, *1*(1), 87–106.

Docquier, F., Lohest, O., & Marfouk, A. (2007). Brain drain in developing countries. *World Bank Economic Review*, *21*(2), 193–218. https://doi.org/10.1093/wber/lhm008

Ekmekci, A., & Gulacar, O. (2015). A case study for comparing the effectiveness of a computer simulation and a hands-on activity on learning electric circuits. *Eurasia Journal of Mathematics, Science and Technology Education*, *11*(4), 765–775. https://doi.org/10.12973/eurasia.2015.1438a

Eneroth, B. (2008). Knowledge, sentience and receptivity: A paradigm of lifelong learning. *European Journal of Education, 43*(2), 229–240. https://doi.org/10.1111/j.1465-3435.2008.00342.x

Eren, E., & Birinci, M. (2013). The effects of strategic management practices on the performance of the universities in Turkey. *Journal of Global Strategic Management, 13*, 17–35. https://doi.org/10.20460/jgsm.2013715673

European Commission. (2002). *European Report on Quality Indicators of Lifelong Learning*. Brussels: Author.

Fortney, J. A. (1970). International migration of professionals. *Population Studies, 24*(2), 217–232. Retrieved from https://www.jstor.org/stable/2172655

Garousi, V., Eskandar, M. M., & Herkiloğlu, K. (2017). Industry–academia collaborations in software testing: Experience and success stories from Canada and Turkey. *Software Quality Journal, 25*(4), 1091–1143. https://doi.org/10.1007/s11219-016-9319-5

Gerstner, S., & Bogner, F. X. (2010). Cognitive achievement and motivation in hands-on and teacher-centred science classes: Does an additional hands-on consolidation phase (concept mapping) optimise cognitive learning at work stations? *International Journal of Science Education, 32*(7), 849–870. https://doi.org/10.1080/09500690902803604

Gökçe, N. (2009). Türkiye'de Öğretmen Yetiştirmede Coğrafya Eğitiminin Sorunları ve Öneriler. *Kuram ve Uygulamada Eğitim Bilimleri/Educational Sciences: Theory & Practice, 9*(2), 721–768.

Gossart, C., & Özman, M. (2009). Co-authorship networks in social sciences: The case of Turkey. *Scientometrics, 78*(2), 323–345. https://doi.org/10.1007/s11192-007-1963-x

Güngör, G., & Göksu, A. (2014). Türkiye'de Eğitimin Finansmanı ve Ülkelerarası Bir Karşılaştırma. *Yönetim ve Ekonomi: Celal Bayar Üniversitesi İktisadi ve İdari Bilimler Fakültesi Dergisi, 20*(1), 59–72. https://doi.org/10.18657/yecbu.15038

Güngör, N. D., & Tansel, A. (2008). Brain drain from Turkey: The case of professionals abroad. *International Journal of Manpower, 29*(4), 323–347. https://doi.org/10.1108/01437720810884746

Güngör, N. D., & Tansel, A. (2014). Brain drain from Turkey: Return intentions of skilled migrants. *International Migration, 52*(5), 208–226. https://doi.org/10.1111/imig.12013

Güzel, S. (2009). Ar-Ge Harcamaları ve Vergi Teşvikleri: Belirli Ülkeler Karşısında Türkiye'nin Durumu. *Eskişehir Osmangazi Üniversitesi İİBF Dergisi, 4*(2), 29–48.

Harteis, C., Gruber, H., & Hertramph, H. (2010). How epistemic beliefs influence e-learning in daily work-life. *Educational Technology and Society, 13*(3), 201–211.

Healey, M. (2005). Linking research and teaching: Exploring disciplinary spaces and the role of inquiry-based learning. In R. Barnett (Ed.), *Reshaping the university: New relationships between research, scholarship and teaching* (pp. 67–78). New York, NY: McGraw-Hill/Open University Press.

Healey, M., & Jenkins, A. (2009). *Developing undergraduate research and inquiry*. York: The Higher Education Academy.

Howell, S. L., Williams, P. B., & Lindsay, N. K. (2003). Thirty-two trends affecting distance education: An informed foundation for strategic planning. *Online Journal of Distance Learning Administration, 6*(3), 1–18.

Işık, N., & Kılınç, E. C. (2011). Bölgesel Kalkınma'da Ar-Ge ve İnovasyonun Önemi: Karşılaştırmalı Bir Analiz. *Eskişehir Osmangazi Üniversitesi İİBF Dergisi, 6*(2), 9–54.

Jenkins, A., & Healey, M. (2005). *Institutional strategies to link teaching and research*. Retrieved from The Higher Education Academy website: http://www.heacademy.ac.uk/assets/York/documents/resources/resourcedatabase/id585_institutional_strategies_to_link_teaching_and_research.pdf

Justice, C., Rice, J., Warry, W., Inglis, S., Miller, S., & Sammon, S. (2007). Inquiry in higher education: Reflections and directions on course design and teaching methods. *Innovative Higher Education, 31*(4), 201–214. https://doi.org/10.1007/s10755-006-9021-9

Kahn, P., & O'Rourke, K. (2004). Guide to curriculum design: Enquiry-based learning. *Higher Education Academy, 30*(3), 1–10. Retrieved from http://www.ceebl.manchester.ac.uk/resources/guides/kahn_2004.pdf

Kaplan, R. S. (2001). Strategic performance measurement and management in nonprofit organizations. *Nonprofit Management and Leadership, 11*(3), 353–370. https://doi.org/10.1002/nml.11308

Karabulut, B. (2010). Think tank ınstitutions in the world and Turkey: A comparative analysis. *Gazi Akademik Bakış, 4*(7), 91–104.

Katz, J. S., & Martin, B. R. (1997). What is research collaboration? *Research Policy*, *26*(1), 1–18. https://doi.org/10.1016/S0048-7333(96)00917-1

Kazu, H., & Demiralp, D. (2016). Faculty members' views on the effectiveness of teacher training programs to upskill life-long learning competence. *Eurasian Journal of Educational Research*, *16*(63), 205–224. https://doi.org/10.14689/ejer.2016.63.12

Kiley, M., & Cannon, R. (2000). *Leap into… Lifelong Learning*. Adelaide: Centre for Learning and Professional Development, The University of Adelaide.

Kireçci, M. A., Bacanli, H., Erişen, Y., Karadağ, E., Çeliköz, N., Dombayci, M. A., … Şahin, M. (2016). The internationalization of higher education in Turkey: Creating an index. *Egitim ve Bilim*, *41*(187), 1–28. https://doi.org/10.15390/EB.2016.6223

Kloot, L., & Martin, J. (2000). Strategic performance management: A balanced approach to performance management issues in local government. *Management Accounting Research*, *11*(2), 231–251. https://doi.org/10.1006/mare.2000.0130

Köksal, N., & Çöğmen, S. (2013). Pre-service teachers as lifelong learners: University facilities for promoting. *Eurasian Journal of Educational Research*, *53*, 21–40. https://doi.org/10.14689/ejer.2013.53.2

Köser-Akçapar, S. (2006). Do brains really going down the drain? *Revue Européenne Des Migrations Internationales*, *22*(3), 79–107. https://doi.org/10.4000/remi.3281

Kuh, G. D. (2008). *High-impact educational practices: What they are, who has access to them, and why they matter*. Washington, DC: Association of American Colleges and Universities.

Kurtulmuş, N. (1992). Gelişmekte Olan Ülkeler Açısından Stratejik İnsan Sermayesi Kaybı: Beyin Göçü. *Sosyal Siyaset Konferansları Dergisi*, 37–38, 205–221. Retrieved from http://dergipark.gov.tr/download/article-file/9622

Kurul-Tural, N. (2007). Universities and academic life in Turkey: Changes and challenges. *International Journal of Educational Policies*, *1*(1), 63–78.

Kyvik, S., & Reymert, I. (2017). Research collaboration in groups and networks: Differences across academic fields. *Scientometrics*, *113*, 951–967. https://doi.org/10.1007/s11192-017-2497-5

Lambert, C. (2009). Pedagogies of participation in higher education: A case for research-based learning. *Pedagogy, Culture and Society*, *17*(3), 295–309. https://doi.org/10.1080/14681360903194327

McCarthy, C. B. (2005). Effects of thematic-based, hands-on science teaching versus a textbook approach for students with disabilities. *Journal of Research in Science Teaching*, *42*(3), 245–263. https://doi.org/10.1002/tea.20057

Meyer, C. (1994). How the right measures help teams excel. *Harvard Business Review*, *72*(3), 95–101.

Namal, Y. (2012). Contributions of foreign scientists to the higher education between 1933–1950 years in Turkey. *Journal of Higher Education and Science*, *2*(1), 14. https://doi.org/10.5961/jhes.2012.028

Online Education for Lifelong Learning. (2007). In Y. Inoue (Ed.), *Online Education for Lifelong Learning*. https://doi.org/10.4018/978-1-59904-319-7.ch006

Onursal-Beşgül, Ö. (2017). Translating norms from Europe to Turkey: Turkey in the Bologna Process. *Compare: A Journal of Comparative and International Education*, *47*(5), 742–755. https://doi.org/10.1080/03057925.2016.1273094

Otten, H., & Ohana, Y. (2009). *The eight key competencies for lifelong learning: An appropriate framework within which to develop the competence of trainers in the field of European youth work or just plain politics?* Bonn: Institute for Applied Communication Research.

Ozorhon, B., Arditi, D., Dikmen, I., & Birgonul, M. T. (2007). Effect of host country and project conditions in international construction joint ventures. *International Journal of Project Management*, *25*(8), 799–806. https://doi.org/10.1016/j.ijproman.2007.05.003

Parkinson, A. (1999). Developing the attribute of lifelong learning. *Proceedings - Frontiers in Education Conference*, *1*, 16–20.

Radnor, Z. J., & Barnes, D. (2007). Historical analysis of performance measurement and management in operations management. *International Journal of Productivity and Performance Management*, *56*(5–6), 384–396. https://doi.org/10.1108/17410400710757105

Salmi, J., & Hauptman, A. M. (2006). *Innovations in tertiary education financing: A comparative evaluation of allocation mechanisms* (Working Paper Series No. 4). Washington, DC: World Bank. https://doi.org/10.1142/9789813278752_0011

Schaal, S., & Bogner, F. X. (2005). Human visual perception—Learning at workstations. *Journal of Biological Education*, *40*(1), 32–37. https://doi.org/10.1080/00219266.2005.9656006

Scruggs, T. E., & Mastropieri, M. A. (2007). Science learning in special education: The case for constructed versus ınstructed learning. *Exceptionality*, *15*(2), 57–74. https://doi.org/10.1080/09362830701294144

Sebatane, E. M., Ambrose, D. P., Molise, M. K., Mothibeli, A., Motlomelo, S. T., Nenty, H. J., ... Ntoi, V. M. (2000). *Review of Education: Sector Analysis in Lesotho 1978–1999*. Paris: Working Group on Education Sector Analysis, UNESCO.

Slaughter, S., & Leslie, L. L. (1997). *Academic capitalism* (p. 421). Baltimore, MD: Johns Hopkins University Press.

Speckbacher, G. (2003). The economics of performance management in nonprofit organizations. *Nonprofit Management and Leadership*, *13*(3), 267–281. https://doi.org/10.1002/nml.15

Spronken-Smith, R., & Walker, R. (2010). Can inquiry-based learning strengthen the links between teaching and disciplinary research? *Studies in Higher Education*, *35*(6), 723–740. https://doi.org/10.1080/03075070903315502

Su, A., & Karadağ, E. (2018). *Türkiye'de Yükseköğretimin Değişen Rolü ve Karakterine İlişkin Bir Analiz* (pp. 163–164). Afyonkarahisar: International Congress on Science and Education.

Swigger, K., Alpaslan, F., Brazile, R., & Monticino, M. (2004). Effects of culture on computer-supported international collaborations. *International Journal of Human-Computer Studies*, *60*(3), 365–380. https://doi.org/10.1016/j.ijhcs.2003.10.006

Tansel, A., & Güngör, N. D. (2004). *Türkiye'den Yurt Dışına Beyin Göçü: Ampirik Bir Uygulama*. Ankara: Middle East Technical University.

Turk. Const. art. 278. (1963). Türkiye Bilimsel ve Teknolojik Araştırma Kurumu Kurulması Hakında Kanun.

Ünal, T., & Seçilmiş, N. (2013). Ar-Ge Göstergeleri Açısından Türkiye ve Gelişmiş Ülkelerle Kıyaslaması. *İşletme ve İktisat Çalışmaları Dergisi*, *1*(1), 12–25.

Üstüner, M. (2004). Geçmişten Günümüze Türk Eğitim Sisteminde Öğretmen Yetiştirme ve Günümüz Sorunları. *İnönü Üniversitesi Eğitim Fakültesi Dergisi*, *5*(7), 63–82.

Uzunboylu, H., & Hürsen, Ç. (2011). Lifelong learning competence scale (Llcs): The study of validity and reliability. *Hacettepe Egitim Dergisi*, *41*, 449–460.

Wächter, B. (2004). The Bologna Process: Developments and prospects. *European Journal of Education*, *39*(3), 265–273. Retrieved from https://www.jstor.org/stable/1503854

Wang, C. Y. (2008). Enhancing the interactive relationship between lifelong learning and social changes to carry out a learning society in Taiwan. *International Journal of Lifelong Education*, *27*(5), 535–542. https://doi.org/10.1080/02601370802051702

CHAPTER 3

UNIVERSITY PARTNERSHIPS FOR DEVELOPING RESEARCH AT THE UNIVERSITY OF PRISHTINA, KOSOVO

Arlinda Beka

ABSTRACT

University partnerships have been promoted and implemented a good deal in Europe since the approval of the Bologna Declaration of June 19, 1999 (Bologna Declaration, 1999). Over the past two decades, the University of Prishtina has developed many bilateral and multilateral initiatives to strengthen cooperation and partnership among universities from different countries and regions (University of Prishtina, 2004, p. 2). The University of Prishtina embraced the Bologna Declaration in 2001, and since then has established several partnerships aimed at strengthening its capacities and improving the quality assurance of its higher education (Brunnhofer, 2010, p. 107). In the recent years, the University of Prishtina has given priority to the area of research, aiming to increase the quality and quantity of research conducted by its faculty. The quality and relevance of the international partnerships of the University of Prishtina is the main focus of this paper, including the current state of research among the faculty. The researcher used a qualitative method for conducting this research. It shows the institutional and individual benefits of those partnerships. Finally, it presents the impact of cooperation on developing research and improving the quality of education in Kosovo.

Keywords: University partnership; research; University of Prishtina; Kosovo; higher education; cooperation; education reform; transformation; higher education; research collaboration; professional development; staff exchange; international partnerships; joint project; inter-university programs; faculty development; academia

INTRODUCTION

Kosovo education has changed considerably over the last two decades (Beka, 2015). Kosovo institutions have worked hard to integrate their education system with the region and the world through many international partnerships, initiatives, and different projects. It has been beneficial not only for those who benefited directly but also for their institutions and the whole education system. To achieve their goal of modernizing the education system, Kosovo's institutions have worked together with their international partners to reform, change, adapt, and restructure its higher education institutions (H.E.I.s). A part of the positive changes was the approval of the Development Strategy for Higher Education in Kosovo (2005–2015) by Kosovo's government (Ministry of Education Science and Technology [MEST], 2005). This strategy's goal was to contribute toward the modern system of higher education in Kosovo and to enhance the country's development (MEST, 2005). This strategic document emphasized which points of the higher education system needed improvement and development, identifying them as strategic goals. These strategic goals are challenging tasks that require strenuous efforts from all who are either directly engaged in higher education or interested in its development (MEST, 2005). Part of the changes and reforms included: improving the focus of H.E.I.s on the development of international cooperation and research as a critical factor in improving and integrating Kosovo' education regionally and internationally. In particular, these changes follow the European Union (E.U.) guidelines and regulations as a part of Kosovo's institutions' commitment to being a part of the E.U. in the future (Beka, 2015).

The University of Prishtina is considered the leading H.E.I. in Kosovo that is involved in cooperation and research partnerships at national and international levels (University of Prishtina, 2004, p. 2). One of the main focuses of the University of Prishtina as well as different international agencies and organizations working with Kosovo's H.E.I.s was the internationalization of the work of the University. International partners of the University of Prishtina recommended making efforts to "enhance research activity and support for the internationalization of research" (OSCE, 2008, p. 6). The Regional Research Promotion Program-Western Balkans (RRPP, 2013) provided a brief policy document about research at the University of Prishtina. A part of their recommendations was that:

> The University of Prishtina lacks the necessary human capacity to apply for international projects and absorb international funds... There is a lack of research institutes and partnerships with other universities and academic institutions in the region. (RRPP, 2013, p. 18)

However, it should be emphasized that one of the key factors why the University was not well received in international cooperation networks was the political situation in Kosovo. This situation changed with the end of the war (1999) and better opportunities for regional and international cooperation, partnerships in Europe, and the world opened up.

The Kosovo Education Strategic Plan 2017–2021 approved by the MEST, envisages improvement of the quality of university work by strategic objective no. 7: "Upgrading the quality and competitiveness of higher education through the promotion of excellence in teaching, scientific research, artistic creation, innovation, and internationalization" (MEST, 2016, p. 17).

Through bilateral and multilateral partnerships, universities can achieve internationalization. Moreover, the University of Prishtina has already developed some crucial partnerships in the last two decades. The strategy and Action Plan of the University of Prishtina consider international partnerships as crucial factors for the globalization and internationalization of the research work of the University. Increasing global partnerships and joint study programs are some of the activities that should be a part of the University of Prishtina (University of Prishtina, 2016).

One of the essential international partnerships of the University of Prishtina is the Fulbright Exchange Program of the United States:

> United States government in partnership with more than 160 countries worldwide, through the Fulbright Program offers international educational and cultural exchange programs for passionate and accomplished students, scholars, artists, teachers, and professionals of all backgrounds to study, teach, or pursue important research and professional projects. (ECA, 2019)

Through this program, many professors have visited American universities for short periods, gaining different professional, cultural, and social experiences, which they implemented to their work with students upon returning, thus bringing changes to the work of the University of Prishtina.

Another international project of the University of Prishtina is the United States of America International Development (USAID) supported project called Transformational Leadership Program-TLP. Through this program USAID:

> ...Works with the University of Prishtina – the largest public University in Kosovo – to enhance its overall management, financial viability, and sustainability, improve teaching methodologies, strengthen institutional support for research, and improve career orientation services for graduates and alumni. This partnership accomplished through partnerships and academic exchanges with American universities that improve teaching, research, curriculum, and course development at the University in key development areas: engineering, education, agriculture, and economics. (USAID, 2019)

The project is implemented in partnership with the Government of Kosovo's Ministry of Education, Science, and Technology. The overarching program goal is to develop a cadre of leaders that drive significant changes in Kosovo's priority economic, political, and social areas (USAID, 2019). In addition, the project aims to develop the capacity of Kosovars to bring about transformational change through opportunities for advanced education, leadership development, and technical assistance. According to the website of the Transformational Leadership Program, the critical results among others were:

> University Partnerships established between the University of Prishtina and Arizona State University, Indiana University, the University of Minnesota, and Dartmouth College in the United States. This project, envisaged helping faculty in increasing the quality and quantity of research projects and external funding at the university through University of Prishtina's Centre for Research. (USAID, 2019)

Furthermore, as a part of this project, professors and teaching assistants at the University of Prishtina had the opportunity to create local and international cooperation through training, exchange visits, or the implementation of joint research projects.

Apart from those two international partnerships with the United States, the University of Prishtina was involved with the Tempus project through E.U. funding. One of the first projects was Modernizing Teacher Education at the University of Prishtina "Med@UP." (This project was supported and co-financed by the European Commission, established in 2013 to modernize and improve the university preparation of teachers in Kosovo.) The overall idea of this project was to help the Faculty of Education at the University of Prishtina, to develop human resources capacities and to enhance quality assurance in teaching, learning, administration, and research. The activities of Med@UP, therefore, fit into this framework, pursuing teacher training according to European standards, objectives, and models (University of Bologna, 2016).

Another E.U.-funded project that supports Kosovo's H.E.I.s is the Erasmus + Program, which contributes to the achievement of the objectives of the Europe 2020 Strategy in terms of education target and cooperation in education and training. Promotion of European values, cooperation among the youth, sustainable development of partner countries in the field of higher education (Erasmus, 2019).

These and many other projects have helped the University of Prishtina to get involved in international cooperation networks, allowing the faculty and students to gain new experiences advance professionally and bring changes to their institutions.

LITERATURE REVIEW

Changes in higher education at the global level are enormous and rapid (de Wit, 2017). Competition to be attractive and thriving in the labor market has created the need to gain new experiences through international partnerships (Takahara, 2018). Partnerships were increasingly aimed at bringing changes and professional development to the faculty, enhancing the quality of study programs as well as better preparing students (Darling-Hammond, 2017). These trends are not only a requirement of developing countries, whose goal is to increase the quality of their work. Nowadays, they are also considered a global trend, even in the universities of developed countries who are increasingly lobbying for international cooperation between the Universities. Through partnerships and cooperation come positive changes for the parties involved (Childress, 2009). According to Billot (2010) and Archer (2008), understandably, such cataclysmic shifts in the higher education landscape, especially the intense competition that has generated in attracting international students, have led to the emergence of new types of educational organizations and hybrid partnerships (Kaktins, 2018). The need for cooperation between different universities has made study programs more attractive, but at the same time brought about significant changes in the work performance of teachers and students (Association of European Border Regions, 2004).

Therefore, the rise of international education is a part of a global rise in trade within a highly competitive environment (Gillett, 2011, p. 29). It affects a multiplicity of H.E.I.s internationally, as well as the academics and administrators working within them (Kaktins, 2018). Creating opportunities for collaboration between University institutions has brought about many positive changes. It has enabled individuals involved in collaborations to create new opportunities, not only at the personal level but also at the institutional level (Tremblay, Lalancette, & Roseveare, 2012).

The creation of bridges of cooperation has opened the door to opportunities for the professional development of teachers and administrative staff and has also had a direct impact on enhancing the quality of performance of university institutions (Choi & Kang, 2019). According to Cozza and Blessinger (2016), the international program collaborations, by definition, require going beyond boundaries within institutions and involve reaching out to build bridges with other global communities. There is a growing demand for mutually beneficial partnerships that arise from interventions between higher education and international development (Cozza & Blessinger, 2016). Creating opportunities for collaboration with global communities impact the comparison and measurement of personal and professional performance outcomes with those of different communities. Dealing with different cultures makes us aware of the changes taking place in the international arena (de Wit, 2020). It motivates us to initiate changes related to our work within the institutions we operate (de Wit, 2020).

This experience has amplified the need for increased interest among academia and H.E.I.s in order to increase research partnerships and regional and international cooperation (Posselt, Abdelkafi, Fischer, & Tangour, 2019). Those supporting this idea consider it fundamental to improve research and to expand the sharing of information and experiences (Maltais, Weitz, & Persson, 2018). Hilliard (2012) considers that:

> There are many incentives for universities to partner with another university or share their community resources. Partnerships create a culture of collaboration and innovation. University partnering with other universities can create a framework for improved teaching, learning, research, program development, leadership, and services and improve the quality of academic programs. The new and improved knowledge learned through university collaboration can contribute to the higher performance of faculty and students. Partnerships could cause each University to target improved ways of conducting professional development activities for faculty, students, and staff to improve teaching, learning, and research in broader communities. The university partnerships through innovative research and development can enhance the use of technology. (Hilliard, 2012)

Creating bridges of cooperation between Universities, whether locally or internationally, enables all parties to develop new experiences by bringing innovation to their home institutions (Woldegiyorgis, Proctor, & de Wit, 2018). Changes that occur as a result of cooperation have a long-term impact (de Wit, Rumbley, Craciun, Mihut, & Woldegiyorgis, 2019). According to Coburn, Penuel, and Geil (2013), research partnerships can provide a long-term relationship and bring positive results (Coburn et al., 2013).

It is often the case that universities that are most in need of investment in quality development and enhancement are the ones that benefit the most from international partnerships and research cooperations (Coburn et al., 2013). In fact, during the collaboration of Universities, benefits are mutual because partnerships involve faculty and administrative staff. In general, these partnerships create experiences for all stakeholders (Dodds, 2015). Experiences continually bring about change within institutions and thus improve the performance and quality of activities and programs (Hobbs & Campbell, 2018). The biggest benefits that a faculty gets from partnerships are the possibilities of the development of joint research. Šiška, van Swet, Pather, and Rose (2013) consider that international partnerships have a major impact on our professional roles and identities on the developmental needs of all involved (both students and staff), add culturally responsive dimensions to our teaching, research, and scholarship (Šiška et al., 2013).

The research assesses the current situation on findings and comparisons of results between Universities to initiate changes aimed at improving the current situation. Hall, Tandon, and Tremblay (2015) support this approach by considering that research partnerships are key to ensuring a dynamic and collaborative research agenda and to breaking free from traditional disciplinary and other boundaries in order to research excellence (Hall et al., 2015). Similarly, Boekholt, Edler, Cunningham, and Flanagan (2009) see that the internationalization of research has been most influential in growing and developing science (Boekholt et al., 2009). Sharing and exchanging information and experiences has enabled H.E.I.s, faculty, and researchers to build their future research on better foundations (Dodds, 2015). The flow of information and open access to it is perhaps most visible in the growth of a global science system (Boekholt et al., 2009).

According to Watson, Hollister, Stroud, and Babcock (2011), "the transformative potential of our community sector organizations and our higher education institutions is enhanced when we combine our collective knowledge, global connections, skills, and resources" (Watson et al., 2011). The global demand for knowledge, skills, new and attractive opportunities, and constant change have always aroused interest, as well as the need to forgo new collaborative links (Bennet, Bennet, & Lewis, 2015). Therefore, collaboration nowadays is considered as a way for change to improve the lives of each individual who is on the path of professional development and preparation for the labor market (Bennet et al., 2015). Various scholars see the opportunity for inter-university collaboration as an extraordinary opportunity (Steel, Thompson, & Wright, 2018). Partnerships can influence all parties involved in numerous ways: First, they encourage the creation of innovative partnerships to improve instructional delivery services to diverse groups of candidates or individuals. Second, they use the whole concept of partnership to bring into being new and improved educational programs.

Finally, they expand opportunities for faculty members to engage in collaborative research project activities (Hilliard, 2012). Inter-university cooperation is taking place on all continents, making it intercontinental networking (Steel et al., 2018). Universities in Europe had been discussing cooperation and partnerships for decades by the end of the 20th century. Finally, they approved the Bologna Declaration of June 19, 1999, which followed the fundamental principles laid down in the Bologna Magna Charta Universitatum of 1988 (Bologna Declaration, 1999). Essential points of the Bologna Declaration were: commitment to achieve the agreed goals and priorities of the European Higher Education Area, the place of European higher education in the world, and the social dimension of higher education (Bologna Declaration, 1999).

New experiences across European countries and beyond summarize the field of education as a whole, with a common goal of creating attractive opportunities for knowledge and skills as well as being able to integrate easily into the networks of the global labor market (Bennet et al., 2015). To reach this point, various organizations around the world have allocated funds that aim to create opportunities for the mobility of teachers, students and all stakeholders involved in H.E.I., and to create more significant opportunities for societies of different countries (Rob van Tulder, 2013).

According to Hilliard (2012), international partnership initiatives can provide faculty and students with the opportunity to participate in collaborative activities in multicultural settings, which could add to participants' knowledge and skills (Hilliard, 2012). Faculty and students could enrich their own experiences academically, socially, and culturally by having an international partnership (Hsiao-Ping, Garza, & Guzman, 2015). The partnering universities could: participate in promising international research and scholarship, particularly that which incorporates and expands student scholarship opportunities; help in the development of innovative curricula that strengthen the preparation of faculty and student scholars for an increasingly global future; expose underserved students to study in programs at universities abroad; increase international and multicultural respect and understanding of previously underserved constituencies in the University's communities; expand recruitment or meaningful engagement of international students in scholarly studies and research; serve as goodwill ambassadors ... in other parts of the world (Hilliard, 2012).

These forms of collaboration make it possible for teachers and students to feel a part of different global networks (Hsiao-Ping et al., 2015). It is also a form of collaboration in which positive attitudes are created for different cultures, viewing themselves as part of a global society (Hall et al., 2015). These forms of cooperation also affect society's acceptance awareness of different ethnicities, religions, and nationalities and serve to remove inter-social prejudice (Watson et al., 2011).

All these forms of cooperation bring about changes in the relevant institutions of which the University of Prishtina is a part. These partnerships and cooperation launch changes that almost always bring about reforms of the education system, unification, and equilibration of education systems globally (Dodds, 2015). Nevertheless, to make sure that the changes are positive, the attention of all parties involved in the cooperation must be focused on quality assurance (de Wit, 2020).

According to Adams (1998), Fiocco (2005), and Gillett (2011, p. 29), an overarching issue in corporate/university partnerships relies upon is quality. Gillett explains, "It is essential that quality is maintained while sustaining the commercial viability of the programs" (Gillett, 2011, p. 29). In other words, both the education and commercial imperatives need to have equal weight and deserve equal attention (Castejon, Chakroun, & Coles, 2011). Because of the nature and context of these collaborations, such a delicate balance may not be achieved (Kaktins, 2018).

RESEARCH METHODOLOGY

The purpose of this research was to look at the quality and relevance of the international partnerships of the University of Prishtina and the current state of research among the faculty. The research was conducted using qualitative methodology.

The data were collected through questionnaires with a group of faculty and semi-structured interviews with another group who are also involved in the leadership roles of their academic units. This research involved 30 professors from different units of the University of Prishtina. Interviews were held mainly with the management personnel of the 5 faculties/academic units.

RESEARCH QUESTIONS

This research was based on the following research questions:

RQ1. How involved is the academic staff in various international projects/programs?

RQ2. To what extent have projects/programs influenced the quality of work in teaching and scientific research?

RQ3. How have the projects/programs influenced the promotion of cooperation at local and international levels?

RQ4. In what areas have the academic units been of the greatest benefit?

RQ5. How are the projects/programs conceived by the academic staff?

RESEARCH RESULTS

The results of the study present the impact that international projects/programs have had on the professional development of teachers, enhancing the quality of teaching methodology, scientific work, collaboration, infrastructure, etc. These results show the institutional and individual benefits of those partnerships. Therefore, this is the impact of partnerships on developing research and improving the quality of education in Kosovo.

This research involved a total of 30 teachers (professor and teacher assistant). Of these, 66.7% were female and 33.3% were male. The highest percentage of respondents (46.7%) is 35–44 years old. About 33.3% belonged to the 45–54 age groups, while the rest were younger or older.

In terms of the working experience of the respondents, the majority of respondents (37.7%) have more than 30 years or more of experience. Almost the same number of respondents (30%) has 16–20 years of working experience. Between 21 and 25 years of working experience are 20% of the respondents and lowest number of respondents (13.3%) have 26–30 years of working experience.

From 13 academic units (faculties), research was answered by professors from 7 academic units: School of Education, Philology, School of Arts, Department of Medicine, School of Mathematical-Natural Sciences, School of Law, and School of Physical Education and Sport.

From the survey data, about 93.3% of the respondents stated that they were a part of various international projects/programs, while the rest did not participate for various personal reasons.

RESULTS OF THE SURVEY

The results of the survey have shown that the project that has had the greatest impact on higher education is TEMPUS. This project included collaborations with European universities, the creation of new master programs, training held by different Universities, study visits, equipping of tools and materials, organizing conferences, publications. Of the survey respondents, 63.3% stated that they were involved in the TEMPUS project, respectively, in the component of training or study visits to one of the partner universities. Respondents' answers show that 60% of them were also a part of the Erasmus + program. Another program involving teachers was the Transformation Leadership Program (T.L.P.), which is supported by the US and Kosovo Governments. From the respondents, 53.3% were a part of the training organized in Kosovo in the framework of this project, while 40% were also a part of the study visits organized in the United States under the T.L.P. A small number of respondents, 10% were also beneficiaries of the Fulbright Scholar Program, and 3.3% of them were also a part of the different project – Erasmus + program.

Respondents found their involvement in various international projects/programs to be very useful (86.7%) either for developing and enhancing the quality of the programs, teaching methodology, or even in the field of scientific research. A number of them felt that these projects brought valuable benefits (13.3%) to their professional development, to their teaching, researching, and managerial skills.

During the interview, respondents listed a large number of the benefits they received from their involvement in international projects/programs. They identified teacher professional development as a great achievement for them. Then they stimulated cooperation at the local and international levels. Enhancing the quality of the programs, advances in research, applying advanced teaching, and learning methodologies were the advantages they had gained. At the same time, respondents have been in various international projects/programs (42%).

About 90% of the respondents expressed that their participation in international projects/ programs has greatly improved the quality of their work in their academic unit. About 10% of the respondents did not feel that collaboration and partnership changed the quality of their work. About 86.7% of respondents felt that due to the involvement of academic staff in international projects/programs, there is a clear improvement in the quality of study programs within their academic units. The new experiences and models exchanged between them and colleagues from international universities provided this opportunity. Improvement of their cooperation with colleagues of the respective academic unit is very important in terms of the benefits they have had in the respective academic units. About 66.6% of respondents thought that their participation in scientific projects/programs had influenced them to reflect and open the door to new opportunities for collaboration within their academic units. About 20% of the respondents considered involvement to have had affected the establishment of cooperative relationships between the academic staff of the relevant units but to a lesser extent. The rest thought that inclusion had not helped them at all, or they had no consistent opinion about this component. Nevertheless, one thing that stood out is that the involvement of academic staff in international projects/programs has influenced the creation of excellent cooperation between faculty and the students. The majority of respondents (89%) shared this attitude.

This percentage clearly shows that any teacher involvement in international projects/programs implies a change in the teachers themselves, beginning with changing mindsets, approaches, world views, and adopting new methods of collaboration. This change can be a slow process but one of great value to the faculty and students in the long term. According to the respondents, their participation in international projects/programs helped the development of inter-institutional cooperation relationships. It has also led to the development of infrastructure within the academic units in these projects. Therefore, respondents stated that collaboration within international projects/programs has brought many positive changes in the infrastructure of their institution. The majority of respondents 74.2% think that there have been tremendous changes in infrastructure improvement, while 22.6% notice this change but to a minimal extent. According to these respondents (22.6%), the changes have been small, and they have not changed the pace of their work because they participated in international partnerships. They share the same opinion for the tools and materials that the academic unit has been able to provide through international projects/programs.

For example, the School of Education has managed to equip various laboratories (with tools and materials), create libraries for students and professors, equip contemporary literature titles, and provide computers for students. However, the largest percentages of respondents think they had an enormous benefit in the provision of tools and materials (64.6%). Some consider that there were innovations, but that they did not have so much impact (25.8%). While, 9.7% of the respondents, who participated in the international partnerships, saw their participation as not beneficial in helping them with the tools and materials they could use in their student work.

The involvement of academic staff has brought great benefits in the area of their research and publications in scientific journals. More than half of the respondents, 58.1% stated that their involvement in international projects/programs had created opportunities for new research. According to those respondents, research has been carried out in collaboration (co-authorship) with their international colleagues and published in various scientific journals. A quarter of the respondents, 25.6%, think that there have been positive but small changes. Approximately a dozen respondents (16.1%) have either a neutral stand on this issue or have failed to conduct any research in collaboration with their international colleagues.

Seeing that their involvement in international projects/programs is very lucrative, the respondents in this research stated that they are willing to not only partake as participants/beneficiaries but to also be involved in the project preparation. Most of the respondents, 98.8%, are willing to contribute to the preparation of materials for various international projects/programs.

The faculty's willingness to prepare projects/programs for them to be involved with not only as individuals but also as institutions is because of their attitudes toward institutional involvement or even personal involvement. They consider it an excellent opportunity for their professional development and an indispensable opportunity for enhancing professional performance. International networking is seen as essential for professional development as well as for enhancing the quality of study programs. Some respondents think this is the only way to advance the education system in the country. One of the interviewed professors declared: "They are the most effective mechanism for opening the horizon for the personal, professional, and institutional development of the academic (and administrative) staff involved in the university" (Interview #4).

The difference before the professors' involvement in international projects and after is clearly evident. Those changes include the professors' approach to teaching (Interview #3). Partnerships provided more experiences and those who participated adopted more contemporary teaching approaches. They are more open-minded about collaborating with students and other colleagues, therefore creating a culture of collaboration in research and publications (Interview #2).

CONCLUSIONS

The results of the research show that a considerable number of university teachers are involved in international projects/programs. All international projects/programs implemented within academic units are endorsed by the University of Prishtina through formal approval for the implementation of these projects/programs. The involvement of the University of Prishtina in international projects/programs has been influential in every academic unit involved because it has helped the University fulfill its vision and mission for students, faculty, and the scientific field.

The results of the research indicate that the changes that occurred consequently to their academic units being a part of the projects/programs were essential to their professional development. Several faculties have managed to be a part of international program exchanges and training has helped them improve their work with contemporary teaching practices. It has enabled them to reflect and change approaches to the application of teaching and learning methodologies.

In addition to facilitating their work, it has also made it easier for students to get involved and engaged in class.

Additionally, it was vital that academic units had the benefit of equipping laboratories and classrooms with various tools and materials. It has also given teachers more significant opportunities to apply contemporary teaching approaches, engaging students in various research projects, and allowing them to develop creativity during the learning process.

Another significant benefit that has emerged as a result of the involvement of professors in international projects/programs is the research conducted by the faculty of the University of Prishtina. These research projects that were carried out in inter-collegiate collaboration at local and international levels have helped professors as well as the University of Prishtina. Each research project that has been published in international journals has improved the ratings of the University on various academic platforms.

The creation and promotion of study programs in collaboration with partner Universities have also been one of the benefits considered highly crucial by University professors. It has given students new, contemporary study opportunities that have been demanded by the labor market.

The long-term stay of professors in the United States through the Fulbright Program, their involvement in research projects, and the teaching and learning process have provided beneficiaries with a completely different work system. Dealing with different cultures has provided the professors of the University of Prishtina with an experience that will directly impact their quality of teaching, learning, and contemporary research.

Finally, professors feel that their engagement in international projects/programs is essential not only for their professional development but they are also ready to contribute to the preparation of projects and their ongoing implementation.

REFERENCES

Adams, T. (1998). The operation of transnational degree and diploma programs: The Australian case. *Journal of Studies in International Education, 2*(1), 3–23.

Archer, L. (2008). Younger academics' construction of "authenticity", "success" and professional identity. *Studies in Higher Education, 33*(4), 385–401.

Association of European Border Regions. (2004, April 20). Retrieved March 13, 2020, from https://www.aebr.eu/files/publications/KoopUnivBericht15Apr04GBling.pdf

Beka, A. (2015). The Kosovo education for sustainable development's role in promoting the decade of education for sustainable development in Kosovo. *Applied Environmental Education & Communication, 14*(2), 126–131.

Bennet, A., Bennet, D., & Lewis, J. (2015). *Leading with the future in mind: Knowledge and emergent leadership.* Frost, WV: MQIPress. doi:10-0-9798459-8-X

Billot, J. (2010). The imagined and real: Identifying the tensions for academic integrity. *Higher Education Research & Development, 29*(6), 709–721.

Boekholt, P., Edler, J., Cunningham, P., & Flanagan, K. (2009). *Drivers of international collaboration in research.* Manchester: Technopolis Group.

Bologna Declaration. (1999). Retrieved from https://web.archive.org/web/20080211212119/http://www.bologna-bergen2005.no/Docs/00-Main_doc/990719BOLOGNA_DECLARATION.PDF)

Brunnhofer, M. (Ed.). (2010). *Higher education in South Eastern Europe. University economy partnerships for enhancing knowledge transfer.* WUS Austria. Retrieved from https://www.wus-austria.org/files/docs/manual5_endps.pdf

Castejon, J. C., Chakroun, B., & Coles, M. (2011). *Developing qualifications frameworks in EU partner countries: Modernising education and training*. London: Anthem Press. doi:10.7135/UPO9780857286581

Childress, L. K. (2009). Internationalization plans for higher education institutions. *Journal of Studies in International Education, 13*(3), 289–309. doi:10.1177/1028315308329804

Choi, J., & Kang, W. (2019). Sustainability of cooperative professional development: Focused on teachers' efficacy. *Sustainability, 11*(3), 585. doi:10.3390/su11030585

Coburn, C. E., Penuel, W. R., & Geil, K. E. (2013). *Research practice partnerships a strategy for leveraging research for educational improvement in school districts*. New York, NY: William T. Grant Foundation.

Cozza, B., & Blessinger, P. (2016). Pioneering approaches in university partnerships: An introduction to university partnerships for international development. In P. B. Cozza (Ed.), *University partnerships for international development (innovations in higher education teaching and learning* (Vol. 8, pp. 3–17). Bingley: Emerald Group Publishing Limited.

Darling-Hammond, L. (2017). Teacher education around the world: What can we learn from international practice? *European Journal of Teacher Education, 40*(3), 291–309. doi:10.1080/02619768.2017.1315399

de Wit, H. (2017). Global: Internationalization of higher education: Nine misconceptions. In G. Mihut, P. G. Altbach, & H. de Wit (Eds.), *Understanding Higher education internationalization. Global perspectives on higher education* (pp. 9–12). Rotterdam: Sense Publishers.

de Wit, H. (2020). Internationalization of higher education the need for a more ethical and qualitative approach. *Journal of International Students, 10*(1), i–iv. doi:10.32674/jis.v10i1.1893

de Wit, H., Rumbley, L. E., Craciun, D., Mihut, G., & Woldegiyorgis, A. (2019). *International mapping of national tertiary education internationalization strategies and plans (NTEISPs)* (CIHE Perspectives no. 12). Boston, MA: Center for International Higher Education. Retrieved from www.bc.edu/cihe

Dodds, F. (2015). *Multi-stakeholder partnerships: Making them work for the post-2015 development agenda*. New York, NY: ECOSOC, United Nations.

ECA. (2019, September 30). Retrieved from https://eca.state.gov/fulbright

Erasmus. (2019, September 6). Retrieved from http://erasmuspluskosovo.org/en/erasmus/overview-and-objectives/

Fiocco, M. (2005). *'Glonacal' contexts: Internationalisation policy in the Australian higher education sector and the development of pathway programs* (Doctoral thesis). Perth: Murdoch University.

Gillett, R. A. (2011). *Steering in the same direction? An examination of the mission and structure of the governance of providers of pathway programs* (Doctoral thesis). Perth: Edith Cowan University.

Hall, B., Tandon, R., & Tremblay, C. (Eds.). (2015). *Strengthening community university research partnerships: Global perspectives*. Victoria: University of Victoria and PRIA.

Hilliard, A. (2012). Sharing resources: Benefits of university partnerships to improve teaching learning and research. *Journal of International Education Research, 8*(1), 63–69.

Hobbs, L., & Campbell, C. (2018). Growing through partnerships. In L. Hobbs, C. Campbell, & M. Jones (Eds.), *School-based partnerships in teacher education* (pp. 139–169). Singapore: Springer.

Hsiao-Ping, W., Garza, E., & Guzman, N. (2015). International student's challenge and adjustment to college. *Education Research International, 2015*, 202753. 9 pages. doi:10.1155/2015/202753

Kaktins, L. (2018). The impact on academic staff of the collaboration between a pathway provider and its partner university: An Australian case study. *Journal of University Teaching & Learning Practice, 15*(1), 1–19.

Maltais, A., Weitz, N., & Persson, A. (2018). *SDG 17: Partnerships for the goals. A review of research needs. Technical annex to the Formas report Forskning för Agenda 2030: Översikt av forskningsbehov och vägar framåt*. Stockholm: Stockholm Environment Insitute. Retrieved from https://www.sei.org/wp-content/uploads/2020/01/sdg-17-review-of-research-needs-171219.pdf

Ministry of Education Science and Technology (MEST). (2005). Retrieved 2018, from www.masht-gov.net/advCms/documents/Strategy_EN.pdf

Ministry of Education Science and Technology (MEST). (2016, July 13). Retrieved November 26, 2018, from https://masht.rks-gov.net/uploads/2017/02/20161006-kesp-2017-2021-1.pdf

OSCE. (2008). Retrieved from https://www.uni-pr.edu/getattachment/8f855abd-07f6-4c02-8dc4-03c711429639/Research-at-the-University-of-Prishtina,-ROADMAP.aspx

Posselt, T., Abdelkafi, N., Fischer, L., & Tangour, C. (2019). Opportunities and challenges of Higher Education institutions in Europe: An analysis from a business model perspective. *Higher Education Quarterly, 73*, 100–115. doi:10.1111/hequ.12192

Rob van Tulder. (2013). *Universal access to education: A study of innovative strategies*. Rotterdam: Erasmus Research Institute of Management (ERIM).

RRPP. (2013). Retrieved 2018, from http://www.rrpp-westernbalkans.net/en.html

Šiška, J., van Swet, J., Pather, S., & Rose, D. (2013). From vision to reality: Managing tensions in the development and implementation of an international collaborative partnership programme for institutional change and sustainable development in inclusive education. *International Journal of Inclusive Education, 17*, 336–348.

Steel, K. M., Thompson, H., & Wright, W. (2018). Opportunities for intra-university collaborations in the new research environment. *Higher Education Research & Development, 38*(3), 638–652. doi:10.1080/07294360.2018.1549517

Takahara, Y. (2018, May 30). Retrieved March 30, 2020, from https://purehost.bath.ac.uk: https://researchportal.bath.ac.uk/en/studentTheses/a-management-approach-to-successful-international-partnerships-off

Tremblay, K., Lalancette, D., & Roseveare, D. (2012). *Assessment of higher education learning outcomes – Feasibility study report*. OECD. Retrieved from http://www.oecd.org/education/skills-beyond-school/AHELOFSReportVolume1.pdf

University of Bologna. (2016, May 9). Retrieved from https://site.unibo.it/almagoals/en/projects/med-up-modernizing-teacher-education-at-university-of-prishtina

University of Prishtina. (2004, July 5). Retrieved 2018, from https://www.uni-pr.edu/inc/doc/statuti1.pdf

University of Prishtina. (2016). Retrieved 2018, from https://www.uni-pr.edu/inc/doc/PLANI-STRATEGJIK2.pdf

USAID. (2019, February 6). Retrieved from https://www.usaid.gov/kosovo/fact-sheets/transformational-leadership-program-scholarships-and-partnerships

Watson, D., Hollister, R., Stroud, S. E., & Babcock, E. (2011). *The engaged university: International perspectives on civic engagement. International studies in higher education*. Florence, KY: Routledge.

Woldegiyorgis, A. A., Proctor, D., & de Wit, H. (2018). Internationalization of research: Key considerations and concerns. *Journal of Studies in International Education, 22*(2), 161–176. doi:10.1177/1028315318762804

CHAPTER 4

INTEGRATED APPROACHES FOR SUPPORTING ACADEMIC RESEARCH: MODELS THAT REVEAL THE FUTURE WHILE PROMOTING SUCCESS

Russell Carpenter, Jonathan Gore, Shirley O'Brien, Jennifer Fairchild and Matthew Winslow

ABSTRACT

Research models and practices change rapidly. While evidence of such changes includes cross-campus collaborations and multi-authored scholarship, faculty development opportunities also signal what is to come. In this case study, authors representing diverse disciplines examine what faculty development programs reveal about the future of academic research. The authors offer an analysis of faculty support programs across the country as a foundation, and then provide an examination of initiatives in place at their four-year regional comprehensive institution in the United States. The authors then report on the outcomes of these programs for research productivity, with a focus on opportunities that were available to all faculty across the university. Finally, the authors offer perspective on the future of academic research based on findings from examining these programs. The authors suggest that the future of research will focus on (1) collaborative design(s) of research-related support, (2) support structures and programs that encourage and facilitate cross-campus and interdisciplinary research collaborations and sharing, (3) incentive for integrating areas of research with teaching and service, and relatedly (4) programs that encourage faculty to span academic research with industry or community partnerships and collaborations, especially ones that can generate revenue or produce future research, development, or funding streams.

Keywords: Academic ranking of world universities; collaboration; collaborative functional teams; Eastern Kentucky University; faculty advancement; faculty development; faculty productivity; Faculty Scholars Institute; faculty support programs; faculty recognition; innovation research grants; innovative research universities; paper sprint; National Taiwan University; regional comprehensive university; research; scholarship of teaching and learning; scholarship of teaching and learning awards; teacher-scholar; University of Florida; University of Hawai'i at Manoa; University of Michigan; University of Washington; University of Waterloo

INTRODUCTION

Institutions around the world are exploring new ways of producing academic research of high quality and value for a variety of audiences. Technology, web-based tools, and social media have expanded access to academic research – including recent publications – in ways that would be difficult to imagine just years ago. Academic research models and practices are evolving, partly in response to changes in the academy and availability of funding streams (Rouse, Lombardi, & Craig, 2018).

Higher education institutions of a variety of sizes and contexts are facing myriad challenges to research productivity (Knox, 2019). Although the contexts and trajectories of colleges and universities internationally can differ significantly in meaningful ways that impact the long-term and day-to-day work of their local communities, generally the goal is to create prepared minds by educating students (Fortino, 2012). Conducting academic research is participating in the culture and process of this endeavor by remaining current in one's disciplinary field and, more broadly, about trends in higher education. For this chapter, research is considered the process of bringing new knowledge into the institution and shaping it through offering perspective on the ideas of others. The process often involves an ongoing scholarly dialogue with information flowing in and out of the institution, rather than insular or unidirectional approaches. The choice not to conduct academic research, however, can present challenges to the major tenets of higher education culture – the purpose of higher education.

Although inquiries into the future of academic research can provide valuable exercises and insights for any classification of the institution, regional comprehensive universities – those that prioritize highly effective teaching – are of particular interest for their goal(s) of balancing teaching with research. Moreover, the regional comprehensive, which requires academic publication for promotion and tenure paired with strong and rigorous teaching in the classroom along with academic mentorship of undergraduate and graduate students, is an interesting and valuable configuration to consider. The culture, while different from the contexts and situatedness of a research-focused institution where teaching loads provide pathways for and incentivize scholarly productivity, allows for a unique and valuable perspective. Participation in research is being part of a broader understanding of the field – including teaching – and contributes to confidence in the classroom and a larger "world view" of research inside and outside of disciplinary boundaries. Although the current climate of higher education is challenging across institutional contexts (Guthrie, 2019; O'Brien, n.d.; Selingo, Clark, & Noone, 2018), research and scholarship are valuable contributions to collegiality and culture, even at colleges and universities that require heavy teaching loads.

Higher education is in a time of transition, a point at which institutional missions could be under scrutiny prompting leaders – alongside faculty – to reconsider the ways in which goals can be accomplished. Aspects of central significance to higher education institutions in a variety of contexts and sizes are teaching and research in the many forms in which they are designed and implemented. Many interesting and valuable models for scholarly production exist among colleges and universities of varying types and classifications, each with different degrees of success and history. Programs that support or advance these models would benefit from further analysis and investigation so that others can adapt these initiatives for their own contexts. As a variety of institutions design and implement programs and resources to support their own campus communities while enlisting their wisdom and perspective to navigate change and, at the same time, prepare for what they consider to be the future of academic research, the timing for investigation into the future of academic research is ideal.

While many institutions have designed efforts to support faculty, the authors in this chapter anticipate a rethinking of the way(s) academic research is coordinated and designed. These approaches are becoming more inclusive of and responsive to collaborative practices. As a guidepost for this case study, the University of Michigan offers a prominent example of the changes emerging in academic research. The School of Public Health's Center for Evaluating Health Reform and Institute for Health Care Policy and Innovation's "How to Conduct Paper Sprints" outlines a compelling, productive, and, perhaps, futuristic model for producing and publishing academic research. Described as, "A more collaborative, efficient and fun way to write academic papers," the paper sprint represents, the authors argue, an important move in academic research worthy of detailed exploration, analysis, and application across a variety of institutional types, sizes, and contexts (Ryan, Kerppola, & Verhey-Henke, n.d.). This model suggests the value placed on efficiency, reliability, and replicability. That is, there are fewer questions about "how" research is conducted and published, often hidden from plain view or seen as a rite of passage for experienced or successful scholars. In this model, there is value placed on transparency, which at the authors' institution, can reduce or remove barriers while encouraging cross-disciplinary, cross-department, cross-college, or cross-institutional collaborations to emerge that preference productivity.

Higher education will need to seek new ways of designing and producing academic research. The authors in this case study take this unique moment in history to examine and analyze programs that advance academic research at their institution, which values high-quality teaching, the scholarship of teaching and learning, and community engagement.

The authors examine academic research initiatives at a four-year, public regional comprehensive university in the United States of approximately 14,000 students located in the southeast. Three programs designed to increase academic research productivity and success are introduced and analyzed: Innovation Research Grants (https://cedet.eku.edu/eku-board-regents-innovation-fund-II), Scholarship of Teaching and Learning Awards through the Noel Faculty Awards Program in the Noel Studio for Academic Creativity (https://studio.eku.edu/noel-faculty-awards-program), and the Faculty Scholars Institute (FSI, https://studio.eku.edu/faculty-scholars-institute). These three programs offer faculty resources and support in different, complementary ways. Resembling the goals of the paper sprint, however, these programs also support faculty academic research in several ways by:

- encouraging productivity via academic research projects as defined by publications and presentations,
- reducing barriers to production and publication of academic research, and
- aligning collaborations that enhance academic research processes.

As the authors argue, based on their analysis – and specific examples from this case study – the future of academic research will depend on high-functioning, accountable, collaborative research teams that thrive on clearly articulated, mapped, planned, and documented outcomes and goals, resembling the transparency and productivity of "paper sprints" (Ryan et al., n.d.). Collaborative teams will emerge as critical in the development and advancement of academic research. Future academic research will be focused on issues of large-scale value, wide applicability, and broad-based readership. The authors, in this case, offer specific examples from faculty research support programs that reveal productive practices applicable across a wide range of institutions. Specifically, the authors will provide insights into the most impactful examples, such as cross-disciplinary mentoring and collaboration that reveal the future of academic research.

Faculty work emphasizes finding ways to produce high-quality research efficiently in order to publish. In this chapter, we examine the

- types of academic research produced,
- processes for production, and
- initiatives that support academic research.

By exploring these areas in more depth, the authors offer a look at the future of academic research. To better understand faculty development programming's role in the future of research, questions the authors consider include:

- What programs incentivize academic research?
- What initiatives support academic research?
- What processes prepare academicians for the future of academic research?
- In what ways might faculty support programs suggest the future of academic research?

LITERATURE REVIEW

The future of research has been explored by a number of scholars and establishes a foundation for this case study. As Blessinger (2017) explained, "Broadly defined, research is the process of systematic inquiry" (n.p). Higher education institutions often define research for their students, faculty, and communities in line with the mission and vision statements. For Western Sydney University (n.d.), research is defined as:

> the creation of new knowledge and/or the use of existing knowledge in a new and creative way so as to generate new concepts, methodologies and understandings. This could include synthesis and analysis of previous research to the extent that it leads to new and creative outcomes. ("Definition of Research")

The University of Florida Office of Research (n.d.) offers specific definitions for Applied Research, Basic Research, and Developmental Research via a "Purpose and Project Type Definitions" statement. Texas Woman's University (n.d.), however, defines research as

> a systematic investigation designed to test hypotheses, evaluate programs, draw conclusions, or contribute to generalizable knowledge. Research is usually described in a formal protocol that sets forth objectives and a set of procedures designed to reach those objectives. ("Definition: Research")

The University of Waterloo (n.d.) offers a definition of course-based research. Of note within this definition are several points:

- While pedagogical in nature, results intend to reflect scholarly or academic traditions and customary approaches used in the discipline;
- Process used is systematic, rigorous, and intended to generate knowledge according to scholarly or academic traditions within the discipline; and
- Findings and results are typically not disseminated beyond the classroom or department but are of sufficient quality that it could be via posters, seminar presentations, articles.

Importantly, for the context of this chapter, the University of Waterloo (n.d.) acknowledges the complexity of not only the research process but also the dissemination of results, outcomes, and data. In addition, it suggests an integrated – woven into classrooms, processes, and student engagement programs – approach of expressed value to the academic institution within which it is situated. That is, there is value placed on the benefit(s) of outcomes and directly to the institution. Research is suggested to have outcomes that enhance classrooms and pedagogy. Innovative Research Universities (IRU) is a consortium of seven research universities situated across Australia. As the IRU Purpose (n.d.) statement explains:

> The IRU members' research focus is on the translation and commercialisation of research on issues of critical importance to the communities in which they are based and addressing problems of national and global scale. Over time our members have developed their own particular research strengths, with multiple areas of research at and well above world standard.

This statement suggests multiple complementary points of value when investigating the future of academic research, and closely related to the claims made in this chapter, including these threads of significance to our line of inquiry in this case study:

- Translation and commercialization of research;
- Research importance to local communities;
- Research that addresses national or global issues; and
- Complementary research strengths across academic institutions engaged in cooperation, data sharing, and continuous collaboration.

Although many definitions exist, and each institution places a different value on research, several threads emerge that span institutions: program support to align with institutional goals, programs focused on the advancement and retention of faculty, initiatives that encourage faculty resilience and grit, and opportunities for scholarship of teaching and learning as research practice.

Research Initiatives and Faculty Advancement

Many of these efforts are in place to support faculty advancement and reduce barriers to research. Klaib (2011) identified research obstacles among faculty at Zarqa University, including financial and moral support. Higher education institutions will continue to explore new, innovative approaches for supporting faculty research, which can present major challenges across institutional contexts, including placing research in highly competitive publication venues (Johnson, Wagner, & Reusch, 2016).

Related support initiatives promote currency and rigor. Higher education institutions will continue to provide programs to support research in a variety of forms, especially as they place more emphasis on scholarly production by, for example, asking faculty and administrative units to report the number of books, chapters, articles, and other research published. Some higher education institutions have put into place assessment metrics (Altbach, 2015) focused on the quantity of research published, while others compile this material for internal annual reports. In some cases, this information is used as an attempt to raise the research profile of the institution, especially by way of national (or international) ranking or institutional classification. These metrics can be valuable for numerous reasons, including not only institutional profile but also access to external grants, faculty recruitment, and future research funding. A prominent example of such a ranking system is the Performance Ranking of Scientific Papers for World Universities (also known as the NTU Ranking), published and released by National Taiwan University and provides rankings by six fields (Agriculture, Engineering, Life Sciences, Medicine, Natural Sciences, and Social Sciences). "This ranking system is designed to evaluate research universities' achievements in scientific research by using objective indicators" (NTU Ranking, n.d.). More specifically,

> This ranking system evaluates the performance of scientific papers, and the indicators are designed to compare both the quality and the quantity of scientific papers in each university. Through examining long-term performance and short-term research efforts, we look forward to providing a more objective ranking as a reference for diverse research performance in universities worldwide. (NTU Ranking, n.d.)

Many institutions recognize and celebrate this ranking through various forms of institutional media and publicity. For example, the University of Washington, located in Seattle in the United States, issued a release via university channels noting its performance in the 2019 NTU rankings (UW Medicine, n.d.), while the University of Hawai'i at Manoa published a similar release (University of Hawai'i at Manoa, n.d.). In addition, the Academic Ranking of World Universities (ARWU, n.d.)

> includes every institution that has any Nobel Laureates, Fields Medals, and Highly-Cited Researchers. In addition, major universities of every country with significant amount of articles indexed by Science Citation Index-Expanded (SCIE) and Social Science Citation Index (SSCI) are also included. (ARWU)

Transformational Research

Taylor (2013) suggested that research can be transformative for meaning-centered education, recognizing that it is culturally situated. While Taylor searched for teaching moments in research development among graduate students, other scholars have examined strategies for managing the challenges associated with research. The process of advancing research through publication can be challenging and even productive scholars need support. Turner, Brown, and Edwards-Jones (2014) examined some of the challenges associated with academic publication, with persistence being among them. Berk (2018) defined grit within the context of faculty development, acknowledging the multitude of challenges faced by the modern faculty researcher. In addition, Berk provided a sampling of grit studies while also examining results that predict lifelong success. In a two-part series, though, Stivers and Cramer (2017a, 2017b) coach faculty through the process and strategies for moving on from painful rejections in the publication process.

Teacher-scholar

Scholars have recast the idea of the teaching scholar as being more integrated than previously conceived or clearly delineated roles as teachers or researchers. Kuh, Chen, and Laird (2007) coined the term "teacher-scholar" as those who are

> committed to high-quality undergraduate education, pursue an active program of research and scholarship, and are presumed to enliven and enrich their teaching and the student experience by incorporating insights from their own research into their instructional activities, student advising, and related work. (n.p.)

The authors ask several questions regarding the teacher-scholar, but most importantly,

> [a]t institutions where faculty members report participating in activities characteristic of the teacher-scholar model, are students more engaged overall, do they more frequently work with faculty members on research, and are they more involved in educationally purposeful activities?

Finally, the authors found that,

> for students to get involved in research, the faculty members on a campus must make a conscious effort to involve undergraduates in their research activities and believe that such involvement is important. They also must take the time to work with undergraduates directly and emphasize deep approaches to learning in the classroom. (n.p.)

This move was important in its time but is now over a decade old. The integration of teacher-scholar roles, though, is critical for understanding the future of academic research. Kuh et al. (2007) were not alone, of course, in taking interest in the research lens of scholarship of teaching and learning (SoTL). Numerous scholars have examined the place of SoTL within the national landscape of research and scholarship and valuation in the promotion and tenure process (Marcketti & Freeman, 2016; Simmons, 2016).

Similarly, researchers have explored strategies for supporting the scholarship of teaching and learning (SoTL) specifically (Myatt, Gannaway, Chia, Fraser, & McDonald, 2018; Peters, Schodt, & Walczak, 2008), including conceptual frameworks applicable across institutional contexts. One of the approaches for supporting and advancing scholarship is grants (Morris & Fry, 2006); however, numerous models have proved successful in supporting research more broadly (Gayle, Randall, Langley, & Preiss, 2013), while commonly supported through faculty development programs (Kalish & Stockley, 2009; Skarupski & Foucher, 2018). Kalish and Stockley (2009), for example, examined two movements: SoTL and Faculty Learning Communities, specifically the ways in which the Carnegie Academy for the Scholarship of Teaching and Learning (CASTL) facilitated and cultivated SoTL. The authors offered an example of the ways in which a multi-institution faculty learning community defined and contextualized SoTL via ongoing planning and collaboration. Skarupski and Foucher (2018) coined the concept of writing accountability groups (WAGs) as an approach for faculty with ambitions of scholarly productivity. The authors outline the process of designing and implementing WAGs at their own institutions. Research support – especially in the form of publication – has yielded valuable scholarship recently, practical and applicable approaches for scholars at a variety of stages in their careers. To this end, writing support via faculty development programs have also offered scholars needed resources for advancement (Brantmeier, Molloy, & Byrne, 2017; Gray, Madson, & Jackson, 2018; Sweet, Blythe, Carpenter, & Phillips, 2017; Weaver, Robbie, & Radloff, 2013), which includes individualized mentor programs (Hubball, Clarke, & Poole, 2010) and professional learning communities (PLCs) (Sweet, Blythe, O'Brien, & Carpenter, 2019). Sweet et al. (2019) examined a SoTL PLC that provided the resources and support for faculty to plan and design scholarly publications. The authors survey PLC participants and argue that the experience was transformational in its productivity.

Faculty Recognition and Productivity

In addition to programming, faculty recognition of scholarly accomplishments is well documented. Cruz, Ellern, Ford, Moss, and White (2009) offered a case study of SoTL efforts – including recognition and rewards – at a regional comprehensive university, Western Carolina University. The authors organized the study by examining sample promotion and tenure documents. As part of the study, the authors examine load balance, scholarly outlets, peer review, SoTL vs scholarly teaching, and SoTL valuation in promotion and tenure documents. At Willingham-McLain's (2015) institution, the incentive program rewards faculty for innovations in the scholarship of teaching and learning.

A recent emphasis on collaboration also highlights new opportunities for research productivity. Initiatives and resources such as the paper sprint (Ryan et al., n.d.) have the potential to transform the approaches researchers use to advance scholarly agendas, noting the potential for efficiency. Serving as a notable example, Ryan et al. designed this process to support faculty interested in coordinating effective team-based collaborations focused on scholarly productivity (emphasizing publication). The guide takes readers through a multi-step approach from beginning to end. This approach could inspire cultural changes across teaching and research institutions alike as faculty explore approaches for designing, implementing, and publishing research. It is also a futuristic approach, as it values efficiency and distributed effort that aligns, primarily through the emphasis on collaboration with that of Weaver, Robbie, Kokonis, and Miceli (2012). Similarly, Ryan and Ellimoottil (n.d.) designed an insider's guide for writing and publishing manuscripts. This guide reveals how accomplished scholars have structured manuscripts while also providing practical examples of use to a variety of writers and researchers. Similarly, other scholars have offered advice to researchers (see Gibbs, 2016; Schrager & Sadowski, 2016). Schrager and Sadowski (2016), however, offered strategies focused on increasing scholarly productivity of use for all scholars. Noteworthy among these strategies is "the art of using day-to-day work as scholarship" (see Table 6). The authors provide readers with suggestions for time management to allow for scholarly productivity, including strategies for approaching non-priority tasks (such as email). Strategies and supports have become more prevalent at higher education institutions, providing a worthwhile platform for further analysis.

DESCRIPTION OF WORK GROUPS

Research support opportunities are offered in a variety of forms and take on a different look from institution to institution. They are often designed to meet the priorities of faculty based, in some cases, on input or evidence of need. In other cases, programs, often indicative of priorities for research and related areas such as teaching, are intended to support practices deemed productive.

In this case study, the authors examine the results of faculty work groups formed through campus-wide initiatives designed to foster and promote research and related activities among faculty based on several criteria, including eligibility for all faculty members at the institution regardless of discipline; promotion of research or related academic activity; and inclusive of faculty across traditional ranks (assistant, associate, and full professor). The initiatives analyzed for this case study support research across the institution and include Innovation Research Grants, FSI, and Faculty Innovation Awards.

Innovation Research Grants

Description
Recognizing that Kentucky has urgent and formidable societal and economic challenges that have persisted for generations, Eastern Kentucky University

(EKU) is positioned to play an important role for the economic, intellectual, and cultural vitality of our service region, the commonwealth, and our global society. This natural purpose creates and maintains dynamic programs, provides the building blocks for the inventors of the future, and aspires to translate ideas and talents into new products, services, robust employment, and societal advancement for all. At the June 2018 Board of Regents meeting, the Board formally approved a $250,000 faculty and staff innovation pool that advocates, encourages, and incentivizes new innovations that can be executed. Innovation Research Grants are offered by EKU's Office of Sponsored Programs, while the Faculty Innovation Awards are offered through the Office of Research and administered through the Board of Regents.

The fund is available to all EKU faculty and staff (including collaborations between faculty and staff), competitively awarded and a strong preference given to applications that demonstrate an innovative or entrepreneurial solution that

1. demonstrates an ability to generate a return on investment within a reasonable period of time,
2. demonstrates an ability to create operating efficiency resulting in cost savings, and
3. is related to Kentucky priorities.

These funds can be used for larger matching grants, like Small Business Innovation Research (SBIR) program; research that has demonstrable commercial value, scale, and stability; research and development related to Kentucky priorities (Board of Regents, n.d.; Table 1).

Faculty Scholars Institute (FSI)

Description
Offered once per year, at the end of each spring semester, the FSI helps faculty build momentum on summer research projects (Table 2).

Expected outcomes of the FSI include

Table 1. Innovation Research Grants.

Classification	Campus Grant
Information	https://regents.eku.edu/insidelook/faculty-innovation-awards

Table 2. Faculty Scholars Institute.

Classification	Research Support Program
Information	https://studio.eku.edu/faculty-scholars-institute

- strengthened skills applicable in the production of scholarship;
- increased knowledge of cultural competency approaches applicable across a wide range of scholarly endeavors;
- enhanced knowledge of approaches to producing, managing, submitting and enhancing scholarly projects;
- improved skills for those pursuing scholarship and preparing for the promotion and tenure process;
- enhanced ability to identify meaningful scholarly projects as well as their potential structures; and
- development of writing skills necessary for producing high-quality scholarship.

Faculty Awards

Description

Faculty awards provide incentive for areas of priority for the university focused on innovative scholarship of teaching and learning. These awards provide university-wide recognition for faculty recipients and allow for cross-sharing of research methodologies, approaches, and results across colleges and departments throughout the year using the following criteria (Noel Studio for Academic Creativity, n.d.; Tables 3–5).

Table 3. Annual Faculty Awards.

Classification	Annual awards given to incentivize academic innovation among faculty from across disciplines
Information	https://studio.eku.edu/annual-faculty-awards

Table 4. 2017–2018 Awards and Departmental Representation.

Award	Department of Recipient
High-Impact Practice Teaching Award	Management
High-Impact Practice Teaching Award	Criminal Justice
Faculty Innovation in Teaching Award	Psychology
Faculty Innovation in Teaching Award	Agriculture
Faculty Scholarship of Teaching and Learning Award	English
Faculty Leadership Award	Spanish

Table 5. 2018–2019 Awards and Departmental Representation.

Award	Department of Recipient
High-Impact Practice Teaching Award	Homeland Security
High-Impact Practice Teaching Award	Government
Faculty Innovation in Teaching Award	Justice Studies
Faculty Innovation in Teaching Award	History
Faculty Scholarship of Teaching and Learning Award	Curriculum & Instruction
Faculty Leadership Award	Psychology
Inclusive Excellence Faculty Award	Curriculum & Instruction

High-Impact Practice Teaching Award (two awards given each year)

- The overall quality of the impact
- The effectiveness on learning and/or impact on student success
- The ability to facilitate learning outside the classroom
- The ability to enable meaningful interactions between faculty and students
- The ability to encourage collaboration

Faculty Innovation in Teaching Award (two awards given each year)

- The overall quality of the innovation
- The effectiveness on learning and/or impact on student success
- The creativity or novelty of the innovation
- The currency of the innovation, or to what degree the innovation can be determined to be cutting edge

Faculty Leadership Award (one award given each year)

- The overall impact of the leadership at the University
- Quality and insight into the leadership philosophy

Inclusive Excellence Faculty Award (two awards given each year)

- Evidence of exemplary culturally responsive instructional practices (e.g., assignments, tools, resources used in the classroom, and/or syllabi modifications); and
- Student evaluations which measure motivation and engagement

Faculty Scholarship of Teaching and Learning (SoTL) Award (one award given each year)

- Systematic investigation regarding teaching, student learning and instructional conditions which promote learning, or similar pedagogic research; and
- Dissemination by published peer-reviewed scholarly work that leads to new knowledge in teaching and learning.
- Strategies for new or innovative methods for determining the impact of teaching practices on student learning and/or knowledge retention.
- Incorporation of student voices, from a culturally relevant perspective within design, collaboration, and dissemination in scholarship.
- Adapting or enhancing SoTL strategies from the literature to further enhance student learning and/or knowledge retention.

Overview of Award Recipients

Several threads emerged when examining the work groups from these programs, which promote partnership and collaboration, defined in many ways, and are outcome driven. In addition to forging new partnerships or collaborations, researchers who received the awards are expected to produce and disseminate research outcomes.

Integrated Approaches for Supporting Academic Research

Outcomes of Work Groups

Outcomes of the work groups were analyzed using the metrics in Table 6, which tracks and describes the different stages of academic research. The column on the left documents the stage of the scholarly process, while the column on the right indicates the tasks that this stage includes.

Table 6 offers a transferable tracking process while also allowing for an exploration of ways in which research is developed and distributed. Examining the stages can allow for a better understanding of ways in which faculty development programs might suggest the future of academic research.

Table 6. Stages of Scholarship.

Stage	Tasks Include
1. Development and Planning	• Familiarizing yourself with the topic • Reading, summarizing, evaluating past work • Determining what still needs to be done • Creating/identifying data collection materials • Recruiting a research team • Securing funding • Obtaining IRB approval
2. Information Gathering, Coding, and Entry	• Developing coding and scoring system • Training research assistants for collection, coding, entry • Gathering data from participants • Gaining access to equipment • Obtaining samples • Traveling to collection sites
3. Information Analysis	• Identifying analysis strategy • Training on analysis technique • Cleaning, managing the data • Conduct analyses/evaluation of gathered information • Presentation plan for results (tables, figures, etc.)
4. Writing and Revising	• Develop writing schedule • Pre-writing/outline • Delegating writing responsibilities to team • Writing assigned portion of manuscript • Reviewing own and others' portions of manuscript • Revising assigned portion of manuscript
5. Submission and Proofs	• Identifying publication outlet options • Tailoring paper's rationale/implications to outlet • Final review of paper before submission • Submitting paper to outlet • Organizing reviewer comments • Delegating revision responsibilities to team • Revising based on reviewer comments • Developing response letter • Resubmitting to outlet/Submit to new outlet • Reviewing and submitting proofs
6. Dissemination	• Identifying and submitting to professional conference opportunities • Identifying and pursuing social media outlets • Identifying and pursuing radio and television outlets • Identifying and pursuing speaking engagements • Writing and submitting a press release

RESULTS

Overall, career longevity/career age is a factor in understanding and accessing the six stages of scholarly inquiry. A 46% return rate was received of the faculty surveyed from the three types of awards at the institution. Overall, faculty understood the steps of Developing and Planning, Information Gathering, and Coding Data. Faculty commented on engaging in several projects at the same time, with funding identified as a challenge. Interestingly, new faculty were still establishing relationships for collaboration, and often continued to work independently, which is not an efficient strategy. Two of the five funded Innovation Research Grants involved teams, working toward the desired outcome as collaborators. Information Analysis is a step where 66% of non-tenured, tenure track faculty in the Faculty Scholars Group reported the need for support, stating "this is my sticking point." Delegation was a task in the Writing and Revising area, where experienced faculty understood the importance (72% of those receiving Annual Awards for Teaching/Leadership and 100% of those receiving campus incentive grants). Submission and Proofs and Dissemination were clearly understood by all surveyed. Dissemination, however, continues to take the shape of traditional measures (e.g., articles, books, presentations, etc.). One faculty member commented on scholarship as a non-linear process, which reinforces the complementary nature of collaboration and engagement across units.

IMPLICATIONS

The results from our brief survey suggested that generating ideas is in no short supply, but faculty may experience considerable challenges as they progress through the research process. The two most commonly identified challenges in the survey were (a) funding for the project and (b) information analysis. Although more funding and more training might appear to be the solution, more integrated collaboration across disciplines may also help resolve these challenges. These may include a university-wide resource list that includes funding sources, personnel, equipment, software, and experts (esp., data analysis) that could be shared and integrated across multiple research programs to offset the needs for any given project. To foster accountability, each contributor should be assigned a particular task and function, and in turn, be held responsible for implementing that task. Although this integrative process may divide resources in too many directions, it could also foster more interdisciplinary work to tackle broader and larger issues.

Another way to offset costs for personnel would be to incorporate research tasks in the classroom and delegate to students through mentorships for course credit. By training students to become researchers through scaffolded teaching strategies, research projects could be analyzed through class-wide exercises, and promising students could be offered collaborative roles in publications and future projects. This would also encourage a more ingrained process for developing teacher-scholars (Kuh et al., 2007) at the institution.

Some additional recommendations include (1) fostering collaborative design(s) of research-related support, (2) creating support structures and programs that encourage and facilitate cross-campus and interdisciplinary research collaborations and sharing (such as WAGs or Boot Camps), (3) creating formalized incentives (e.g., promotion and tenure standards) for productively integrating areas of research with teaching and service, and relatedly (4) encouraging research programs that merge with industry or community partnerships and collaborations, especially ones that can be productively revenue generating or can produce future research, development, or innovation funding streams. Institutions can use communications or public relations outlets to assist and promote faculty scholarly contributions in social media or other news outlets, which will broaden an understanding of scholarly contributions within the public domain and local communities.

FURTHER RESEARCH

A recent study examined plausible research futures (Elsevier & Ipsos MORI, 2019). The report found three possibilities: Brave Open World, Tech Titans, and Eastern Ascendance. These findings are especially interesting and relevant for the perspectives offered in this chapter. In a climate where higher education institutions are often in search of new sources of funding, state funders and philanthropic organizations will become more integral to supporting academic research. In addition, research will be accessible in modular forms (or "bite-sized publications" and "dynamic notebook-style articles") available via open-access venues (p. 11). Technology will also play a more prominent role in the future of research, with artificial intelligence being employed in phases of the publication process (p. 17). While some of these future trajectories could be on the distant horizon, much remains to be learned.

Whitney (2018) organized future trends into three areas: Business of Research, Researchers, and IT. For this study, "representatives from 60 of the top North American research institutions shared their predictions for the future of research" (Whitney, 2018). To summarize, this study suggests that future research funding will come from the private sector and areas other than the federal government. In addition, technologies will continue to change the ways higher education institutions will manage research and data, with more being situated within the cloud. Also of interest, future research will be generated by interdisciplinary teams. Converging interests in technology, along with industry collaboration, will also necessitate further inquiry moving forward as Renault (2006) suggested.

As these studies suggest, the future of research will continue to be an important topic of conversation for academicians – and researchers – in the years to come. As higher education institutions continue to change, evolve, and adapt, research will respond to both needs and opportunities.

For the purposes of this chapter, the authors focus on four areas of future research. These broad areas can be explored by scholars at a variety of institutions across international contexts:

1. Examining research requirements from institutions of multiple types, goals, and levels;
2. Designing cross-institutional studies involving research support intended to increase faculty productivity;
3. Exploring large-scale faculty productivity practices; and
4. Exploring the role of open access in research production and productivity.

Higher education institutions will continue to quantify outcomes in terms of research productivity, impact, and selection rate. However, other metrics will become valuable to track as well, including the number of collaborators, number of collaborators from different institutions (perhaps of varying sizes and contexts), and academe-industry partnerships. Within the context of academe-industry partnerships, however, profits for businesses based on research productivity will be of interest and, perhaps, shape future collaborations that span these sides. The question of when you know your research has "arrived," though, could become more complex. Historically, it might mean publishing in a high-tier journal or securing high-dollar grants to support your research. In the future, stakeholders will have different definitions of success. Participating in the scholarly conversation could mean situating ideas, theories, practices, or data within the context of local, regional, national, or international business. Thus, research protocol, goals, and outcomes will be negotiated across multiple stakeholders spanning ranges of experiences and expectations. Moving forward, though, this will mean opportunities for innovation and new practices to emerge.

Participating in scholarly conversations moving forward will look different for researchers in the future. More data will be available via open-access sources, creating new opportunities for accessing – and contributing to – research. Higher education institutions will continue to develop and adapt support models to ensure that faculty are situated to contribute to these venues as well, although these supports will become more integrated and networked as faculty continue to communicate, share results, and make processes more transparent. New opportunities to reassess the difference between partnership and collaboration will also emerge, and researchers will have the opportunity to establish the parameters of these emerging designs. Furthermore, corporate entities and the private sector will become more invested or involved in research support programs, practices, and outcomes.

RECOMMENDATIONS

The results are transferable across higher education institutions in a variety of contexts and for a variety of goals. Here we offer considerations for adapting and implementing these approaches.

1. The stages of research in Table 6 can be adapted to fit institutional contexts. Each stage is an opportunity for support and development. In addition, it is also an opportunity to determine how – or to what extent – the research process is progressing. All too often, research is seen as holistic – just the resulting publication – while overlooking the stages or phases of the process. Each phase of research needs to be understood in ways that are meaningful and replicable. At each stage, progress toward the goal in that stage or objective allows researchers to track – and reflect on – their progress and outcomes.
2. The stages available in Table 6 also offer guidance for researchers to provide unique scholarly contributions at every level, while also avoiding unproductive situations, strategies, or relationships.
3. Support structures can be implemented at each stage and faculty provided with the incentive to track the stages carefully in their own processes. This process can enable preparation for the future of research among all researchers.
4. Programming can be intentionally designed to promote cross-disciplinary investigations. Collaborative functional teams can be formed through research-related programs and initiatives. Support systems can help institutions create highly productive research collaboratives wherein research processes are tracked transparently and that other researchers or research teams can benefit from learning best practices. Thus, fewer barriers exist among researchers or research teams.

Envisioning the future of research – via related support programs – opens up opportunities to examine – or reexamine – processes and practices. The future will be determined by decisions and processes designed and created now.

Programs that are designed with cross-campus collaboration, technology, and cloud-based software(s) stand to prepare researchers for future practices. These programs can intentionally establish criteria for success and share – via multiple channels – the processes that have proven successful. Any necessary structures can be built on needs, interests, and goals of researchers while reducing barriers to research success.

Five key themes for the future of research emerge:

1. The future will align skills and strengths with resources.
2. Funding increasingly will come from outside of the institution and from local, regional, or national partners.
3. Partnership outside of the institution will propel research in new ways.
4. Venues for sharing and distributing research will become more modular with component pieces of research becoming available via technologically rich and sophisticated channels that are freely available.
5. Data and results will be available rapidly by researchers and research teams around the world while, as the University of Michigan Department of Surgery's slogan states, collaboration will become the new competition.

As Lee (2011) and Kyvik and Reymert (2017) argued, approaches for aligning support with possibilities of the future of research will present new ways of working across or among areas of the institution and, in some cases, industry. For example, collaborative partnerships can be designed based on research, skills, and record of success. The value of contributions will be in their merit, weight, or transferability in (1) solving problems, (2) creating efficiencies, and (3) innovating practices. The future of research – with these developments – will move much more rapidly than research has in the past as the concept of publication continues to transform toward more accessible and applicable outcomes.

CONCLUSION

A major predictor of the future of research is the way in which faculty development and support opportunities are designed and configured to be responsive to the needs, expectations, challenges, and working patterns of researchers. The collaborative, cross-campus configurations of the support programs examined in this chapter, complemented by a review of recent literature in areas such as faculty development, suggests several key takeaways regarding the future of research. The future of research involves:

- Integration of programs and opportunities that unite faculty for the advancement of research;
- The thoughtful design of incentive structures and programs that integrate research with teaching and other central activities of the higher education institution;
- The design of programs that span academe-industry or community partnerships; and
- Open-access and freely available research via cloud or web-based sources, even social media.

Research will be supported through programs designed to facilitate cross-campus collaboration, to showcase (and share) important discoveries and data, and encourage further conversation and analysis beyond the traditional publication. Furthermore, future research will be shared in smaller, more portable or transferable forms, even outside of venues such as peer-reviewed journals. Results will be available in accessible forms, even visual forms shared in mass. The collaborative culture will continue to drive research support and processes, while also shaping the venues in which it is distributed.

REFERENCES

Academic Ranking of World Universities. (n.d.). *ARWU field methodology*. Retrieved from http://www.shanghairanking.com/ARWU-FIELD-Methodology-2011.html

Altbach, P. C. (2015). What counts for academic productivity in research universities? *International Higher Education, 79*, 6–7.

Berk, R. (2018). Grit 2.0: A review with strategies to deal with disappointment, rejection, and failure. *Journal of Faculty Development, 32*(3), 91–104.

Blessinger, P. (2017, June 11). *Transforming learning through student research*. [Blog post]. Retrieved from http://www.patrickblessinger.com/transforming-learning-through-student-research/

Board of Regents. (n.d.). *Faculty innovation awards.* Board of Regents. Retrieved from https://regents.eku.edu/insidelook/faculty-innovation-awards

Brantmeier, E., Molloy, C., & Byrne, J. (2017). Writing renewal retreats: The scholarly writer, contemplative practice, and scholarly productivity. *To Improve the Academy, 36,* 137–155. doi:10.1002/tia2.20061

Cruz, L., Ellern, J., Ford, G., Moss, H., & White, B. J. (2009). Recognition and reward: SoTL and the tenure process at a regional comprehensive university. *Mountain Rise, 5*(3). Retrieved from https://www.viu.ca/sites/default/files/recognitionandreward.pdf

Elsevier & Ipsos MORI. (2019). *Research futures: Drivers and scenarios for the next decade.* Elsevier. Retrieved from https://www.elsevier.com/__data/assets/pdf_file/0007/847960/Research-Futures_Summary.pdf

Fortino, A. (2012). The purpose of higher education: To create prepared minds. *The EvolLution: A Destiny Solutions Illumination.* Retrieved from https://evollution.com/opinions/the-purpose-of-higher-education-to-create-prepared-minds/

Gayle, B. M., Randall, N., Langley, L., & Preiss, R. (2013). Faculty learning processes: A model for moving from scholarly teaching to the scholarship of teaching and learning. *Teaching and Learning Inquiry: The ISSOTL Journal, 1*(1), 81–93.

Gibbs, A. (2016). Improving publication: Advice for busy higher education academics. *International Journal for Academic Development, 3,* 255–258. doi.org/10.1080/1360144X.2015.1128436

Gray, T., Madson, L., & Jackson, M. (2018). Publish & flourish: Helping scholars become better, more prolific writers. *To Improve the Academy, 37,* 243–256. doi:10.1002/tia2.20081

Guthrie, K. M. (2019). *Challenges to higher education's most essential purposes.* ITHAKA S+R. Retrieved from https://sr.ithaka.org/publications/challenges-to-higher-educations-most-essential-purposes/. https://doi.org/10.18665/sr.311221

Hubball, H., Clarke, A., & Poole, G. (2010). Ten-year reflections on mentoring SoTL research in a research-intensive university. *International Journal for Academic Development, 2,* 117–129. doi.org/10.1080/13601441003737758

Innovative Research Universities. (n.d.). *IRU Purpose. About.* Retrieved from https://www.iru.edu.au/about/purpose/

Johnson, M. R., Wagner, N. J., & Reusch, J. (2016). Publication trends in top-tier journals in higher education. *Journal of Applied Research in Higher Education, 8*(4), 439–454. https://doi.org/10.1108/JARHE-01-2015-0003

Kalish, A., & Stockley, D. (2009). Building scholarly communities: Supporting the scholarship of teaching and learning with learning communities. *Transformative Dialogues: Teaching & Learning Journal, 3*(1), F1A–F13A.

Klaib, F. J. (2011). Trends among Zarqa University faculty members regarding research obstacles and the ways of overcoming them according to their points of view. *Journal of Applied Research in Higher Education, 3*(1), 61–76. doi.org/10.1108/17581181111150919

Knox, L. (2019, June 18). 'These cuts have real consequences': A new study surveys the damage of state disinvestment in public universities. *Chronicle of Higher Education.* Retrieved from https://www.chronicle.com/article/These-Cuts-Have-Real/246516?key=bweE60uWq0JcB8LxAhRzLgBTfkMgOv3bmErYc6dG9_8o-YfY7ooCXr5fr8ZhoIsTTUdyU1RYZTJQbUVxY3dEX1p0WVp0NFloeHVaUEFQY3BGQlQtc1A2M2phaw

Kuh, G. D., Chen, D., & Laird, T. F. N. (2007). Why teacher-scholars matter: Some insights from FSSE and NSSE. *Liberal Education, 93*(4), 40–45. Retrieved from https://www.aacu.org/publications-research/periodicals/why-teacher-scholars-matter-some-insights-fsse-and-nsse

Kyvik, S., & Reymert, I. (2017). Research collaboration in groups and networks: Differences across academic fields. *Scientometrics, 113*(2), 951–967. doi.org/10.1007/s11192-017-2497-5

Lee, Y. S. (2011). The sustainability of university-industry research collaboration: An empirical assessment. *The Journal of Technology Transfer, 25,* 111–133. https://doi.org/10.1023/A:1007895322042

Marcketti, S. B., & Freeman, S. A. (2016). SoTL evidence on promotion and tenure vitas at a research university. *Journal of the Scholarship of Teaching and Learning, 16*(5), 19–31. doi:10.14434/josotl.v16i5.21152

Morris, C., & Fry, H. (2006). Enhancing educational research and development activity through small grant schemes: A case study. *International Journal for Academic Development, 1,* 43–56. doi.org/10.1080/13601440600579001

Myatt, P., Gannaway, D., Chia, I., Fraser, K., & McDonald, J. (2018). Reflecting on institutional support for SoTL engagement: Developing a conceptual framework. *International Journal for Academic Development, 2*, 147–160. doi.org/10.1080/1360144X.2017.1346511

Noel Studio for Academic Creativity. (n.d.). *Noel faculty awards program*. Retrieved from https://studio.eku.edu/noel-faculty-awards-program

NTU Ranking. (n.d.). *Introduction*. NTU Ranking: Performance Ranking of Scientific Papers for World Universities. Retrieved from http://nturanking.lis.ntu.edu.tw/about/introduction

O'Brien, C. (n.d.). *10 challenges facing UK higher education in 2019*. Digital Marketing Institute. Retrieved from https://digitalmarketinginstitute.com/en-us/blog/10-challenges-facing-uk-higher-education-in-2019

Peters, D., Schodt, D., & Walczak, M. (2008). Supporting the scholarship of teaching and learning at liberal arts colleges. *To Improve the Academy, 26*, 39–52. doi.org/10.1002/j.2334-4822.2008.tb00501.x

Renault, C. S. (2006). Academic capitalism and university incentives for faculty entrepreneurship. *The Journal of Technology Transfer, 31*, 227–239. https://doi.org/10.1007/s10961-005-6108-x

Rouse, W. B., Lombardi, J. V., & Craig, D. D. (2018). Modeling research universities: Predicting probable futures of public vs. private and large vs. small research universities. *Proceedings of the National Academy of Sciences of the United States of America, 115*(50), 12582–12589. doi:10.1073/pnas.1807174115

Ryan, A., & Ellimoottil, C. (n.d.). *The ultimate guide to writing manuscripts*. Retrieved from file:///Users/carpenterru/Downloads/Manuscript_Manual.pdf

Ryan, A., Kerppola, M., & Verhey-Henke, A. (n.d.). *How to conduct paper sprints*. Retrieved from file:///Users/deployeduser/Downloads/Paper_Sprint_Manual%20(3).pdf

Schrager, S., & Sadowski, E. (2016). Getting more done: Strategies to increase scholarly productivity. *Journal of Graduate Medical Education, 8*(1), 10–13. https://www.ncbi.nlm.nih.gov/pmc/articles/PMC4763375/. doi:10.4300/JGME-D-15-00165.1

Selingo, J. J., Clark, C., & Noone, D. (2018, July 19). *The futures of public higher education: How state universities can survive – and thrive – in a new era*. Retrieved from https://www2.deloitte.com/content/dam/insights/us/articles/4726_future-of-higher-education/DI_Future-of-public-higher-ed.pdf

Simmons, N. (2016). Synthesizing SoTL institutional initiatives toward national impact. *New Directions for Teaching and Learning, 146*, 95–102. doi.org/10.1002/tl.20192

Skarupski, K., & Foucher, K. C. (2018). Writing accountability groups (WAGs): A tool to help junior faculty members build sustainable writing habits. *Journal of Faculty Development, 32*(3), 47–54.

Stivers, J., & Cramer, S. F. (2017a). From rejected to accepted: Part 1 – Preparing a rejected manuscript for a new journal. *Journal of Faculty Development, 31*(1), 57–59.

Stivers, J., & Cramer, S. F. (2017b). From rejected to accepted: Part 2 – Preparing a rejected manuscript for a new journal. *Journal of Faculty Development, 31*(2), 63–65.

Sweet, C., Blythe, H., Carpenter, R., & Phillips, B. (2017). *Scaling the scholarship mountain: Achieving scholarly productivity*. Stillwater, OK: New Forums Press.

Sweet, C., Blythe, H., O'Brien, S., & Carpenter, R. (2019). A new goal for professional development: A case study of how a professional learning community produced transformative faculty learning. *Learning Communities Journal, 11*, 55–73.

Taylor, P. C. (2013). Research as transformative learning for meaning-centered professional development. In O. Kovbasyuk & P. Blessinger (Eds.), *Meaning-centered education: International perspectives and explorations in higher education* (pp. 168–185). New York, NY: Routledge.

Texas Woman's University. (n.d.). *Definition: Research*. Retrieved from https://twu.edu/research/definitions/definition-research/

Turner, R., Brown, T., & Edwards-Jones, A. (2014). Writing my first academic article feels like dancing around naked: Research development for higher education lecturers working in further education colleges. *International Journal for Academic Development, 2*, 87–98. doi.org/10.1080/1360144X.2013.792729

University of Florida Office of Research. (n.d.). *Purpose and project type definitions*. UF Research. Retrieved from http://research.ufl.edu/dsp/proposals/definition-of-research-instruction-and-other-sponsored-activities.html

University of Hawai'i at Manoa. (n.d.) *UH Ranked among top universities for excellence in scientific publications*. School of Ocean and Earth Science and Technology. Retrieved from https://www.soest.hawaii.edu/soestwp/announce/press-releases/uh-ranked-among-top-universities-for-excellence-in-scientific-publications-3/

University of Waterloo. (n.d.). *Definition of course-based research*. Research. Retrieved from https://uwaterloo.ca/research/office-research-ethics/research-human-participants/pre-submission-and-training/human-research-guidelines-and-policies-alphabetical-list/definition-course-based-research-0

UW Medicine. (n.d.). *UW Medicine, and UW overall, score highly in NTU rankings*. UW Medicine | Newsroom. Retrieved from https://newsroom.uw.edu/postscript/uw-medicine-and-uw-overall-score-highly-ntu-rankings

Weaver, D., Robbie, D., Kokonis, S., & Miceli, L. (2012). Collaborative scholarship as a means of improving both university teaching practice and research capability. *International Journal for Academic Development*, *3*, 237–250. doi.org/10.1080/1360144X.2012.718993

Weaver, D., Robbie, D., & Radloff, A. (2013). Demystifying the publication process – A structured writing program to facilitate dissemination of teaching and learning scholarship. *International Journal for Academic Development*, *3*, 212–225. doi.org/10.1080/1360144X.2013.805692

Western Sydney University. (n.d.). *Definition of research*. Research Services. Retrieved from https://www.westernsydney.edu.au/research/researchers/preparing_a_grant_application/dest_definition_of_research

Whitney, G. (2018). *Top research leaders predict the future of research*. Huron. Retrieved from https://www.huronconsultinggroup.com/resources/higher-education/research-leaders-predict-future-of-research

Willingham-McLain, L. (2015). Using a scholarship of teaching and learning approach to award faculty who innovate. *International Journal for Academic Development*, *1*, 58–75. doi.org/10.1080/1360144X.2014.995661

CHAPTER 5

UNIVERSITY POLICIES AND ARRANGEMENTS TO SUPPORT THE PUBLICATION OF ACADEMIC JOURNALS IN CHILE, COLOMBIA, AND VENEZUELA

Jorge Enrique Delgado

ABSTRACT

Peer-reviewed indexable journals have expanded in recent decades as a result, in part, of the value given to research productivity (measured through citations). Latin American journals have grown prompted by the open access (OA) movement, the emergence of regional repositories/indexes, and policies linking institutional rankings and faculty salaries/promotions to indexed publications. This study's aim was to map the ways Chilean, Colombian, and Venezuelan universities support journal publication. This qualitative study uses Margison and Rhoades' (2002) Glonacal Agency Heuristic to describe factors that shape higher education (i.e., global, national, and local dimensions), adding university as unit of analysis. Semi-structured in-depth interviews from a previous study, current institutional documents, and websites of 12 major universities from Chile, Venezuela, and Colombia conformed the data of the study. Besides the most prestigious global indexes (Web of Science and Scopus) three regional repositories/indexes, Latindex, SciELO, and RedALyC, have played an important role as countries link faculty salaries/promotions and university ranking systems to publications included in one or more of these services. Latindex collaborates with national science and technology agencies, SciELO has country chapters based at universities (Colombia and Venezuela), and RedALyC works with individual institutions and journals. At the national level, Chile has mechanisms to provide funding for the publication and/or upgrade of journals and incentives to institutions for publications in indexed journals. Colombia's journal evaluation system Publindex links articles in indexed journals to salary increases in public universities, standard that is also used by private institutions to grant monetary incentives to faculty for publications. Venezuela used to have a funding and publication incentive system that was discontinued in the last decade. Latin American journals are mainly published by universities. Institutions in this study have implemented strategies to support journals such as institutional repositories, discontinuation of print journals, technology support for OA publication, and funding mechanisms.

Keywords: Academic capitalism; academic journals; bibliographic analysis services; Chile universities; Colombia universities; competitiveness; electronic publication; faculty productivity; funding; Glonacal Agency Heuristic; higher education systems; institutional arrangements; institutional policies; journal indexation; Latin America; national journal evaluation systems; open access; research policies; faculty promotion; faculty salaries; scholarly journals; science; technology; and innovation systems; university journals; university research; Venezuela universities

Academic, peer-reviewed, scientific, learned, and scholarly journals are common terms used to denote periodical publications that publish original research articles and/or reviews (Haustein, 2012). Two additional features characterize journals: articles are evaluated by peer referees and journals are included in specialized bibliographic databases, that is, indexes (Delgado, 2011a). These characteristics are standard, just as presses to be the structure of research articles and methodologies across disciplines and research traditions (Pivovarova, Power, & Fischman, 2020). In this time of academic capitalism that emphasizes productivity and competitiveness (Jessop, 2018), journals are becoming more important for researchers since systems to determine quality, impact, value of research, and even faculty salaries use information from journals (e.g., impact factors).

Publishers (mainly private corporations and academic associations) and journal management models are more developed in countries and institutions where research is more established. However, they do not have necessarily the same organizational characteristics and traditions in regions like Latin America where journals are published predominantly by higher education institutions and academic units (Altbach, 2005; Delgado, 2011a, 2014; Delgado & Fischman, 2014; Rama, Uribe, & de Sagastizábal, 2006). Journals are widely used to provide information for decision-making but organizational characteristics of such journals have not been much studied (Alperín, Fischman, & Willinsky, 2008; Delgado, 2011a). In a previous publication, Delgado (2014) mapped university actors involved in the publication of journals and their roles in a number of universities from Venezuela, Chile, and Colombia. In some cases, new actors have emerged to play roles that traditionally would have been attributed to university press units, which have been described as weak in Latin America by authors such as Rama et al. (2006).

The present chapter aims to add to Delgado's (2014) findings by responding two questions: (1) What types of policies and institutional arrangements have universities from Chile, Colombia, and Venezuela implemented to support peer-reviewed journal publication? (2) How do university institutional journal support policies and arrangements respond to national, regional, and global contextual factors? The purpose is to map the unique and common ways in which Chilean, Colombian, and Venezuelan universities have responded to global, regional, and national trends and pressures to support the publication of journals. Using as a framework Margison and Rhoades' (2002) Glonacal Agency Heuristic, which identifies three intersecting dimensions and forces that shape higher education, that is, global, national, and local, this chapter adds higher education institution (university) level as unit of analysis (Delgado, 2011a, 2011b, 2014).

INTERNATIONAL, REGIONAL, AND NATIONAL CONTEXTS INFLUENCING JOURNAL GROWTH

As it was mentioned above, unlike countries in the global North, journals in Latin America are mainly published by academic units within universities. Journals have experienced an impressive growth worldwide in the last 25 years, particularly in this region (Delgado, 2011a, 2011b; Delgado-Troncoso & Fischman, 2014; Fischman, Alperín, & Willinsky, 2010). There are several reasons that explain such growth. Globally, electronic publication has replaced printing, the movement for public access to knowledge has prompted the development of open access (OA) initiatives, and the emphasis on productivity has influenced the creation of faculty rewards systems for publications in indexed journals. Regionally, the creation of repositories and bibliographic analysis services such as the Regional Online Information System of Scientific journals from Latin America, the Caribbean, Spain, and Portugal (Latindex), the Scientific Electronic Library Online (SciELO), RedALyC (multidisciplinary), LiLACS (health sciences), and the Latin American Council for Social Sciences (CLACSO) has prompted mechanisms of collaboration between initiatives, countries, and institutions, reaching different levels of progress. Nationally, countries have implemented journal evaluation systems (e.g., Qualis in Brazil and Publindex in Colombia), journal funding mechanisms (e.g., Mecesup in Chile and formerly FONACIT in Venezuela). As a result, the number and quality of journals have grown, and some awareness about the value of knowledge and regional research as well as academic collaborations has increased (Aguado López, Rogel Salazar, Garduño Oropeza, & Zúñiga, 2008; Aguado-López, Becerril García, & Godínez-Larios, 2018; Alperín & Fischman, 2015; BIREME/OPS/OMS, 2010; Cetto, 2015; Cetto & Alonso-Gamboa, 2014; Delgado, 2011a, 2011b, 2014; Packer, 2009).

National science, technology, and innovation (STI) systems are connected with higher education through the generation (research), dissemination (communication), and usage (transfer) of knowledge in a wide range of fields, not only in STEM disciplines or specific economic sectors. In Latin America, most of the research and scientific endeavors are concentrated in the largest and most prestigious universities (mainly public and some traditional private) and some research institutions rather than the productive sector (Delgado, 2011a; Didriksson, 2008). However, the scale of the region's research output and impact has been modest when compared to more advanced regions and nations. With the high value given to research and innovation for economic development through policy and expenditures on research and development and STI (Organisation for Economic Co-operation and Development [OECD], 2012), there has been some improvement region-wide. Nevertheless, there are also remarkable differences between countries (Lemarchand, 2015).

Policies and reforms to strengthen and even reform STI and higher education in Latin America have been influenced by international organizations such as the World Bank, the Inter-American Development Bank, and UNESCO, as well as regional initiatives and the most advanced countries within the region such as Brazil and Chile. Several governments have upgraded or created new agencies to coordinate the STI and higher education systems. For instance, the Dominican Republic created in 2001 the Ministry of Higher Education, Science, and Technology, and Chile established a new Ministry of Science, Technology, Knowledge, and Innovation in 2018 (OECD, 2012).

At the national level, trends include faculty professionalization (e.g., growing numbers of academics with higher credentials such as master's and doctoral degrees) and increased focus on research productivity (e.g., projects, publications, and patents). In countries such as Bolivia or Peru, many university professors only hold undergraduate degrees (Pontificia Universidad Católica del Perú, 2019; Vale, 2018). In those cases, policy intends to increase faculty credentials to improve human resources and productivity indicators. As a result, policies can promote the creation of masters and doctoral programs and/or provide scholarships for faculty to pursue graduate education nationally and/or abroad. For instance, in 2014, Peru enacted a new University Law No. 30220 that requires professors to have at least master's degrees (Superintendencia Nacional de Educación Superior Universitaria [SUNEDU], 2014).

In the 1970s and 1980s, policy tended to prioritize research infrastructure development. In the 1990s, the focus of STI policy switched to research outputs as a measure of productivity and even quality (Lemarchand, 2016). As a consequence, journal evaluation systems (journal articles have become more important than books productivity-wise) and patent application indicators have gained relevance (Delgado, 2011a, 2011b, 2014; Salatino, 2017). Research productivity policy often links productivity statistics to faculty salaries. In some countries, there is increasing funding for research in targeted fields and on promoting innovation as well as technology and knowledge transfer (e.g., startup creation and work with communities). Likewise, some countries have attempted talent repatriation mechanisms with still unclear results (Aguirre-Bastos & Gupta, 2009;

Table 1. Population, Higher Education, and Journal Indicators of Chile, Colombia, and Venezuela.

Indicator		Country		
		Chile	Colombia	Venezuela
Population[a] (millions)		18.7	49.6	28.9
Higher education institutions[b] (count)	Public	17	78	45
	Private	47	169	32
	Total	64	247	77
Gross enrollment ratio in higher education (2017)[a]		88.9	56.4	79[c]
Journal Titles in Latindex[d]		2,218	1,149	532

[a]UNESCO Institute of Statistics (2020). http://uis.unesco.org/. 2018 data.
[b]International Association of Universities (2020). https://www.whed.net/home.php.
[c]World Bank data (2020). https://data.worldbank.org/. Most recent data, 2009.
[d]Latindex (2020). https://www.latindex.org/latindex/. 2020 data.

Crespi & Dutrénit, 2013; Hall, Aguirre-Bastos, & Matos, 2014; Holm-Nielsen, Thorn, Brunner, & Balán, 2002; Lemarchand, 2010, 2016).

Scientific journals in three South American countries, Venezuela, Chile, and Colombia, started to experience notable growth in the mid-1990s. The three countries developed evaluation systems for the recognition of international and accreditation of national journals. Publications in accepted indexed journals turn into salary increases (Colombian public universities) or one-time bonuses (some Colombian and Chilean private universities and Venezuelan public universities until the early 2010s) (Delgado, 2011a). Unlikely journals in Chile and Colombia that have continued to increase, Venezuelan journals, after a period of growth and international visibility, have decreased in number and lost visibility as a result of lost funding and government support related to the country's current political and economic crisis. Table 1 shows some indicators of the three countries.

METHODS

This is a qualitative study (Neuman, 2006) that retrieves findings from semi-structured in-depth interviews conducted with key university informants between 2009 and 2011 to depict the initial policies and arrangements established in a group of selected major universities from Chile, Venezuela, and Colombia. It also includes reviews of institutional documents and websites to identify changes or new policies between 2011 and 2019. The sample consisted of 12 universities, four from each country (Table 2). The unit of analysis was the universities and the policies and arrangements were analyzed through the institutional, national, regional, and international contexts.

All Chilean universities in the study are members of the Council of Chilean University Presidents, also known as traditional universities (Departamento de Evaluación, Medición y Registro Educacional [DEMRE], 2019). Three universities are private, Pontifical Catholic from Santiago, Austral from Valdivia,

Table 2. Universities Included in the Study and Information About Their Journals.

Country	University	Number of Titles	Publication Platform	Publishing Unit	Portal(s)
Chile	Austral U.	13 (11)	OJS	Library System (Mingaonline) – SiBUACh	http://revistas.uach.cl/, http://mingaonline.uach.cl/scielo.php
	Pontifical Catholic U.	35	OJS, SciELO, other formats	UC Libraries	http://guiastematicas.bibliotecas.uc.cl/
	U. Chile	89	OJS, SciELO	Library System – SISIB	https://revistas.uchile.cl/
	U. Concepción	12	OJS	UdeC Press	http://revistasacademicas.udec.cl/
Colombia	National U.	68	OJS	SIUN	https://revistas.unal.edu.co/
	Pontifical Javeriana U.	27	OJS	Javeriana U. Press	https://revistas.javeriana.edu.co/
	U. Antioquia	57	OJS	Programa de Integración de Tecnologías a la Docencia	http://aprendeenlinea.udea.edu.co/revistas/
	Valle U.	17	OJS	Programa Editorial	http://revistas.univalle.edu.co/
Venezuela	Andrés Bello U.	12	OJS	Saber UCAB	http://revistasenlinea.saber.ucab.edu.ve/
	Central U. Venezuela	65	OJS	Saber UCV	http://saber.ucv.ve/ojs/index.php
	Andes U. Mérida	101	OJS	Saber ULA	http://www.saber.ula.ve/revistas_electronicas
	Zulia U.	37	OJS	RevencyhLUZ	https://produccioncientificaluz.org/

and Concepción from Concepción, while the University of Chile is public. The Colombian cases include three public universities, National (UNal) from Bogota, Antioquia from Medellín, and Valle (Univalle) from Cali, and one private Pontifical Javeriana. Three public universities, Central University of Venezuela (UCV) from Caracas, Zulia from Maracaibo, and Andes from Merida, and one private, Catholic Andrés Bello, are the Venezuelan institutional cases in this study. Initial interviews and document reviews were carried out between 2009 and 2011. As the project of which this article is part has evolved and the socio-political conditions and STI context have changed in the three countries, follow-up findings and new documents are being incorporated to provide an up-to-date understanding of the current situation and changes that have occurred in the publication of journals in Venezuela, Colombia, and Chile.

Interviews were audiotaped, transcribed, and translated from Spanish into English. Coding included a priori (global, regional, and national context) and a posteriori categories (those that emerged from the transcriptions). The review of documents and websites followed the categories identified from the interviews. The next section, Findings, is structured in three parts: regional context, national context, and institutional policies and arrangements to support the publication of journals.

FINDINGS

Regional Context: Latin America

One of the most determinant factors in the growth and evolution of scientific journals in Latin America has been the creation since the 1990s of three bibliographic services: Latindex, SciELO, and RedALyC. They have played a relevant role as they have established region-wide journal inventories (Latindex); provided OA journal repositories (SciELO and RedALyC); implemented inclusion criteria and performed impact and alternative analyses of publications (Latindex, SciELO, and RedALyC); created forms of collaboration with STI agencies in the region (Latindex); and established country chapters to gather and manage journals (SciELO) (Alonso Gamboa, 2017; Alperín & Fischman, 2015; Delgado, 2011a, 2011b). Governments have used them in different ways to make promotion-and-tenure decisions and faculty productivity evaluations.

The oldest initiative, Latindex, was created in 1995 with the purpose of gathering and analyzing information about journals published in the region that meet international publication criteria. Its mission is to disseminate research findings and increase the accessibility and quality of Latin American scientific periodical publications and serial monographs of Latin American countries. Housed at the National Autonomous University of Mexico, Latindex has two services. The first one is the Directory that provides a general inventory/panorama of journals that meet 33 basic criteria of the International Serial Data System. The second one is the Catalogue that shows those publications that meet high-quality standards. In most cases, national science and technology agencies provide Latindex the information for the Directory and Catalogue (Amaro, Silva, & Carvalho, 2017; Latindex, 1995). One of the Latindex's recent developments is the *Portal de Portales* that provides access to 16 OA repositories (Latindex, 2011). Even though Latindex has the most comprehensive journal inventory in the region, the quality and accuracy of information of individual publications vary from country to country, because of the pace and frequency STI agencies provide updated information to Latindex.

The second service, SciELO, is a multidisciplinary OA platform for the publication of scientific periodicals (and peer-reviewed books in Brazil), whose purpose is to increase the visibility and universal access to journals that meet international standards. It also includes use and impact measures. SciELO started in 1997 as a collaboration between the Sao Paulo State Research Support Foundation and the Pan-American Health Organization in Brazil. Since 2002, SciELO is supported by the Brazilian Council for Scientific and Technologic Development. SciELO works in collaboration with partners to publish country chapters and one thematic site on public health (Alperín & Fischman, 2015; Delgado, 2011a, 2011b; SciELO, 2019). In addition, SciELO has been building collaborations with other services such as Web of Science, Scopus, LiLACS, Medline, ReadCube, ScienceOpen,

Figshare, Public Knowledge Project, and Publons. Similar to Latindex, SciELO country chapters have different levels of development. In Chile, it is managed by the National Commission for Scientific and Technological Research (CONICYT). In Colombia, UNal's School of Medicine operates SciELO and includes most journals in the category B or A of Publindex. In Venezuela, SciELO is housed at Fundasinadib, a foundation of the UCV's Institute of Experimental Medicine. Until around 2009, journals included in the Venezuelan list of top journals received funding to be included in SciELO. However, public policy changes and the economic crisis have deterred that support and SciELO Venezuela has shrunk (Delgado, 2011a, 2011b).

The Scientific Information System RedALyC is an independent initiative based at the Autonomous University of the State of Mexico. It was founded in 2003 to provide full-text OA journals mainly in the social sciences and humanities (Alperín & Fischman, 2015; Delgado, 2011a, 2011b). RedALyC started as a repository (PDFs) and has grown to become an index that includes alternative metrics and communication infrastructure (AmeliCA). In 2019, RedALyC transitioned to a new model that promotes editorial and scientific quality through peer-reviewing, publication using XML-JATS technology to mark structure and semantic of research articles, OA policy (at no cost for publication and/or processing), and signing the San Francisco Declaration on Research Assessment – DORA to avoid using journal-based metrics (e.g., impact factor) (RedALyC, 2019). The RedALyC repository could shrink as a consequence of the new policies and it is unclear what will happen with the publications that were included before in the database.

There are other bibliographic services with regional scope. One in the health sciences is LiLACS (Latin American Health Science Literature), an index of journal articles that is managed by the Medicine Regional Library – BIREME of the Pan-American Health Organization. LiLACS was created in 1979 as the Latin American Index Medicus (Latin American and Caribbean Center on Health Sciences Information [BIREME], n.d.). Another service is CLACSO repository, which is also available through RedALyC. CLACSO publishes different types of studies such as books, journals, and gray literature following the OA principle (CLACSO, 2019).

National Contexts: Chile, Colombia, and Venezuela

Institutional attention to the publication of national academic peer-reviewed journals began in the late 1990s and early 2000s in Latin America with the creation of journal evaluation systems, rankings, and publication funding mechanisms. Policies and programs addressing journal at the national level have been developed in Chile, Colombia, and Venezuela, which have followed different paths. In Chile, CONICYT manages the Scientific Information Program whose goal is to strengthen and assure access to national and international scientific information for research, teaching, and innovation. Some of the services available from CONICYT are the Electronic Library of Scientific Information – BEIC (remote access to more than 5,900 full-text journals), SciELO Chile, the Institutional

Repository of projects funded by CONICYT, RedCiencia (Latin American network of researchers), the Researcher Portal (i.e., profiles and productivity of researchers), the Productivity Portal (monitoring national publications in Web of Science and Scopus), and the Fund for Publication of Chilean Scientific Journals (having supported 453 projects since 1988) (CONICYT, 2019). The Chilean government has also granted incentives to those universities in top-ranking positions and publications in internationally recognized bibliographic indexes. The national journal lists in Chile are SciELO and Latindex (Delgado, 2011a, 2011b).

Colciencias, the Colombian Administrative Department (Ministry, since late 2019) of STI manages the National Journal Indexation and Homologation System – Publindex, which validates international publications and bibliographic information services and ranks national journals. Information of Publindex is used, as established in Decree 1279 of 2002, by public higher education institutions to assign scores to faculty publications, turning them into points for salary increments (Delgado, 2011a, 2011b; Presidencia de la República, 2002). Private universities often use Publindex information for faculty promotion-and-tenure purposes as well. In 2016, Colciencias reformed the model to evaluate national journals increasing the thresholds for each category of the rank (A1, A2, B, and C). An innovation of the most recent version of Publindex is considering quartile information from the Journal Citation Reports, Scimago Journal Rankings, and Google Scholar H5 Index (Colciencias, 2016). The reform seeks to better position Colombian journals in top international indexes. However, it is seen also as a measure to contain the fiscal burden caused by increased numbers of public university professors with doctoral degrees and faculty productivity growth (Redacción Vivir, 2018).

Of the three countries here described, Venezuela's research and science communication is the only that experienced a setback in the last decade. Until 2009, the government's Researcher Support Program (known as PPI, *Programa de Promoción al Investigador*) used to grant monetary bonuses to faculty and researchers from public universities for articles published in recognized national and international journals. The PPI became the Research and Innovation Support Program. Also, FONACIT, the Venezuelan Fund for STI, used to manage a journal registry and provide funding for national journals recognized by its journal evaluation system (Delgado, 2011a, 2011b, 2014). With the recent economic downturn in Venezuela, those programs have contracted or revoked. At one point, the government also restricted funding for the internet, which affected the electronic publication of journals, even if they were OA. In consequence, many journals are not up to date, some changed domains in order to survive, and others have turned to the Venezuelan Journal Index and Electronic Library – Revencyt (created in 1991) that is housed by Andes University (Índice y Biblioteca Electrónica de Revistas Venezolanas de Ciencias y Tecnología [Revencyt], 2019). The Venezuelan chapter of SciELO has also endured challenges.

Institutional Policies to Support Journals Published by Universities
In Latin America, journals are published mainly by universities. A search of publishers among SciELO journals (October 15, 2019) showed that the Venezuelan

chapter included 60 journal titles of which 37 were up to date. 23 of them, that is, 62% were published by universities. SciELO Chile listed 127 titles. 111 were up to date of which 75.7% were published by post-secondary education institutions. In SciELO Colombia there are 230 up-to-date journals out of 239 titles. 204 journals (88.7%) were published by higher education institutions. This section presents and analyzes the strategies that universities have implemented to support their institutional journals.

Groundbreaking Journals and the Beginning of Journal Support Policies

In general, pioneer university journals have paved the road for other peer-reviewed periodicals to obtain institutional support. When achieving national and/or international prestige, some journals have drawn institutional attention and prompted discussions on journal relevance and successful models, which ended up in the implementation of journal support policies. Peer-reviewed periodicals have become prestigious after being included in bibliographic indexes of national (e.g., Publindex in Colombia and FONACIT in Venezuela), regional (Latindex, SciELO, and RedALyC), and international (Medline, Web of Science, and Scopus) levels. For instance, in Chile, *EURE*, a journal on regional and urban studies was the first publication of the Pontifical Catholic University to be included in the Web of Science and one of the first ones in SciELO. Likewise, the Austral University has two emblematic journals that prompted institutional support. One is *Archivos de Medicina Veterinaria*, one of the first Chilean publications in the Science Citation Index, Medline (biomedical sciences), and SciELO. The other journal is *Estudios Filológicos*, the first journal from that university to be indexed in the Web of Science. Both publications contributed to the creation of SciELO Chile (Packer, Irati, & Marão Beraquet, 2001; Prat, 2001). In another case, the University of Concepción maintains a policy of fully funding those journals that are indexed in the Web of Science and SciELO. The oldest journal in Chile, *Atenea* (founded in 1950), is published by Concepción (Delgado, 2011a, 2011b). *Ciencia y Enfermería* was one of the groundbreaking journals at Concepción.

In Colombia, *Cuadernos de Administración* (founded in 1981) and *Universitas Psychologica* (founded in 2001) have played a pioneering role at Javeriana University. Since the early 2000s, lead editors of these two journals have served as advisors to Javeriana University Press (through its journal coordination unit), university authorities, and different schools on topics such as international journal publication trends and the growing challenges to publish international-quality journals (Delgado, 2011a, 2011b, 2014). At UNal, *Revista de Salud Pública* was the groundbreaking journal. Its editor obtained the concession to operate the Colombian chapter of SciELO at their Institute of Public Health. Having SciELO within their main campus allowed UNal to implement strategies to develop its several journals and have them included in this repository-index. As mentioned before, SciELO has played an important role in the recognition of faculty productivity among public universities in Colombia through Decree 1279 of 2002 (Delgado, 2011a, 2011b, 2014). In the city of Cali, *Colombia Medica* (founded in 1970 originally as *Acta Médica del Valle*) is one of the most emblematic journals and stands as a model for the implementation of institutional policies at Univalle. This journal is indexed by Medline, Web of Science, Scopus, and SciELO.

In sum, some journals have served to some extension as triggers for the development of journal policy. In some cases, policies have been created at the university level (i.e., Austral, Concepción, and Javeriana), while in others it has happened at the academic school/department level (i.e., Catholic of Chile and UNal) (Delgado, 2011a, 2011b, 2014).

Diversity of Journal Subjects and Institutional Policy

The 12 universities reviewed in this study are comprehensive institutions that cover diverse fields and different educational levels. Besides pioneering publications reaching bibliographic indexes, academic journals in a wide range of topics are published in each institution. Table 2 lists the number of journals per university in this study. At one point, the complete pools of peer-reviewed periodicals in all universities have prompted the implementation of institutional policies (e.g., Catholic of Chile, Javeriana, UNal, Antioquia, and UCV). As a result of the new journal support policies, the numbers of publications continued to grow, creating the need for specialized journal coordinators (e.g., Javeriana) or expanded functions within university research offices, as it was the case of the councils for scientific and humanistic development at Zulia and Andes universities in Venezuela (Delgado 2011a, 2011b, 2014) until the early 2010s. One of the frequent goals of university policies has been pursuing the inclusion of journals in the most prestigious international indexes (mainly Web of Science and Scopus) and/or regional repositories-indexes (e.g., SciELO). For instance, before the Venezuelan crisis deepened, the University of Zulia sought to get most of its journals in the Web of Science (Delgado, 2011a, 2011b).

Institutional Repositories

Following the international OA-to-knowledge trend, most institutions have created repositories for journals and other documents (Delgado, 2011b). For instance, as it was mentioned above, with the economic and political crisis that has affected Venezuela since the early 2010s, the government support for peer-reviewed journals has declined (Trinca Fighera, 2019). In consequence, universities have struggled to maintain their journals for the lack of funding and some restrictions to access the internet. The Venezuelan Observatory of Science, Technology, and Innovation created in 2016 a National Registry of Scientific Journals (Observatorio Nacional de Ciencia, Tecnología e Innovación [Oncti], 2016). However, the content of the Registry is not available. Luckily, Revencyt in the city of Merida maintains 209 up-to-date journals out of 317 registered titles (Revencyt, 2019). Andes University also has an institutional repository, SaberULA. In another case, Austral University created an institutional repository that uses the SciELO methodology: Minga Online (Delgado, 2011a, 2011b).

Processes to Implement Journal Support Policies at the Universities

In most cases, after recognizing the prestige gained by some of their publications and finding themselves in a new environment that privileges publication in indexed journals, universities started by conducting *inventories and diagnostic evaluations*. That was the case of the Catholic University of Chile, Concepción, Javeriana, and UNal. As a result, universities were able to identify degrees of development of journals, establish funding and management needs, set publication standards, and designate units in charge specific processes (Delgado, 2011a, 2014). For instance, the Catholic University of Chile carried out an inventory and found out there were no publication standards. In response, that unit established publication standards and funding mechanisms, and gave autonomy to editors to manage the journals. With the goal of finding better ways to identify new needs and create new mechanisms to support their journals, universities such as Javeriana and Merida conduct *follow-up and performance evaluations* (Delgado, 2011a). Several universities such as Concepción, Javeriana, Antioquia, UCV, Zulia, and Merida conduct periodically *workshops and trainings* with journal editors, which can be delivered by personnel from the institutions' libraries, press units, and/or technology departments or representatives indexing services, national and/or international experts, and even editors of successful journals (Delgado, 2011a).

Policies on Publication Format

In the past, the main headaches for journal editors were shipping printed journals, attracting subscribers, storing non-delivered copies, and the costs associated with these activities. The growth of *electronic publication and open access* journals have benefitted from cost reduction, expanded readership, and increased visibility. However, new challenges have emerged, including technological capacity requirements, demands for growth and capacity, and resource allocation for both (Delgado, 2011a). Particularly meaningful for the expansion and positioning of journals has been the OA publication. All universities in this study embraced OA. Most of them have used the Open Journal System (OJS) as the management and publication platform that was developed by the Public Knowledge Project at Simon Fraser University in Canada. The Colombian universities in this study grouped their journals using OJS, with a few journals using other platforms. As it was mentioned above, Austral University publishes its journals using Minga Online, their platform based on the SciELO methodology. In Venezuela, journals that lost their publication platforms now use RedALyC or SciELO instead.

Institutional Funding for Journals

The last element to describe in this chapter is journal funding. In the past with print publication, journals attracted, successfully or not, revenue through subscription and advertising. With OA publication, subscriptions are no longer necessary, and it is more difficult to include advertisements. Therefore, universities must provide the funding, which is more demanding as journals grow and gain visibility and international prestige. Universities in this study developed different funding mechanisms. For instance, at the University of Chile funding can come from the schools' budget (e.g., Javeriana and UNal) and some support from the central administration (Andrés Bello). In some cases, funding is only provided to already well-positioned journals as it is the case of the University of Concepción and the Catholic of Chile. The University of Antioquia in Colombia has a stamp whose sales profit is directed to fund research-related activities (Delgado, 2011a).

DISCUSSION

Latin America as a region has been a leader in the emergence of collaborative (e.g., Latindex, SciELO, LiLACS) and independent initiatives (RedALyC) that have prompted the development of OA peer-reviewed scientific journals. At the national level, governments have responded to global and regional trends and pressures with different types of journal support policies and mechanisms (i.e., journal evaluation systems, rankings, incentives and funding for publication, salary mechanisms linked to productivity, etc.). They have evolved in different ways, which depends on the unique contexts and constraints of each country. When looking at the university level, in previous publications, Delgado (2011a, 2014) analyzed the role that traditional and emerging university actors have played in the growth of peer-reviewed journals. As a consequence of the current environment of scientific communication, university press units, technology departments, and libraries have seen their roles redefined and enhanced. Likewise, journal editors and editorial committees are now faced with more intricate responsibilities for which they are not necessarily prepared. Some universities have responded to the emerging needs with training. Often, the need for more personnel, funding, and expertise limits a journal's capacity to grow and be better positioned nationally and internationally. Some of the policies and arrangements include: creation of funding mechanisms (e.g., university-wide, academic/research unit-based, and/or top-journal targeting); conducting inventories, diagnostic, follow-up, and performance evaluations; development of institutional strategies to increase faculty productivity; inclusion of journals in institutional research policies; implementation of electronic publication platforms (disappearance of print publications); embracing OA modes of publication; use of monetary incentives for referees; policies reactive to changing contexts (e.g., journals indexing and economy conditions); and creation of national and institutional repositories. The playfield is not static or even. It changes constantly and governments and institutions respond in different ways depending on their contexts and goals. The communication of knowledge product of research is important for the advancement of science, disciplines, and hopefully societies. It is necessary to think critically about whether they fulfill their mission and how policy can support it.

The combination of journal evaluation systems and rankings, national and international bibliographic indexes, competitive university accreditation and marketing, and university faculty salaries attached to productivity (mainly patents and publications in indexed journals) creates a market that some have named academic capitalism. This market does not necessarily represent research capacity or scientific impact because the value of research is moved from contributions to knowledge and societal needs to a competition for citations and monetary perks. In addition, there is not much evidence that shows how the market of publications is used in teaching and/or to improve education.

Traditionally, mainstream publications originate from professional/academic societies or corporate publishers that have the capacity to involve a wide variety of actors with different affiliations. The most traditional journals in Latin America were created in higher education institutions to disseminate mainly the work of students and faculty. Their scope and capacity to attract external readers, authors, referees, and advisers to build wider networks could be limited or, at least, more challenging. The dynamics are different, and it is unfair to measure them with standards that do not correspond with their realities. Finally, other issues such as the language of publication and where the new knowledge has an impact, that is, the local, national, regional, and/or global levels were not analyzed here. They should be part of future research.

REFERENCES

Aguado López, E., Rogel Salazar, R., Garduño Oropeza, G., & Zúñiga, M. F. (2008). Redalyc: Una alternativa a las asimetrías en la distribución del conocimiento científico. *Ciencia, Docencia y Tecnología, XIX*(37), 11–30. Retrieved from http://www.scielo.org.ar/pdf/cdyt/n37/n37a02.pdf

Aguado-López, E., Becerril García, A., & Godínez-Larios, S. (2018). Asociarse o perecer: la colaboración funcional en las ciencias sociales latinoamericanas. *Revista Española de Investigación en Sociología, 161*, 3–22. http://dx.doi.org/10.5477/cis/reis.161.3

Aguirre-Bastos, C., & Gupta, M. P. (2009). Science, technology, and innovation policies in Latin America: Do they work? *Interciencia, 34*(12), 865–872. Retrieved from https://www.interciencia.net/wp-content/uploads/2018/01/865-GUPTA-8.pdf

Alonso Gamboa, J. O. (2017). Transformación de las revistas académicas en la cultura digital actual. *Revista Digital Universitaria, 18*(3), 1–15. Retrieved from http://www.revista.unam.mx/vol.18/num3/art22/

Alperín, J. P., Fischman, G., & Willinsky, J. (2008). Open access and scholarly publishing in Latin America: Ten flavours and a few reflections. *Liinc em Revista, 4*(2), 172–185. Retrieved from http://www.ibict.br/liinc

Alperín, J. P., & Fischman, G. (2015). *Made in Latin America. Open access, scholarly journals, and regional innovations*. CLACSO. Retrieved from http://biblioteca.clacso.edu.ar/clacso/se/20150921045253/MadeInLatinAmerica.pdf

Altbach, P. G. (2005). Patterns of higher education development. In P. G. Altbach, R. O. Berdahl, & P. G. Gumport (Eds.), *American higher education in the twenty-first century. social, political, and economic challenges* (2nd ed., pp. 16–37). Baltimore, MD: Johns Hopkins UP.

Amaro, B., Silva, D., & Carvalho, T. (2015). A contribuição do Latindex para a promoção e visibilidade das revistas técnico-científicas da Ibero-América: a história dos seus 20 anos. *Ciência da Informação, 44*(2), 229–238. Retrieved from http://revista.ibict.br/ciinf/article/view/1773/2368

BIREME/OPS/OMS. (2010, November 30). LILACS conmemora 25 años. *Newsletter BVS*, 130. Retrieved from http://newsletter.bireme.br/new/index.php?lang=es&newsletter=20101130#1

Cetto, A. M. (2015). Las revistas científicas en América y el acceso abierto (AA). *Espacio I+D Innovación más Desarrollo, IV*(7), 9–30. Retrieved from https://www.espacioimasd.unach.mx/articulos/num7/pdf/acceso_abierto.pdf

Cetto, A. M., & Alonso-Gamboa, J. O. (2014). Latindex y el acceso abierto. *Revista Digital Universitaria, 15*(10), 1–11. Retrieved from http://www.revista.unam.mx/vol.15/num10/art76/

CLACSO. (2019). *Acceso abierto al conocimiento*. Consejo Latinoamericano de Ciencias Sociales-CLACSO. Retrieved from https://www.clacso.org/acceso-abierto-al-conocimiento/

Colciencias. (2016, August). *Política nacional para mejorar el impacto de las publicaciones científicas nacionales* (Documento No. 1601). Departamento Administrativo de Ciencia, Tecnología e Innovación-Colciencias, Gobierno de Colombia. Retrieved from https://minciencias.gov.co/sites/default/files/120816-vfpolitica_publindex_2.0_og_ao_miv.pdf

CONICYT. (2019). *¿Qué es información científica?* National Commission for Scientifc and Technological Research-CONICYT, Ministerio de Educación, Gobierno de Chile. Retrieved from https://www.conicyt.cl/informacioncientifica/sobre-informacion-cientifica/que-es-informacion-cientifica/

Crespi, G., & Dutrénit, G. (2013). *Políticas de ciencia, tecnología e innovación para el desarrollo. La experiencia latinoamericana.* México: Foro Consultivo, Científico y Tecnológico, LALICS.

Delgado, J. E. (2011a). *Journal publication in Chile, Colombia, and Venezuela: University responses to global, regional, and national pressures and trends* [Unpublished doctoral dissertation]. University of Pittsburgh. Retrieved from http://d-scholarship.pitt.edu/9049/

Delgado, J. E. (2011b). Role of open access in the emergence and consolidation of refereed journals in Latin America and the Caribbean. *Revista Educación Superior y Sociedad, 16*(2). Retrieved from http://ess.iesalc.unesco.org.ve/index.php/ess/article/view/407

Delgado, J. E. (2014). Scientific journals of universities of Chile, Colombia, and Venezuela: Actors and roles. *Education Policy Analysis Archives, 22*(34), 1–26. (Special issue: The Future of Educational Research Journals). http://dx.doi.org/10.14507/epaa.v22n34.2014

Delgado-Troncoso, J. E, & Fischman, G. E. (2014). The future of Latin American academic journals. In B. Cope & A. Phillips (Eds.), *The future of the academic journal* (2nd ed., pp. 379–400). Oxford, UK: Chandos Elsevier.

Departamento de Evaluación, Medición y Registro Educacional (DEMRE). (2019). *Acerca del DEMRE.* Universidad de Chile. Retrieved from http://www.uchile.cl/portal/presentacion/asuntos-academicos/demre/presentacion/110082/acerca-del-demre

Didriksson, A. (2008). Global and regional contexts of higher education in Latin America and the Caribbean. In A. L. Gazzola & A. Didriksson (Eds.), *Trends in higher education in Latin America and the Caribbean* (pp. 20–50). Caracas: UNESCO IESALC.

Fischman, G. E.; Alperín, J. P., & Willinsky, J. (2010). Visibility and quality in Spanish-language Latin American scholarly publishing. *Information Technologies & International Development, 6*(4), 1–21. Retrieved from https://itidjournal.org/index.php/itid/article/view/639/274

Hall, J., Aguirre-Bastos, C., & Matos, S. (2014). *Shaping national innovation systems for inclusive growth in Latin America. Towards a research agenda.* INCAE Business School.

Haustein, S. (2012). *Multidimensional journal evaluation. Analyzing scientific periodicals beyond the impact factor.* Berlin: De Gruyter Saur.

Holm-Nielsen, L. B., Thorn, K., Brunner, J. J., & Balán, J. (2002). *Regional and international challenges to higher education in Latin America.* The World Bank. Retrieved from https://pdfs.semanticscholar.org/1607/3d999705bf427292a1c08fd26d568e1f319c.pdf

Índice y Biblioteca Electrónica de Revistas Venezolanas de Ciencias y Tecnología (Revencyt). (2019). *Acerca de Revencyt.* Universidad de Los Andes, Venezuela. Retrieved from http://www.revencyt.ula.ve/acercade

Jessop, B. (2018). On academic capitalism. *Critical Policy Studies, 12*(1). Retrieved from https://www.tandfonline.com/doi/pdf/10.1080/19460171.2017.1403342

Latin American and Caribbean Center on Health Sciences Information (BIREME). (n.d.). *History.* BIREME, Pan-American Health Organization. Retrieved from https://www.paho.org/bireme/index.php?option=com_content&view=article&id=33:historia&Itemid=215&lang=en

Latindex. (1995). *Proyecto fundacional.* National Autonomous University of Mexico. Retrieved from https://www.latindex.org/latindex/proyectofund

Latindex. (2011). *Portal de Portales Latindex.* National Autonomous University of Mexico. Retrieved from http://www.latindex.ppl.unam.mx/index.php/about

Lemarchand, G. A. (2010). *National science, technology and innovation systems in Latin America and the Caribbean.* UNESCO. Retrieved from https://unesdoc.unesco.org/ark:/48223/pf0000189823

Lemarchand, G. A. (2015). Latin America. In *UNESCO Science Report. Towards 2030.* UNESCO. Retrieved from https://unesdoc.unesco.org/ark:/48223/pf0000235406

Lemarchand, G. A. (2016). *Los ritmos de las políticas CTI y sus paradigmas tecno-económicos/organizacionales en ALC (1945–2030).* UNESCO. Retrieved from http://www.unesco.org/new/

fileadmin/MULTIMEDIA/FIELD/Montevideo/pdf/PolicyPapersCILAC-PoliticaCientifcas-GAL.pdf

Margison, S., & Rhoades, G. (2002). Beyond national states, markets and systems of higher education: A glonacal agency heuristic. *Higher Education, 43*, 281–309. https://doi.org/10.1023/A:1014699605875

Neuman, W. L. (2006). *Social research methods. Qualitative and quantitative approaches* (6th ed.). Boston, MA: Pearson, Allyn and Bacon.

Observatorio Nacional de Ciencia, Tecnología e Innovación (Oncti). (2016). *Oncti lanza Portal de Registro Nacional para Revistas Científicas*. Oncti, Gobierno de Venezuela. Retrieved from http://www.cendit.gob.ve

Organisation for Economic Co-operation and Development (OECD). (2012, May). *Innovation for development*. OECD. Retrieved from https://www.oecd.org/innovation/inno/50586251.pdf

Packer, A. L. (2009). The SciELO open access: A gold way from the South. *Canadian Journal of Higher Education, 39*(3), 111–126. Retrieved from http://journals.sfu.ca/cjhe/index.php/cjhe/article/view/479/504

Packer, A. L., Irati, A., & Marão Beraquet, V. S. (2001). Hacia la publicación electrónica. *Acimed, 9*(Supl. 4), 7–8. Retrieved from http://scielo.sld.cu/scielo.php?script=sci_arttext&pid=S1024-94352001000400002

Pivovarova, M., Power, J. M., & Fischman, G. E. (2020). Introduction. Moving beyond the paradigm wars: Emergent approaches for educational research. *Review of Research in Education, 44*(1), vii–xvi. https://doi-org.pitt.idm.oclc.org/10.3102/0091732X20909400

Pontificia Universidad Católica del Perú. (2019, May 16). *El docente será magister o o será*. Retrieved from https://vicerrectorado.pucp.edu.pe/academico/noticias/docente-sera-magister-no-sera/

Prat, A. M. (2001). Evaluación de la producción científica como instrumento para el desarrollo de la ciencia y la tecnología. *Acimed, 9*(Supl. 4), 111–114. Retrieved from http://scielo.sld.cu/pdf/aci/v9s4/aci16100.pdf

Presidencia de la República. (2002, June 19). *Decreto 1279*. Ministerio de Educación, Gobierno de Colombia. Retrieved from https://www.mineducacion.gov.co/1759/articles-86434_Archivo_pdf.pdf

Rama, C., Uribe, R., & de Sagastizábal, L. (Eds.). (2006). *Las editoriales universitarias en América Latina*. Caracas: Instituto Internacional para la Educación Superior en América Latina y el Caribe-IESALC, Centro Regional para el Fomento del Libro en América Latina y el Caribe-CERLALC.

Redacción Vivir. (2018, October 10). Las universidades públicas, en la olla. *El Espectador*. Retrieved from https://www.elespectador.com/noticias/educacion/las-universidades-publicas-en-la-olla-articulo-817089

RedALyC. (2019). *¿Qué es Redalyc.org?* Universidad Autónoma del Estado de México. Retrieved from https://www.redalyc.org/redalyc/acerca-de/mision.html

Salatino, M. (2017). *La estructura del espacio latinoamericano de revistas científicas* [Unpublished doctoral dissertation]. Universidad Nacional de Cuyo. Retrieved from https://bdigital.uncu.edu.ar/10720

Scientific Electronic Library Online (SciELO). (2019). *Modelo de publicação eletrônica para países em desenvolvimento*. SciELO. https://wp.scielo.org/wp-content/uploads/Modelo_SciELO.pdf

Superintendencia Nacional de Educación Superior Universitaria (SUNEDU). (2014, July 8). *Ley No. 30220. Ley Universitaria*. Congreso de la República, Gobierno del Perú. https://www.sunedu.gob.pe/wp-content/uploads/2017/04/Ley-universitaria-30220.pdf

Trinca Fighera, D. (2019). Revistas científicas y crisis. *Revista Geográfica Venezolana, 60*(1), 7–9. Retrieved from http://www.saber.ula.ve/bitstream/handle/123456789/46042/editorial.pdf?sequence=1&isAllowed=y

Vale, C. (2018, August 14). Sólo el 4% de los docentes de la "U" tiene doctorado. *Correo del Sur*. Retrieved from https://correodelsur.com/local/20180814_solo-el-4-de-los-docentes-de-la-u-tiene-doctorado.html

PART II

EMERGING TRENDS IN RESEARCH

CHAPTER 6

HUMANIZING A TEACHER EDUCATION PROGRAM IN A SMALL LIBERAL ARTS UNIVERSITY

Edith Ries, Ellina Chernobilsky and Joanne Jasmine

ABSTRACT

Educational training programs, at times, are criticized for inadequately addressing issues that occur in the field (Brydon-Miller, Greenwood, & Maguire, 2003). This omission in relevancy might possibly be attributed to the fact that teacher education faculty no longer engage with K-12 students on a daily basis. We have decided to fill that relevancy void through our graduate student action research projects. Action research projects, undertaken by graduate students within our program, not only foster reflection upon the needs of the students within their K-12 classrooms, but also inform us, as education faculty, as we prepare our undergraduate students for the world of teaching. In this chapter, we outline action research as a framework of inquiry. We argue in the chapter that engaging students in the individualized action research projects has benefits for multiple stakeholders ranging from the learners in K-12 classrooms to students in pre-service teacher education programs. Using four case studies, we illustrate how the action research process works and the ways it fosters inclusivity in classrooms at numerous levels. We will discuss the benefits and challenges to our approach and will conclude by discussing the lessons that can be learned from our experiences in humanistic education.

Keywords: Action research; humanistic education; pre-service teacher; graduate education; pedagogy; teacher preparation

INTRODUCTION

As we review and study recent national data, it becomes abundantly clear that the United States is experiencing a significant demographic shift at all levels of education. This shift has become a reality to those of us in higher education as we observe more and more students from differing ethnic, cultural, socioeconomic, and racial backgrounds gravitating to our institutions. The pattern is even more apparent at the K-12 level. These students bring with them to their classrooms varied experiences, cultures, and expectations. This change in student demographics requires that educators develop a sensitivity to and an understanding of individual and cultural differences at all levels and embrace these differences in both inclusive and just ways.

In the United States, traditional teacher preparation programs centered on the knowledge and culture of the white females who were the backbone of the profession. The teachers were prepared to address diverse learning needs simply by lessons and activities introduced by higher education faculty throughout the preparation program (Gist, Jackson, Nightengale-Lee, & Allen, 2019). These efforts at addressing diversity, Gist et al. argue, are often additive approaches that are not central to the mission of today's teacher preparation programs. The additive approaches do not address cultural and individual differences. Moreover, these approaches do not embrace student differences in a humanizing way.

If we wish to improve schooling and education, Muessig and Cogan (1972) suggest, we must think in terms of humanizing education. These authors provide us with a list of suggestions that address ways in which educators can humanize schools and bolster relationships between teachers and students. For example, Muessig and Cogan suggest schools hold family-style lunches weekly so that the students can get to know their faculty better. While we wholeheartedly support Muessig and Cogan's recommendations for humanizing classrooms, we feel compelled to point out that these suggestions rely heavily upon policy-wide, broad societal and cultural changes. We suggest that educators can indeed humanize education, address diversity, and bring about cultural understanding in a more rapid and just fashion in smaller one-on-one settings, one teacher and one student at a time. In essence, we subscribe to the view advanced by Bartolome (1994), who believes that the first thing teachers must do when choosing an instructional methodology is to engage in a critical analysis that will assist them in understanding who the students in the classroom really are – taking into consideration their socio-historical and cultural realities. This critical analysis will help teachers to engage in humanistic practices and assist them in applying teaching methods that are best suited for the particular student or group of students being taught. This humanistic approach to education advocated by Bartolome requires not only flexible teaching but flexible curriculum as well.

In our work, we are guided by Bartolome's (1994) philosophy. Our ultimate goal as educators of pre-service teachers is to have our students gain an understanding of this multifaceted flexibility with regard to teaching and curriculum in order to humanize their approach to teaching. In this way, K-12 students experience a just and equal education. To achieve this goal with our in-service and pre-service teachers we rely upon and embrace action research as a humanizing process.

Action Research

Action research is teacher engagement in inquiry, the type of inquiry that enables practitioners to take action and then act upon the results (Dana, 2013). Dana points out that, historically, the action research process asks teachers to reflect upon individual learners, student learning styles, and/or classroom structure with the goal of gathering information that will enable a teacher to develop reflective practice, effect positive change in the classroom and in the school, develop educational practice, and create a classroom environment that is qualitatively different from environments that exist in test-driven classrooms. In order to properly adhere to this all-encompassing definition, we believe that it is our role as pre-service teacher educators to provide opportunities for our students so that they may become the change agents, decision-makers, consultants, and reflective practitioners to which Dana refers (Larrivee, 2008; Stewart, 2018).

This, we suggest, can be done by requiring graduate education students to participate in action research. Moreover, we further suggest that the current emphasis on reflective teaching practices makes action research important to use, primarily because the action research process itself enhances one's own quest for improvement (Neapolitan, 2000). Action research is not imposed upon teachers by someone else, but is a self-directed process (Putman & Rock, 2017); therefore, it allows the practitioner to express his/her own unique identity as a teacher (Dana, 2013) while at the same time addressing the diverse needs of all students. As an action researcher, one reflects upon the results of the data collected. While this reflection is paramount to improving teaching and learning in the K-12 classroom, it is also helpful to higher education faculty as they prepare teacher educators and consider the structure of their teacher education programs.

Some educational training programs are criticized as inadequately addressing issues that occur in the field (Brydon-Miller et al., 2003). This omission in relevancy might possibly be attributed to the fact that teacher education faculty no longer participate in the daily activities of K-12 classrooms. Consequently, we have decided to fill that void through our graduate student action research projects. Our graduate students, who are all practicing teachers, design humanistic interventions for pertinent issues that arise in their classrooms. They collect the data to understand whether the intervention was successful. Students then analyze the data they have collected for their specific study. Once the data are analyzed and interpreted, our students discuss the implications of these data to improve teaching and learning in their classrooms.

It is at this point that we as teacher educators come together with our graduate students, who are practicing, in-service teachers, to reflect upon the results of their research, to learn from their experiences, and to point out the benefits of this humanistic approach to teaching and learning. In an attempt to inform our undergraduate pre-service teachers with regard to the complexities of the profession, we then use this action research as an illustration of the form that humanistic education can and should take in today's classrooms.

In this paper, we present four cases that highlight this approach. In each case, we show how the intervention affected the in-service teachers and the classrooms in which they worked. We then discuss how we use the results of these studies with pre-service teachers in our teacher preparation program.

METHOD

Sources of Data

The data analyzed in this chapter comes from four cases that the authors examined following the teaching of a year-long action research course for master students in a small private university in the Northeastern United States. All students in the course were practicing in-service teachers. The goal of the research course was to have each student develop and execute an action research study in their respective classrooms.

The four cases presented in this paper are illustrations of how each action research project provided pedagogical insights not only to the teachers who executed the project but also to the higher education faculty who teach pre-service education students.

Case 1
Setting. A study of student motivation and comprehension was conducted in a middle school social studies classroom during a unit on culture and society in the ancient world. The teacher decided to implement game-like learning strategies during the unit. Game-like learning is based on the principle that learning can successfully happen through the use of games. Cards, board games, puzzles, or simulations are all examples of games that could be used. In this particular case, the teacher's goal was to improve comprehension and retention of information in his middle school students as well as address the needs of young adolescents in the areas of socialization, cooperation, and higher-level thinking. Middle school-aged students have high levels of cognitive function and language ability. They also have a strong need for peer social interactions and critical self-examination. Recognizing this, the teacher-researcher determined that a different approach to the teaching of specific information was necessary.

Eighth-grade students participated in a different game activity each week. Examples included a puzzle game based on the understanding of the impact of Hammurabi's Laws and a discussion-based game whereby students were required to determine the various themes demonstrated by mythological figures. Students engaged in puzzles and discussion games 2-5 days a week. By providing activities that address the needs of his students, the teacher incorporated a humanistic approach to learning, one that encouraged and fostered group work. At the same time, the students learned to become responsible for their own learning.

During this study, the in-service teacher collected field notes identifying the level of student participation during each activity. At the end of the study, students completed a comprehension post-test on the unit, and a teacher-created survey that assessed motivation. Two weeks after the conclusion of the study, students completed a follow-up test to determine the retention of content.

Findings. Post-test and retention test mean scores and standard deviations revealed that most students understood and retained the content of the unit. Test results ($M = 82.76$, $SD = 9.56$) demonstrated that most students learned the content in a coherent fashion. Retention testing ($M = 79.00$, $SD = 11.89$) showed that students were able to retain the content 2 weeks later with only a slight drop in mean test scores.

Results indicated that students believed that the puzzle-based and discussion-based activities helped them understand the information taught in the unit. They perceived that this approach motivated them to think more deeply and to remember information longer. Many students commented that they could remember more content because the game experiences were memorable. Students also believed games helped them to participate in lessons more fully by allowing them to engage closely with the material and to help each other. Least favorite games were those that did not allow students full participation and/or were too fast-paced. Field notes indicated that student participation depended on student interest as well as on the level of difficulty of the game. Students who believed a game was too difficult withdrew from participation. This indicated to the in-service teacher that he needed to ensure that all students were prepared to participate so that the activity is meaningful. Although students did prefer classroom games over traditional lectures and readings, students recognized that class games did not prepare them for a test better than traditional review methods. Rather, students believed that the games-lecture combination was beneficial because it was the lecture that prepared them for a traditional assessment.

Implications for in-service teachers. The results of the study indicated that many students enjoyed the educational and social aspects of game-like learning. The in-service teacher plans to continue to use these activities as one of many approaches to engage students in learning social studies content. However, the in-service teacher learned that in order for students to be engaged and on-task, he needed to assign their roles during each activity. In addition, the in-service teacher recognized the need to evaluate the academic level of each activity prior to implementation. Some activities were too easy which limited engagement and others were too challenging which caused anxiety among some students, each requiring more teacher preparation and better facilitation.

By reflecting on the results of this game-like learning study in such an in-depth way, the in-service teacher began to recognize individual differences in the way his students learned. He became more aware of student abilities and interests. This awareness and reflection allowed him to humanize his classroom and to reach all of his students so they can learn successfully.

Implications for pre-service teacher educators. This study illustrated that in addition to understanding the cognitive aspect of learning, pre-service teachers must take into account the age of their students and adjust activities and lessons to fit the unique needs of the students they will eventually teach.

As higher education faculty prepare prospective teachers to teach middle and high school students, they need to address the learning needs and psychological characteristics of adolescents as a part of the pre-service curriculum. As pre-service teachers learn to develop lesson plans and create learning activities, they need to consider, among other things, the adolescent need for social interaction. Thus, faculty teaching pre-service educators should demonstrate ways to transform a traditional lecture and its respective activity into an interactive and participatory experience for students at the K-12 level. Using this action research study as an example, it becomes imperative that higher education faculty model ways in which group activities at the middle school level can be differentiated to include participants of varied abilities.

An unexpected outcome of this particular study was the realization that time was a factor for teachers to consider when incorporating active learning in the classroom. Therefore, as educators of pre-service teachers, we are reminded that pacing and momentum are a part of the teaching process. Pre-service teachers must learn to monitor and adjust teaching not only to keep students engaged, but also to make sure that the needs of all students are addressed, thus, humanizing our teaching practices.

Case 2

Setting. Understanding the age and capabilities of learners enables teachers to consider a more humanistic way to address teaching, accentuating the needs of learners in the classroom.

The in-service teacher in this action research study wanted to implement creative dramatics into mathematics instruction. She wanted to determine the extent to which it helped her second-grade students solve multi-step mathematics word problems. Creative dramatics is similar to reader's theater whereby students act out scenarios to help with comprehension (Ulubey, 2018). It is a form of role-playing that helps students visualize a problem by making it more concrete.

Second-grade students progressed from following a teacher-created role-playing script to solve problems to the point where they began to create their own scripts that led them to a solution. For example, a problem might be "The baseball team had 81 games this season. They won 43 games. How many did they lose?" Student groups were to create a plan and script for how they would solve the problem. The groups would then use creative dramatics to perform the word problem for the class. This gave students an opportunity to demonstrate their own understanding of the problem and to ensure a shared all-class understanding. Following the performance, the students in the group would solve the problem. The class then would discuss the elements in the dramatic presentation that aided them in arriving at the correct answer.

The introduction of creative dramatics in the classroom demonstrates an understanding of the nature of young children and their need for movement and physical activity during the course of a school day (Morrison, 2012). Since creative dramatics is a form of role-playing, students are able to visualize the problem, making it more concrete. A majority of second-grade students have difficulty grasping abstract concepts (Piaget & Inhelder, 1969). Thus, using various modalities increases the chance for students to correctly solve the word problems. The researcher analyzed the end of unit math test and collected student feedback on the new teaching method.

Findings. The results of this action research project indicate that students enjoy acting out word problems. The results also suggest that using creative dramatics may help students in math comprehension ($M = 78.57$, $SD = 18.75$). Raw data showed that half of the students mastered the content while half of the students continued to struggle. In addition, results revealed that students found acting out problems to be a fun activity. It also provided opportunities for movement while learning. This opportunity to act out math problems enabled second graders to see the relationship between problem and solution.

Students indicated a desire to continue using creative dramatics in mathematics class as doing so helped them learn. Although the test data revealed that only half of the participants fully mastered the mathematics concepts taught in the unit, the use of creative dramatics is a method that should be an integral part of the teaching process to address different ways students learn.

Implications for in-service teachers. The results of this project indicated to the in-service teacher that creative dramatics can be effective in math instruction for primary students. In conjunction with traditional teacher-led instruction, this teacher plans to continue to use this strategy in her math class. The in-service teacher realized that students in her classroom were motivated to participate in their own learning. Providing an opportunity for students to take charge of their own learning stems from the desire to create a humanistic classroom environment where everyone has a chance to learn.

Implications for pre-service teacher educators. As teacher education faculty, we need to emphasize, through our actions, that instruction cannot be one-size-fits-all (Tomlinson, 2017). We must acknowledge that active participation is a prerequisite to successful learning. As teacher educators, we need to provide our pre-service teachers with ample opportunities to practice building lessons that incorporate active student participation. This study also provides evidence that we as pre-service teacher educators must acknowledge and share the idea that a positive classroom environment helps to foster the goal of student participation. This will enable the pre-service teachers to address individual needs in a humanistic manner.

Case 3

Setting. One of our graduate students was confronted with a group of fifth graders who were unable to focus during math class. She noted that her students were restless, distracted, and off-task during this particular class period especially on days when they did not have a scheduled physical education period. The teacher had an understanding of the need for young children to have movement for physical health but also for cognitive wellbeing. In a humanistic approach, one must seek to address the affective and physical side of learning as well as the cognitive aspect of learning.

Aware of this need, the in-service teacher elected to incorporate brain breaks, mental and physical refocusing activities, at the beginning of math lesson. Her goal was to see if the movement integration strategy would help students release energy through physical activity and, in so doing, introduce a calm classroom atmosphere. The movement integration upon which she relied included aerobic exercises, stretching, yoga, and dance. The teacher then chose to study four students who demonstrated the most off-task behaviors during the baseline assessment. At the conclusion of the study, all students in the class completed a teacher-designed survey regarding the brain break activities.

The in-service teacher introduced one of her brain break activities at the beginning of each math lesson. Then the math instruction began. Students sat with a partner, reviewed homework, and worked together on assigned math practice problems. Following this, students began an independent activity during which the off-task behaviors of the four students were noted in the observation checklist.

Findings. Data revealed that there was a decline in off-task behavior of the four students under study. Moreover, the observation checklist indicated that three of the four students under study had zero incidences of off-task behavior on multiple occasions over the course of the study. Survey data suggested that most students believed that brain breaks helped them focus and get ready to learn. Further, students believed that the participation in physical activity at the beginning of each lesson got them "ready to learn" and helped them to pay attention to the lesson. However, when introducing physical brain breaks, it is important that the teacher understand the interest and comfort levels of the students, as some students expressed discomfort when asked to dance in class.. This is the goal of humanistic education.

Implications for in-service teachers. The teacher realized that the implementation of brain breaks depended on students need to get up and move. The brain breaks may happen at any time during a lesson or the school day. Having introduced this innovation into the classroom, the in-service teacher enhanced her own knowledge of student development and learning. The results of this action research project enriched her teaching repertoire for keeping students focused, engaged, and ready to learn.

Implications for pre-service teacher educators. Pre-service teachers spend a great deal of time creating lesson plans and units that are filled with strong content and hands-on activities. But pre-service teachers also need to recognize the importance of movement for learning. Two takeaways from this study are evident:

(1) Pre-service teacher educators need to model and explain how the affective side of learning can be incorporated into daily activities. Brain breaks are but one strategy. Pre-service educators also need to be aware of the characteristics of children at different ages and appropriately incorporate this knowledge into their instruction.
(2) Pre-service teachers should anticipate any possible off-task behaviors of students they may encounter in their classrooms. Pre-service teacher educators need to intentionally speak about such activities as brain breaks when discussing classroom management.

We believe that this study teaches us, as pre-service teacher educators, to convey to our students the importance of being knowledgeable about student growth and development as well as sensitive to student needs and interests in order to be successful educators in the 21st century.

Case 4
Setting. Recently, a student in our graduate action research class came to realize that she needed to consider a different instructional approach for her three second-grade ESL students, each of whom was having difficulty in the area of writing. In this case, the students under study came from three different cultural backgrounds, spoke little English, and had extensive reading and writing challenges. Fortunately for these three students, this in-service teacher recognized that learning is fundamentally human and that humans are unique. She was sensitive to the fact that these students would have great difficulty keeping up with their peers if they were required to take part in whole-class, large group writing instruction.

Relying on her desire to humanize instruction and recognizing the needs of these three ESL students, the in-service teacher created a structure that enabled the three students to work together in a small-group setting. She then designed this particular intervention as an action research project. This peer-review structure enabled the students to become individual writers and peer reviewers at their own pace. As expected, in its early stages, the instructional model called for extensive teacher oversight and modeling. However, as the three students became more independent both in their writing and in their ability to question their peers, the teacher became the helpful observer.

The original goal of this study was to measure student growth in the following writing areas: organization of content, sentence structure, writing mechanics, and writing conventions. The in-service teacher was anxious to determine if a small-group, peer-review writing format would improve student writing skills and, at the same time, increase student confidence levels in the area of writing. The in-service teacher provided the three students with a daily writing topic, allocated writing time, and then gave them the opportunity to share their writings and become peer editors for each other. In their role as editors, students had an opportunity to pose questions and evaluate the writing of the peer author. This questioning and evaluation on the part of the students were accomplished through the use of a teacher-created checklist and rubric.

Initially, the teacher-created checklist included only three writing criteria for peer evaluation. As the study progressed, more items were added. At the conclusion of the study, the checklist incorporated 10 specific writing criteria that were to be applied by the two students who were editing the work of the third peer. As editors, the students in this study were required to ask questions of their peer author and, at the same time, make verbal suggestions that would help improve the writing submitted for review. Those peer suggestions led to revisions of the written work by each of the authors. This revision process was followed by an additional peer evaluation. In order to assist the three students as they began taking on peer evaluation responsibilities, the in-service teacher provided each with editorial sentence starters that assisted them as they began to offer revision advice to the author. Those sentence starters were classified as "compliments," "suggestions," or "corrections." For example:

- I really liked the way you...
- You have really strong reasons for...
- Maybe you can go back to add...
- I think you should add another reason for...
- This is a good place to correct...
- It looks like you are missing a ...

All three students relied on these sentence starters as they began their peer evaluation process. However, as the students became more confident in their ability to question their peers, reliance on the teacher-created sentence starters was no longer necessary.

Findings. As a result of being given the opportunity to work in a small peer-review group, each of the three ESL students showed considerable growth in the writing areas that were being addressed in this study, namely: content organization, sentence structure, writing mechanics, and writing conventions. The pre- and post-assessment scores for each of the three students can be seen in Table 1.

The in-service teacher felt that these results indicated that the intervention was successful and that the students under study improved in their writing skills. She also found this intervention increased student English-speaking skills. As noted above, initially the students under study relied on teacher-created sentence starters in order to pose questions and suggestions to their writing peers. As the weeks progressed, however, the students became more comfortable relying on their own

Table 1. Pre- and Post-Assessment Writing Rubric Scores for Three ESL Students Under Study.

Students	Rubric Writing Scores		Score Percentage	
	Pre-test	Post-test	Pre-test	Post-test
Student A	20/40	34/40	50.00%	85.00%
Student B	19/40	23/40	47.50%	57.50%
Student C	14/40	30/40	35.00%	75.00%

questions in order to assist their peers in writing and revising their written work. They continued to ask questions of each other and their own English-speaking skills began to improve. They became more comfortable going off-script as they asked questions and made revision suggestions to one another. Another important outcome of the project was greater communication between the three ESL students and other students within this third-grade class. In her evaluation of this action research project, the in-service teacher stated the following:

"As English-speaking skills improved, the students under study gained more confidence in their ability to converse with all of their peers and they began to enjoy the opportunity of meeting in order to discuss their writings."

Implications for in-service teachers. In this particular case, the action research experience noted above gave this in-service teacher an opportunity to "evaluate my teaching practices." She felt that this study provided her with a wonderful professional opportunity in that she was able to interact with and understand the needs of her ESL students in an in-depth way. This in-depth interaction with ESL students gave the in-service teacher not only greater sensitivity to their academic and social needs, but also greater insight as to ways in which she can make them feel comfortable in the classroom.

Implications for pre-service teacher educators. The results of this action research project provided us with an opportunity to share with our pre-service teachers the importance of planning for the diversity that will exist within their own classrooms, the task of bringing ESL students into the mainstream in creative ways. In this case, the in-service teacher thought in terms of the needs of each student in her class. In essence, she humanized her approach to education. She made a point of understanding the characteristics and the needs of each of the students within her classroom.

And finally, this action research project taught us one more thing, that is, if our goal is to assist ESL students to speak English with greater confidence then we must encourage them to speak English on a daily basis. We must allow them to speak English with their peers and provide opportunities for them to model correct grammar and proper sentence structure. In structuring classroom instruction in such a flexible and sensitive manner, the in-service teacher succeeded in helping the three ESL students to improve their English writing and speaking skills, thus providing an opportunity for these students to gain confidence in both areas.

DISCUSSION

The goal of action research is to improve both student learning and teacher pedagogy (Arends, 2007). Action research gives one an opportunity to gather and analyze student data, and thus, empowers teachers as they take action within the classroom and address learning differences (Ornstein, Pajak, & Ornstein, 2015). We further suggest that action research provides the same reward for those of us in higher education. As we bring these examples into our pre-service education classes, we are confident that our pre-service teachers have gained new perspectives. Therefore, the cases presented above, allow us to showcase three pedagogical implications for pre-service teacher educators.

Implication 1: Modeling of Best Practices Should Happen at all Academic Levels, Including Pre-Service Classrooms

All case studies presented here show that pre-service teacher educators should include modeling of various strategies into their instruction. Moreover, this modeling of novel ideas, skills, and strategies in the classroom must happen intentionally and explicitly at the pre-service level. It is also important to show pre-service teachers how activities and assessments align with course objectives and the standards that are being applied in K-12 classrooms. To achieve this, it is necessary that higher education faculty maintain their connections to the K-12 environments in order to keep current with best practices in authentic instruction environments. Action research projects undertaken by graduate students and overseen by university faculty provide another opportunity for university instructors to keep current with issues arising in classrooms today.

At the same time, it is important to remember that modeling requires that we make pre-service teachers aware of the time it takes to implement changes within the classroom. Case studies 1 and 2 speak to this issue. Each in-service teacher in these case studies recognized the fact that it takes time and reflection to prepare and present material in novel, exciting, and interesting ways. Thus, recognizing the need to humanize one's own teaching approaches must go hand-in-hand with the knowledge that doing so takes time, effort, dedication, and energy on the part of the teacher. Action research projects that address improvement within one's classroom answer this need to humanize our approach to teaching and give the teacher an opportunity to address the specific needs of the students within his/her class within a short period of time. These types of short-term, dedicated projects offer manageable and data-rich ideas for improving one's teaching and add to student learning, one small step at a time.

Implication 2: Pre-Service Teachers Need to be Cognizant of the Idea that in Some Instances the Approach, Whether Social or Academic, Needs to be Individualized

Spending the time to understand the needs of individual students who sit in our classrooms enables teachers to design instruction that results in true learning. Case study 4 illustrates this implication with clarity. The students who participated in this peer-editing study were given extensive scaffolding and individual writing opportunities in order to grow as writers. Thus, it follows that in order for individualized, humanistic approaches to be successful, the teacher has to understand the specific strengths, weaknesses, and interests of each student.

When discussing strategies that are intended to address the needs of students, it is important that pre-service teacher educators point out the fact that teaching strategies frequently applied to the special needs population may also be helpful in addressing the learning needs of students within the general education population. Doing so helps future teachers to become sensitive to the needs of all students. Case studies 1, 2, 3, and 4 demonstrate that thinking about all students in a critical way helps teachers understand both the social and academic needs of a particular group of students.

These creative approaches to education cannot take place unless pre-service teacher education faculty spend the time to present and share with pre-service teachers the results of actual 21st-century classroom research. In that way, we suggest, humanistic approaches addressing the educational needs of all students will become an integral part of the pre-service student experience.

Implication 3: Pre-Service Teachers Need to Understand that Meaningful Innovation Transcends the Classroom and Leads to School-Level Change

Humanizing education starts with teachers working with one child in one classroom. However, when teachers are encouraged to work collaboratively, humanistic practices have an opportunity to transcend and spread beyond just one classroom. Replicating their success in other classrooms and with other children eventually allows these small pedagogical changes to grow into a larger cultural shift on a school-wide level.

Thus, pre-service teachers need to realize that they are a part of a collaborative system. When they work together, solve problems together and come up with innovative solutions to address the needs of the students in their classrooms, they are using the system resources available to them and setting the stage for a humanistic approach to their teaching. To prepare for this pedagogical collaboration, higher education faculty need to become involved in action research at the graduate level and, at the same time, take the time to share the results of the research with future teachers. In that way, we can demonstrate to future teachers the importance of action research as well as the importance of becoming part of a team that is emphasizing holistic, humanistic, and 21st-century state-of-the-art approaches to educating each child.

CONCLUSION

Action research is a powerful tool that can and should be used by teachers in the classroom. Requiring graduate students to develop action research projects in order to complete their graduate degree, has become a positive experience not only for the graduate students, but also for those of us who teach in the pre-service teacher education program at our university. As pre-service education faculty working with graduate students, we have an opportunity to continuously reflect upon and analyze the various interventions and innovations that our graduate students have applied in their respective K-12 classrooms. Doing so allows us to introduce our undergraduate students to new and innovative teaching strategies that have been successful in a K-12 classroom. The four action research projects that we have highlighted here illustrate our own learning and the learning experiences that have been shared with our undergraduates in the university's teacher education program. This learning and sharing cycle enables us to personalize and humanize education for our graduate and undergraduate students, and, by extension, the K-12 students for whom they are responsible.

REFERENCES

Arends, R. (2007). *Learning to teach* (7th ed.). New York, NY: McGraw-Hill.

Bartolome, L. I. (1994). Beyond the methods Fetish: Towards a humanizing pedagogy. *Harvard Educational Review, 64*(2), 173–194.

Brydon-Miller, M., Greenwood, D., & Maguire, P. (2003). "Why action research?" *Action Research, 1*(1), 9–28. http://journals.sagepub.com/doi/pdf/10.1177/14767503030011002

Dana, N. F. (2013). *Digging deeper into action research: A teacher inquirer's field guide.* Thousand Oaks, CA: Sage.

Gist, C., Jackson, I., Nightengale-Lee, B., & Allen, K. (2019). Culturally responsive pedagogy in teacher education. In J. Lampert (Ed.), *Oxford research encyclopedias, section education, subject: Education, cultures, and ethnicities.* New York, NY: Oxford University Press. Retrieved on August 1, 2019. doi:10.1093/acrefore/9780190264093.013.266

Larrivee, B. (2008). Development of a tool to assess teachers' level of reflective practice. *Reflective Practice, 9*(3), 341–360.

Morrison, G. S. (2012). *Early childhood education today* (12th ed.). New York, NY: Pearson Publishing.

Muessig, R. H., & Cogan J. J. (1972, October). Humanizing schooling. *Educational Leadership, 30*(1), 34–36.

Neapolitan, J. E. (2000, February). *What do teachers believe about action research as a mechanism for change?* Paper presented at the Annual Meeting of the Association of Teacher Educators, Orlando, FL, February 12–16.

Ornstein, A., Pajak, E., & Ornstein, S. (2015). *Contemporary issues in curriculum* (6th ed.). New York, NY: Pearson.

Piaget, J., & Inhelder, B. (1969). *The psychology of the child.* New York, NY: Basic Books.

Putman, S. M., & Rock, T. (2017). *Using strategic inquiry to improve teaching and learning.* Los Angeles, CA: Sage.

Stewart, K. L. (2018). *The role of growth mindset and efficacy in teachers as change agents.* Moraga: Saint Mary's College of California.

Tomlinson, C. A. (2017). *How to differentiate instruction in academically diverse classrooms.* Alexandria, VA: ASCD.

Ulubey, Ö. (2018). The effect of creative drama as a method on skills: A meta-analysis Study. *Journal of Education and Training Studies, 6*(4), 63–78.

CHAPTER 7

NAVIGATING TRICKY TERRAIN: EARLY CAREER ACADEMICS CHARTING A RESEARCH TRAJECTORY IN THE NEOLIBERAL UNIVERSITY

Mohamed Alansari, Jennifer Tatebe and Carol Mutch

ABSTRACT

The current book chapter seeks to respond to the existing literature on early career researchers, using an autoethnographic approach to further unravel the crossroads of identity formation, research politics, and successful promotion through the eyes of early career researchers. Combining autobiography and ethnography, we systematically analyze our own experiences to make sense of wider social and political practices. Ellis, Adams, and Bochner (2010) remind us that autoethnography is not to be dismissed as a form of self-therapy but is to be presented in a rigorous manner as other research forms by carefully justifying the data sources and techniques, analyzing the data and crafting the findings. Our sources were both found texts (e.g., university policies) and created texts (our journal entries and personal communications). Using analytic techniques such as highlighting critical incidents or epiphanies, we structured coherent narratives to illuminate the complexity and uncertainty of the lives of early career academics. This chapter's focus on early career researcher experiences makes poignant commentary on neoliberalism's impact on and within higher education. The chapter concludes with the authors' reflections on the dilemmas of academic and research choices made within the limitations of institutional structures, processes, and systems that shape career trajectories.

Keywords: Early career academics; emerging scholars; post-doctoral research; neoliberalism; neoliberal university; higher education; tertiary education; conscious complicity; unwitting complicity; coercive complicity; autoethnography; narrative inquiry

INTRODUCTION

The neoliberal university continues to be a subject of critique (Ball, 2012; Bottrell & Manathunga, 2019a; Cupples & Pawson, 2012; Olssen & Peters, 2005; Shore & Davidson, 2014; Smeltzer & Hearn, 2015). It has been variously described as toxic (Smyth, 2017), feudal (Bergami, 2019), dystopic (Roberts, 2013), and schizophrenic (Shore, 2007, 2010). In finding ways to express feelings of anxiety and frustration with how their roles have changed under a neoliberal regime (Roberts, 2013), academics have turned to more creative forms of expression to enable these emotions to be recognized (see, e.g., Grant, 2019). First, such expression is a cry to be heard, where the emotions are raw, powerful, and cathartic (see, e.g., Andrew, 2019). Second, it is a self-protective move as the academic comes to understand the mechanisms of the neoliberal university for what they are and how they have reshaped academic identity (see, e.g., Vicars, 2019). Third, it provides an opportunity for an overt challenge to the system – now that the mechanisms have been recognized, they can potentially be dismantled (Cupples & Pawson, 2012). Whereas experienced academics are finding spaces to air their concerns and plan their strategies to subvert the system they find so oppressive, early career academics are often left in limbo. They have come into academia with high expectations and yet find the reality of the neoliberal university a hard and bewildering place. As Bottrell and Manathunga (2019b) state, "Early career academics tend to be more vulnerable to exploitation and may find they need to be 'super-heroes' to meet institutional expectations" (p. 8). This chapter gives voice to two early career academics who were part of an emerging scholars' discussion group. Their wish to join the wider academic conversation on constructing an academic identity within the neoliberal university was the genesis of this chapter. Autoethnography gave them the means by which to begin their narrative journey.

This chapter begins by synthesizing some of the literature on the neoliberal university before outlining a theoretical framework, drawn from that literature that will later be used to examine the early career academics' joint narrative. The section that follows the literature review outlines the autoethnographic methodology undertaken and the way in which the co-constructed narrative emerged. The findings section of the chapter shares the early career academics' joint narrative, written in the first person and arranged in three themes: (1) Bifurcations and hierarchies; (2) Identities: Harmonies and clashes; and (3) Game of thrones: Tyrants, gatekeepers, and legends. The chapter concludes with a discussion that draws on Shore and Davidson's (2014) three theoretical concepts – conscious complicity, unwitting complicity, and coercive complicity to place the early career academics' story of navigating the neoliberal university into an explanatory theoretical framework.

LITERATURE REVIEW

Neoliberalism is a contested, fluid, and contradictory term that "reinvents itself in startlingly new and innovative ways" (Cupples & Pawson, 2012, p. 20). For the purposes of this chapter, neoliberalism is seen as a trend in higher education policy and decision making toward individualism, competitiveness, commodification, and managerialism. Neoliberal ideology reinscribes the university as a corporate enterprise where individual customers (students) make choices of products (course, qualifications, or credentials) in order to secure their own and the country's economic security. Because the state provides less financial support to the business of higher education, the products need to be of high quality to compete in a free market environment. This strategy requires efficient and cost-effective production through the commodification of academic labor. Universities develop a brand and market their niche products, in order to attract fee-paying international students. Leadership styles became hierarchical and corporate. Vice-Chancellors became CEOs. A divide occurs between managers and academics; unions are weakened and labor is casualized. Research turns its focus to innovation, entrepreneurialism, and commercialization through patents and consultancies. Higher education moves from a public good to a private investment (Andrew, 2019; Ball, 2012; Bergami, 2019; Bottrell & Manathunga, 2019a, 2019b; Cupples & Pawson, 2012; Mountz et al., 2015; Mutch and Tatebe, 2017; Olssen & Peters, 2005; Shore & Davidson, 2014; Smeltzer & Hearn, 2015). Shore and Davidson (2014, p. 13) note:

> From institutions that were geared to higher learning, the disinterested pursuit of knowledge, public good research and nation building, public universities have been refashioned increasingly to resemble transnational business corporations operating in a global knowledge economy.

The competitive, low-trust neoliberal corporate culture encourages an audit mentality "with its perpetual measurement and evaluation of teaching 'outputs' and research 'inputs', and the displacement of academic values and faculty members' scholarly judgement" (Smeltzer & Hearn, 2015, p. 354) and an increased focus on measurement through "strategic planning, performance indicators, quality assurance measures and academic audits" (Olssen & Peters, 2005, p. 313). Time is compressed, which, when combined with the audit culture, "is designed to elicit compliance without resistance" (Mountz et al., 2015, p. 1242). Smeltzer and Hearn's description (2015, p. 354) resonates with the experience at our university:

> Demands to produce research with monetizable results, the unceasing mantra of innovation, the preoccupation with techno-science, the administrative use of information and communication technologies for the integration of faculty into client-self-service systems, the casualization and increasing tiering of academic labour, the erosion of faculty self-governance, the growth of branch campuses overseas and the overt courting of lucrative international students and their lucrative international fees are other symptoms of the neoliberal university.

In the literature, the authors use a range of theoretical frameworks to explain how neoliberalism operates within higher education. Foucault's concepts of governmentality, surveillance, power, and subjection are often called upon. Olssen and Peters (2005), for example, discuss the difference between *liberal* governmentality which encourages the autonomous professional and *neoliberal* governmentality which favors line management chains and hierarchical structures designed to do the very opposite. Ball (2012) uses Lyotard's notion of performativity to highlight, "a powerful and insidious policy technology that is now at work at all levels and in all kinds of education and public service" (p. 19). Olssen and Peters (2005) also use Lyotard's notion of performativity. They claim that the traditional academic culture of open intellectual debate has been replaced with "an institutional stress on performativity, as evidenced by the emergence of on measured outputs: on strategic planning, performance indicators, quality assurance measures and academic audits" (p. 313).

We, however, were taken by Shore and Davidson's (2014) claim that "Many academics express concern that despite their intellectual critiques of neoliberalism, when neoliberal practices reach their own workplace, they can find themselves as *accomplices* [our emphasis] in various ways." Shore and Davidson discuss this idea using three descriptors – *conscious complicity*, which pertains especially to those who willingly buy into the subjugation and subjectification of their colleagues; *unwitting complicity* which describes those who fail to see "the structural violence and webs of domination in which they are suspended" (p. 14); and *coercive complicity*, which is where the system puts their employment or advancement at risk if they show any act of defiance or resistance. We will return to these descriptors in the discussion section.

METHODOLOGY

This chapter is deliberately subjective. The purpose is to share the experiences of two early career academics in a co-constructed narrative. The narrative was forged through personal journaling and recorded conversations, interspersed with outpourings of frustration, and bursts of laughter. The data gathering process was iterative and emergent drawing on two main qualitative approaches – autoethnography and narrative inquiry.

Autoethnography is more than autobiography. The term itself gives an indication of its purpose – auto (self) + ethno (culture) + graphy (writing) – writing one's own story in order to illuminate social, political, or cultural issues (Denshire, 2014; Ellington & Ellis, 2008). It is described as both a process (the crafting) and a product (the narrative) (Ellis et al., 2011). It borrows from literary traditions of storytelling with setting, plot, characters, action, and dénouement but illuminates the problem being explored within the wider context in which the problem exists (Denshire, 2014; Ellington & Ellis, 2008; Ellis, 1999, 2004). Autoethnography is deliberately self-conscious but not self-indulgent. Autoethnography approaches research as a construction arising out of a researcher's personal history and current position. It has its own internal discipline – part of which is to challenge the objective, positivist stance that is privileged in much research and draws instead on post-modern, interpretivist, and/or social constructionist theories (Wall, 2006). It does not purport to be a truth, as Ellis (1999, p. 673) states, "The truth is that we can never capture experience ... [it is] one selective story about what happened from a particular point in time for a particular purpose." Autoethnography seeks "verisimilitude" rather than truth: "it evokes in readers a feeling that the experience described is lifelike, believable and possible" (Ellis, 1999, p. 674). Anderson describes this as "narrative fidelity" (2006, p. 386) in which the writer aims to give insight into a broader understanding of a social phenomenon that is greater than the narrative itself. It enables the researcher to be more reflexive about who they are, why they are recording their experience and for what purpose (Wall, 2006). By challenging conventions, engaging the reader and holding society up to scrutiny, autoethnography provides an evocative entrée into an authentic lived experience (Andrew, 2019; Denshire, 2014; Ellington & Ellis, 2008; Ellis, 1999, 2004; Ellis et al., 2011; Mutch, 2013;Wall, 2006).

Narrative inquiry is a related field. Narrative researchers use stories, narratives, and descriptions as their object of study as well as their data gathering, sense-making, and sharing techniques (Clandinin & Connelly, 2000; Connelly & Clandinin, 1990; Pinnegar & Daynes, 2007). Both autoethnography and narrative inquiry use a range of narrative techniques. Ellis (1999), for example, lists internal monologue, dialogue, dramatic recall, imagery, and flashback. Denshire (2014) includes testimony, diary excerpts, reflective writing, and poetry. The initial strategy employed by the two early career scholars in this chapter was to journal their own experiences. This way they could record their thoughts and feelings freely, delving into the past and adding more recent commentary. Ellis (1999) supports this approach:

> Memory doesn't work in a linear way, nor does life either, for that matter. Instead, thoughts and feelings circle around us, flash back, then forward; the topical is interwoven with the chronological; thoughts and feelings merge, drop from our grasp, the reappear in another context. In real life we don't know when we know something. Events in the past are always interpreted from our current position. (p. 675)

From their original journal entries, the early career researchers were able to construct, reconstruct and deconstruct vignettes that they were willing to share with each other through a series of focused conversations. In these conversations, they were struck by the similarities of their experiences and yet the different opportunities that these experiences afforded each of them. In autoethnographic terms, their individual vignettes would have been sufficient to fully engage the reader in the lived reality of an early career researcher. This approach is known as "evocative autoethnography" (Anderson, 2006; Ellington & Ellis, 2008; Ellis & Bochner, 2006). Anderson (2006), however, makes an argument for more use of "analytic autoethnography." He discusses the factors that make autoethnography *analytic*, including the researcher's membership of the group being researched, analytic reflexivity, narrative visibility, dialogue beyond oneself, and commitment to theoretical analysis.

The process that began with the early career academics sharing their vignettes took an analytic turn and the result fits neatly with Anderson's (2006) criteria for analytic autoethnography. The autoethnography writers are members of the group they are researching (early career academics); they engaged in reflexivity through each stage of the process – both individually and collaboratively; their product (the findings section of this chapter) is visibly in narrative form; they engaged in dialogue with each other (and their co-author); and they committed to theoretical analysis.

In their analysis, the early career academics conducted a thematic analysis (Mutch, 2013) of their vignettes and the resulting conversations before reconstructing collaborative narratives under the following themes: *Bifurcations and hierarchies, Identities: harmonies and clashes*, and finally, *Game of thrones: Tyrants, gatekeepers, and legends*. Later, they returned to the theoretical framework discussed by Shore and Davidson (2014) to attend to the last of Anderson's criteria and undertake "theoretical development, refinement and extension" (2006, p. 387). The findings section that follows is told in their joint narrative voice.

FINDINGS

Theme 1: Bifurcations and Hierarchies

There are so many systemic, structural barriers within academia that force difficult choices in time-sensitive situations. The systems of recognition, participation, and what "counts" are age-old within a monolithically slow-moving pace of the university. These systems directly contribute to the bifurcation of research and teaching. Being an academic in our university requires staff to spend 40% of their time on research, 40% on teaching, and 20% on service and leadership. Being judged as an academic in my university, therefore, is done holistically on the assumption that a person can excel in all three areas and is able to switch between teaching tasks, research activities, and leadership roles in any given semester, month, week, or day.

The implicit privilege of research over teaching however is firmly entrenched. It is often staff who are described as excellent researchers who are supported to travel abroad, work with colleagues overseas, share their research insights, and establish further research collaborations to advance their academic trajectories. At our institution, as with most others globally, there is an entire office dedicated to supporting academics to secure research grants. The administrative support includes assisting with budgets, grant writing, and seeking external funders, amongst others. I experienced the above first hand in numerous occasions, the unspoken privileges of research. The more I excelled in my research, the more funding I attracted which, in turn, gave me access to assistants to support my research, invitations to join other research teams to contribute with my data analytical expertise, invitations to review manuscripts in top journals in my field, requests to join advisory groups, invited presentations and workshops in other faculties, as well as funding opportunities to buy me out of my teaching (which I equally enjoyed) and focus more on my research.

In contrast, teaching simply does not hold the same value or status in the academy. It is rarely excellent tertiary teachers who receive similar opportunities and support from the same institution to travel abroad, work with tertiary teaching colleagues overseas, share their practice, and establish further communities of tertiary practice. Instead, staff who spend a substantial amount of time perfecting their teaching, supporting their students, and enhancing the teaching and learning environment, are often assumed to not be good researchers by virtue of the time, passion, and resources that they pour into their teaching. There is also no comparable institutional support for teaching. Whereas many institutions do have teaching and learning centers, their support largely comes from limited spaces in ad-hoc workshops on a variety of topics. In contrast with research support, teaching and learning centers do not employ professional staff to help academics with daily teaching activities like developing courses and lecture preparation, course administration and set up, nor do they assist with applying for teaching grants or offer support for writing applications to support teaching buy out, if that option exists at all. Teaching awards similarly do not bring the same status or career propelling outcomes of a major grant. Whereas we may be seeing further attention placed on teaching in academia (see the U21 Teaching Standards Framework, and UK-based Teaching Excellence Framework), strong teaching evaluations do not build a career narrative in the same way research grants do. It's an internal problem perpetuated by universities (coercive complicity). There are clear indications and explicit messages from middle and senior leadership teams that academics are judged holistically, yet it is hard not to believe otherwise. I have had numerous conversations with staff who told me that being good at teaching will not take me far in academia, and that research brings in profit, prestige, and increased rankings, which in turn brings in more students. Despite my excellent record in teaching, I am rarely offered a teaching assistant to support the long hours of marking, dealing with student queries, and tracking their progress both online and in person. I am rarely invited to co-teach in other teams, almost never invited to talk about my tertiary practice locally or internationally, and never receive funding opportunities to improve my teaching practice. In fact, there is no professional development time factored in my workload to improve my teaching capabilities, as these opportunities are seen as add-ons; yet another thing to do on top of an already busy 40-hour week.

Institutions have also helped to create strong research-teaching hierarchies. These hierarchies operate in official and informal capacities. The most visible hierarchy related to the bifurcation of research and teaching are academic titles. Academic titles vary globally. Our institution follows UK conventions with traditional academics moving from Lecturer, Senior Lecturer, Associate Professor, and Full Professor. All academics holding one of these titles has research, teaching, and service components to their positions. Meanwhile, a current global trend of research only and teaching only academic pathways extend the bifurcation of research and teaching. At our institution, Research Assistant and Research Fellow positions are purely research-based. Teaching Fellows are teaching only positions with these academics holding very high teaching workloads and often work exclusively in the university's professional programs. Whilst it can be argued that these two different pathways recognize particular expertise, they offer little potential to address the aforementioned bifurcation of research and teaching. At the same time, they also contribute to hierarchical conversations about the value of research and teaching. Emerging scholars entering academia must also be aware of the challenges of changing pathways. Unless actively (and successfully) pursuing opportunities in the other track, jumping back into a traditional research, teaching, and service position or the opposite track is often difficult.

Theme 2: Identities: Harmonies and Clashes

Being a new and emerging academic staff has always attracted certain colleagues, typically seniors in terms of career progression and generation, to talk to me about my future plans, what I need to focus on as well as who I should be. Being identified as a "newbie," "post-doc," or simply "young" had always contained negative connotations and indirect judgments on my professional capabilities and academic skills. Despite receiving excellent teaching evaluations, and producing a range of research outputs every year, it is messages such as the ones below that are often prevalent in my communication with senior academics:

> "Don't worry about your teaching, it's the research that matters."
>
> "It's okay, one day you won't be as optimistic."
>
> "You're young, you will learn how to play the game properly soon."
>
> "Focus on research, teach when you have to, and engage in one service element as a new academic staff member."

There is no comparable emphasis on teaching. The following quote exemplifies the pressure to develop a research-based identity, I was advised to:

> "Just get through teaching without terrible [teaching] evaluations, and you will be fine. Focus on getting grants instead."

Service is even less valued and thus often omitted from the list as there is no "value" in it. I am often left in an internal clash between how I want to carve an academic career path for myself, and how influential senior academics see that path carved for me. In a way, I did not have a real academic identity until I resolved this clash as I forcefully transitioned out of a "junior academic" state that saw me as fragile, prone to judgments, and individual. Interestingly, professors tend to give advice to new staff more so than their own fellow professors.

Working in a largely professional Faculty further amplifies the tensions between different academic identities. The chasm between those who identify as researchers are often the ones who come from academic and professional backgrounds outside of the traditional education or professional fields. I have found that this group is the most likely to advise to steer away from being "pigeon-holed" as a teacher in favor of being more favorably seen as researchers who "bring in the money." I have regularly been directly advised to forget that I am a teacher, and even refrain from identifying as a teacher in my lectures. Meanwhile, the other tension comes from those proud of their professional identity as a teacher or social worker. Those operating within teacher preparation circles often hold comparable aversion for the researchers and colleagues who do not contribute to professional fields.

Several questions arise from the tension between various contrasting identities. First, what opportunities for change exist within academia to value different types of knowledge and expertise? I have observed the difference between researchers who conduct research in schools, and educational settings more broadly, who lack the knowledge and understanding of the complexity of schools, teaching, and learning. This has led to numerous blunders amongst colliding worlds with competing interests. More specifically, those who research **on** schools, educators, and learners versus those who research **with** and **for** the same three groups. As one school Principal explained, he accepted my research invitation over the 10 + he receives each week because I am a teacher who knows about how schools work, I have connections to the Deputy Principal and teachers, and I made the time to personally meet his full staff at a morning staff meeting to explain my research and answer any questions about the project. Further, I offered to come back and present my findings to his senior leadership team and full staff upon request. In contrast, in this Principal's experience, the majority of researchers "take" from schools, teachers, and learners. Take, in this sense, meaning taking up time, space, energy, and being a disruption. He went on to describe how most researchers come and go without any feedback to those that make the research possible: the participants – or the schools, teachers, and learners.

The second question I ask is, does the divide need to exist? While acknowledging institutional pressures, is it possible to merge these identities into a broad understanding of academics as educators? This tension between the self-perceived and perpetuated academic versus professional identity is unlikely to abate any time soon due to conflicting institutional messages about this divide. On the one hand, our Faculty promotes itself as teaching and learning focussed in its vision statement. However, the Faculty has also developed and supported a system of "comfortable" silos where some staff have little, if any, engagement with undergraduate students and those preparing for a specific profession. Instead, teaching has been conceptualized by some as working exclusively with postgraduate students and teaching on inter-Faculty programs outside of our two main professional programs. A second contradiction is the promotion of the University's identity as a leading "research-intensive" institution. The strategic plan, vision, and other similar strategy documentation make explicit the orientation and emphasis on research. The outcome of contrasting messaging about the Faculty and University priorities underscores the division between teaching and research.

> *I quickly learned that you need to decide very early on what kind of academic you wish to be. It's a hard question because you really don't have much experience to go on except for what you've observed. The classic trope of the career building, career hungry academic who climbs to the rank of Professor as quickly as possible does exist. There are always a few of these touting their own praises in every department. However, the career-driven academic is partly the outcome of the intense pressures of being an academic that we all feel. The "publish or perish" mantra is real. So is the increasing need for "evidence" of all aspects of our work that is inseparable from processes like continuation, promotion, and tenure. The "Professor fast track," as I fondly refer to it, is certainly promoted within particular academic circles but ... at what cost?*
>
> *On the other hand, I have also attracted a number of academic staff who identified with my journey, early career achievements, and aspirations. Indeed, I enjoyed their positivity, support, and intellectual conversations on the state of academia. It is people like them who I prefer to identify with, and it is their insights that made me reflect on who I want to be as an academic in five or even 10 years' time:*
>
> "Don't worry, we've all been there, just stand your ground."
>
> "It's okay, you should hear what they've done to me when I started."
>
> "Just avoid the backstabbers, all they care about is their careers."
>
> *I gained solace listening to their stories, which made me feel like I was not alone in how I experienced my first three years in academia. And yet, I became even more frustrated at the recurring theme: a never-ending vicious cycle of the powerful senior academic "handing over" an identity, a mentality, a predetermined path to follow; a recipe for producing another ruthless academic.*

Theme 3: Game of Thrones: Tyrants, Gatekeepers, and Legends

Institutional power, status, and privilege flourish in academia built on the bifurcation of research and teaching, academic rank hierarchies, and institutional systems that support different academic identities. Add in the neoliberal pressures of competition, choice, and privatization that are present within many public and private institutions, and some academics become tyrants and gatekeepers. This can lead to the hoarding and denial of opportunities. In everyday academic life, this can mean shoulder-tapping instead of widely disseminating advertised positions, inviting certain individuals to meetings while leaving others uninformed leading to the absence of multiple voices on committees; however, there is no better example than selection committees. I have often thought of myself and other new and emerging staff as people with great potential, fresh perspectives, creative ideas, and different ways of problem-solving. And so, I assumed that by virtue of being fresh out of university, that

I would be given the opportunity to serve on university committees, and use my experience of studying in the same college to make a difference from within to other students' (and potentially upcoming academics') professional trajectories. Engaging in leadership opportunities has often given me a sense of pride, challenge, and purpose – all of which are crucial for my sense of self-worth and personal satisfaction. Yet, I was often shocked to find that, despite being confident in my capabilities, that opportunities to lead, impact policy, and change are often predicated on seniority not merit. I needed a few more promotions, a few more publications, and a few more gray hairs, before my expression of interest would be considered for a challenge that I am well-qualified, well-suited, and well-commended, to tackle. All of a sudden, achievements that are irrelevant to opportunities I want to rise to, are now paramount to my survival as an academic. I began worrying that by the time I am given an opportunity to make a difference to any strategic initiatives in my institution, my ideas and arguments might no longer be current, useful, or important to consider. But then, this is how it always has been. It often appears as though academic staff are more concerned with upholding a status quo which has always served them well, more so than one that opens up opportunities and pathways for new practices, initiatives, and new colleagues like us.

Let us be clear – the myth of meritocracy extends to academia. Opportunities and career progressions can be made or broken by individual tyrants and gatekeepers. Academic snobbery is often central to such decisions. Here we come back to the issue of what is valued in academia. As an emerging scholar, I have sat on selection committees for grants standing in for senior academics unable to attend such meetings and I have observed rules become guidelines, exceptions made and academic snobbery at its finest become apparent as personal agendas and vendettas take center stage. "This person is a very low-level academic" is an example of a comment made about a colleague that still rings in my ears. Weaving in another previous thread is how gatekeeping is often tied to academic rank. Academia is interesting in that many selection processes are governed and facilitated by our colleagues. Senior academics are often over-represented on promotion and selection committees, as are those who identify as researchers. This can lead to limited understanding of "generational" understanding of the changing climate of academia for emerging scholars. For example, a well-intentioned, yet out of touch, senior colleague advised me to "finish your PhD and then publish a paper or two." In contrast, most institutions require 3–5 peer-reviewed publications to even apply for an entry-level position. The absence of multiple academic identities including professionally oriented academics may lead to blind spots on promotion committees. After speaking with a mentor I became aware of how some "top" researchers may have limited knowledge of other fields. Commentary from a peer review of a promotion application offers the perfect example of how academic snobbery and the limitation of certain expertise can have long-term career advancement implications. The comment, "well this person has no A star publications or national grants. Clearly, this application cannot go forward" ignored how the applicant's emerging (and innovative)

> field is so new there are no A star publications to publish in. Similarly, the applicant's work is interdisciplinary creating some challenges of "fitting" into traditional academic disciplines and grants.
>
> But what of the legends? Thankfully there are some true legends who use their power, status, and privilege to create space for others. These academic heroes support colleagues formally and personally. They are the ones sitting on the committees who point out the systemic advantages and disadvantages to minority scholars. They create opportunities for their postgraduate students to work on their projects, and insist on mentoring emerging scholars in their research and teaching teams. At conferences, they attend colleagues' presentations and if the presenter is attacked or asked a question that they need more time to think through, they offer an insightful comment. Perhaps, a tertiary environment in which new staff could flourish may benefit from leaders and professors with a pathway-enabling, people-focused, approach that opens up the door for colleagues with potential to grow academically, as opposed to those with a gate-keeping, system-oriented, approach that rewards eliteness over potential, proficiency over growth, and profit over people. If someone had told me this about academia before joining, I would have probably chosen another career pathway. Legends bring us back to a previous question of academic identity ... what kind of academic do you want to be?

Anomalies: Two Academics, Similar Paths, Same Qualifications, Different Opportunities?

In the process of identifying common themes and experiences, one strong anomaly became apparent: How is it that two friends and colleagues, who started their academic careers within three years of each other, with identical qualifications and similar teaching and research records, end up receiving different opportunities to advance their careers?

Author 1
On the one hand, I noticed that I am offered more opportunities to collaborate with others on my teaching (both at the undergraduate and postgraduate levels) and research because I'm both the "smart and a nice guy." I have often felt proud that people thought of me that way, until I realized that other colleagues' initial judgments and expectations of me were not based on my merits and expertise, but instead my doctoral supervisor's merits and expertise, as well as their existing relationships with other colleagues. I have come to realize that the more enemies my doctoral supervisors had (e.g., those who disagreed with their work, had poor working relationships, or simply did not get along with my supervisor), the more enemies I picked up even before meeting any of those so-called enemies. In contrast, those who cherished my supervisors, admired their work, or simply had invested interest, had welcomed me with open arms even before knowing about my skills or knowledge.

I realized that all of the staff who had been condescending, telling me that I would not make it in academia because I am too young or I am not ready yet, have had some issues or turbulence with my supervisors. Conversely, those who no longer saw me as a doctoral student, invited me to work with them, or asked for my expertise on research or teaching matters, are staff who approached my supervisors and valued them in the same areas above. In a way, being supervised by prolific, well-established professors and supervisors had its blessings and curses. I am now blessed to be thought of highly by some, but cursed by others as that one person who was "lucky" to get an academic post because of who he knew, as opposed to what he knew, as one senior tutor attacked me once with these words.

I cannot emphasize enough how political the relationships between one's mentor, supervisor or advisor, and their colleagues can be, including the impact of such relationships on the doctoral student or junior academic being supervised or advised by that staff member. At times, I do wonder whether I am lucky enough to have been surrounded by my previous supervisor's research groups and colleagues who have nurtured me into becoming the academic I am today. At other times, I equally wonder what would have happened to my career if I was supervised by excellent supervisors who were either selfish, disconnected from any professional network, or had many disagreements with colleagues at the same institution.

Author 2

My friend and colleague's story is similar to mine. I too, experienced the double-edged sword of being employed in my first academic position at the same institution where I completed my PhD. One of my former supervisors was in a senior leadership position when I was hired which has drawn many disdainful looks and snide comments from colleagues who felt I got my job out of nepotism. The reality couldn't be farther than the truth. The position was internationally advertised and I successfully won the position against several well-qualified candidates based on the decision of eight selection committee members. Luckily, I am fortunate to have other colleagues who choose to see my skills and abilities as assets and are champions of my employment and work.

Invitations to teach on postgraduate courses and be involved in other research projects are where our stories diverge. Unlike my colleague, in six years, I have yet to be given the opportunity to teach postgraduate research courses. Politics again. I have been told I already "get too many opportunities," that I "have to wait my turn," or that "I'm unqualified" despite having a PhD and all the required skills to teach postgraduate research courses. Again, the legends stepped up and created opportunities to teach on complex undergraduate programs that have advanced my career and university profile. I'm still hopeful that I will teach on a postgraduate research course in the near future. Academic identity returns here as a second contributing factor. As a registered teacher with full-time teaching experience in three global contexts, I primarily teach on our professional undergraduate and diploma programs. I have also not been invited onto colleagues' research projects. Different expertise and areas of interest are relevant reasons yet, tyrants and gatekeepers could have opened the door. It would be remiss to omit how marginalized academic groups within the academy (i.e., ethnic and cultural groups, women, and others) are often further marginalized through inequitable access to professional development opportunities and formal recognition systems like teaching evaluations (Matthew, 2016), and are often given extra service and other similar "invisible" work (Social Sciences Feminist Network Research Group, 2016). Mentoring support of legends and hard work has progressively led from smaller to more significant solo grants and research I strongly value.

Authors 1 and 2
Upon enrollment in any doctoral program, we were told to choose a supervisor whose research area and expertise aligns with ours. No one told us that we also needed to look for someone who is respected, liked, and well connected in the research community. For one of us, had we known what we know now back then, the same supervisors would have been chosen, but the choice to work somewhere where the supervisor isn't well-known would have been made. For the other, the importance of greater awareness of how academic politics work well beyond the PhD would have led to more strategic teaching and research choices from day one.

DISCUSSION

The manner in which the two early career academics recall their experiences in the neoliberal university resonates with the words of Darder (2019) as they found themselves, "ensconced in the dehumanizing ethos of free market supremacy, social surveillance, and community shattering individualism…" (p. 5).

Whereas there might be many theoretical frameworks through which the early career academics' narratives could be interpreted, we have chosen Shore and Davidson's (2014) notions of complicity. Shore and Davidson explain that neoliberal assumptions and ways of operating have become so intrenched in the higher education system that the idea of "collusion loses its intentional, scheming character and becomes a more passive yet willing acceptance of immoral action" (p. 17). Viewed this way, neoliberalism is taken for granted, unquestioned and unchallenged. Yet, academics can, and many do, benefit from the new affordances. To understand how they might achieve this, Shore and Davidson instead use the term *complicity* and see this concept as playing out in nuanced ways – *conscious complicity* – those who willingly buy in to the subjugation and subjectification of their colleagues; *unwitting complicity* – those who fail to see the dehumanizing ethos Darder describes; and *coercive complicity* – where academics dare not risk any act of defiance or resistance.

The strongest of the complicities that the early career academics experienced was that of *conscious complicity*. The stories they tell of their senior colleagues (except for those they title "legends") were of conscious buying into the system for their own ends. The joint narrative talked of "career hungry academics" who used their titles to further their own status and recognition, using tactics such as "academic snobbery" and "hoarding and denial of opportunities." Such academics claim their right to choose the courses they will teach, selectively invite others onto research projects or committees, and overtly deride those who do not meet their narrow criteria for appointment or promotion. Shore and Davidson (2007, pp. 17–18) describe this conscious complicity as:

> ...forms of collusion where individuals are aware of the consequences of neoliberal policies but nevertheless support them. This may be for reasons of apathy or cynicism, but often involves ideological motivations, through which actors might be convinced of the ethics of their position.

These senior academics act as gatekeepers who let in (or keep out) those they deem worthy (or unworthy) of the privileges that they have already amassed. Shore and Davidson continue:

> This class might include the many academics who, attracted by the higher salaries and status (or pushed by the incessant pressures to be "research active"), have joined the ranks of the expanding academic administration.

They become the academic or administrative *elite* who broker new ways of operating and through their roles in the academic or administrative hierarchies, oversee the ensuing policies and procedures that advantage them and disadvantage those who do not know how "to play the game." There are also academics within the system who do not see the managerialist system for what it is but who willingly support the drive for clear delineation, efficiencies, and accountabilities because it plays into their hands.

One of the outcomes of these new hierarchies is "what counts." The Faculty in which the early career academics' work describes itself as "*teaching and learning focussed*," yet research is more highly regarded, and rewarded, than teaching or service. Shore and Davidson explain that this separation (or "bifurcation") between research and teaching leads to "the shrinking scope of academic autonomy and de-professionalization of academics" (p. 23). Because building a research portfolio takes time, established academics stand to benefit and early career academics, such as the two in this chapter, are forced into roles that limit their opportunities. Academics with research track records get the full weight of the university machinery behind them in the form of dedicated support staff, recognition, and rewards. Those burdened with heavy teaching portfolios are not supported in the same manner. Casualization of academic staff and new career tracks, such as professional teaching fellows or research fellows, further inhibit early career academics from gaining a foothold or from speedy career advancement.

The second type of complicity that Shore and Davidson raise is *unwitting complicity*. The two early career academics provided multiple examples of the career advice that they had been given by well-meaning senior academics: "Don't worry about your teaching, it's the research that matters"; "Focus on getting grants instead." Did these senior academics not seem to realize that their advice would only perpetuate an inequitable system? Shore and Davidson state, "Unwitting complicity occurs when the strength of neoliberal norms means that individuals' actions become aligned with the intentions of management" (p. 18). Even though they were all employed in a Faculty whose main focus was preparing teachers and social workers, one of the early career academics was told not to mention their earlier career as a teacher. Such comments deny academics from professional fields the opportunity to be recognized as having knowledge and skill from their applied fields. This constricting advice blocks the recognition of multiple pathways into academia. The early career academics were also given well-meaning but inappropriate advice from academics who did not see that the system had changed before their very eyes.

The third of Shore and Davidson's complicities is *coercive complicity*, which "refers to those situations where individuals are either compelled to comply or do so reluctantly when resistance is clearly futile" (p. 19). The dictates of "publish or perish," the fear of "speaking out" and the need to accept "invisible work," such as extra teaching or service without complaint were among the examples the early career researchers gave. The fact that various layers of committees in the hierarchical system did not seem willingly to engage with early career voices or alternative perspectives also coerced the early career academics into silence by default. Paradoxically, senior academics who find themselves in managerial positions also can find themselves coerced by the neoliberal machinery into acting in ways where non-compliance would find them in breach of their contracts. Thus, Darder's "dehumanizing ethos" becomes self-perpetuating.

However, it is in the very notion of complicity that early career academics can find a safe space to speak back. They can form their own notion of *resistant complicity*, whereby they collude in ways that reject individualism and support compassionate, collective resistance. Ball and Olmedo (2013) suggest that they can act "irresponsibly" as a method of resistance:

> This is not a struggle in the normal political sense. Rather it is a process of struggle against mundane, quotidian neoliberalisms, that creates the possibility of thinking about education and ourselves differently. (p. 85)

In the production of this chapter, two early career academics and one of their supportive mentors have shown that turning the neoliberal story back on itself is a liberating act of defiance. Autoethnography and narrative have been used as Andrew (2019, p. 63) suggests, as a method of resistance "using memory to construct stories of resilience. It enables individual lived experience to be inscribed within a collective critical debate" and through this to empower other early career academics to recognize and take up the challenge.

FINAL WORDS

Unravelling Complexities, De-Glorifying Academia and the Unfiltered Daily Life as an Emerging Academic

Too often, doctoral students (as we once were), think of academia as the golden standard, or a tick-box, that suggests they have "made it." Academia, therefore, is often romanticized as a "post-struggle" utopia for intellectuals. Throughout the chapter, we have spoken about the complexities of being an emerging academic through our personal career journeys. We have intentionally offered an honest approach to what we see as the tricky terrain of early career academics. Our aim in writing this chapter is to offer some advice that we would have found helpful in our PhD and early days in the academy. In sharing our experience with the politics and challenging career choices we have made, we hope to create a much-needed space to be realistic about the pressures of a competitive environment places on new academics. Although fraught with complexities, we conclude on a hopeful note that some of our choices offer insight into ways to persist and resist a system that encourages and even fosters individualism. By presenting a model of collegiality, even through virtue of co-authoring this chapter, we present an alternative and realistic narrative of early career researchers. We conclude this chapter by coming back to the research and teaching that brought us both to academia – it's work that fuels us. When it gets a bit dark in the battles with tyrants, gatekeepers, and inequitable institutional systems, remember the passion that brought you to this place called academia.

REFERENCES

Anderson, L. (2006). Analytic autoethnography. *Journal of Contemporary Ethnography, 35*(4), 373–395. doi:10.1177/0891241605280449

Andrew, M. (2019). Double negative: When the neoliberal meets the toxic. In D. Bottrell & C. Manathunga (Eds.), *Resisting neoliberalism in higher education. Volume 1. Seeing through the cracks* (pp. 54–82). Cham: Palgrave Macmillan.

Ball, S. (2012). Perfomativity, commodification and commitment: An I-Spy guide to the neoliberal university. *British Journal of Educational Studies, 60*(1), 17–28. doi:10.1080/00071005.2011.650940

Ball, S., & Olmedo, A. (2013). Care of the self, resistance and subjectivity under neoliberal governmentalities. *Critical Studies in Education, 54*(1) 85–96. doi:10.1080/17508487.2013.740678

Bergami, R. (2019). Twenty-first century feudalism in Australian universities. In D. Bottrell & C. Manathunga (Eds.), *Resisting neoliberalism in higher education. Volume 1. Seeing through the cracks* (pp. 37–58). Cham: Palgrave Macmillan.

Bottrell, D., & Manathunga, C. (Eds.). (2019a). *Resisting neoliberalism in higher education. Volume 1. Seeing through the cracks*. Cham: Palgrave Macmillan.

Bottrell, D., & Manathunga, C. (Eds.). (2019b). Shedding light on the cracks in neoliberal universities. In D. Bottrell & C. Manathunga (Eds.), *Resisting neoliberalism in higher education. Volume 1. Seeing through the cracks* (pp. 1–34). Cham: Palgrave Macmillan.

Clandinin, D. J., & Connelly, F. M. (2000). *Narrative inquiry: Experience and story in qualitative research*. San Francisco, CA: Jossey Bass.

Connelly, F. M., & Clandinin, J. (1990). Stories of experience and narrative inquiry. *Educational Researcher, 19*(5), 2–14.

Cupples, J., & Pawson, E. (2012). Giving account of oneself: The PBRF and the neoliberal university. *New Zealand Geographer, 68*, 14–23. doi:10.111/j.1745-7939.2012.01217

Darder, A. (2019). Foreword. In D. Botterell & C. Manathunga (Eds.), *Resisting neoliberalism in higher education, Volume 1. Seeing through the cracks* (pp. v–x). Cham, Switzerland: Palgrave Macmillan.

Denshire, S. (2014). On auto-ethnography. *Current Sociology Review, 62*(6), 831–850. https://doi.org/10.1177/0011392114533339

Ellington, L., & Ellis, C. (2008) Autoethnography as constructionist project. In J. A. Holstein & J. F. Gubrium (Eds.), *Handbook of constructionist research* (pp. 445–65). New York, NY: Guilford Press.

Ellis, C. (1999). Heartful autoethnography. *Qualitative Health Research, 9*(5), 669–683. doi:10.1177/104973299129122153

Ellis, C. (2004). *The ethnographic I: A methodological novel about autoethnography*. Walnut Creek: Altamira Press.

Ellis, C., Adams, T. E., & Bochner, A. P. (2011). Autoethnography: An overview. *Historical Social Research, 36*(4), 273–290. doi:10.12759/hsr.36.2011.4.273-290

Grant, B. (2019). Wrestling with career: An autoethnographic tale of a cracked academic self. In D. Bottrell & C. Manathunga (Eds.), *Resisting neoliberalism in higher education. Volume 1. Seeing through the cracks* (pp. 119–143). Cham: Palgrave Macmillan.

Matthew, P. (2016). It's not just us. This is happening everywhere: On CVs and the Michigan women. In P. Matthew (Ed.), *Written/unwritten: Diversity and the hidden truths of tenure* (pp. XI–XVII). Chapel Hill: University of North Carolina Press. Retrieved from http://www.jstor.org/stable/10.5149/9781469627724_matthew

Mountz, A., Bonds, A., Mansfield, B., Lloyd, J., Hyndman, J., Walton-Roberts, M., ... Curran, W. (2015). For slow scholarship: A feminist politics of resistance through collective action in the neoliberal university. *ACME: An International E-Journal for Critical Geographies, 14*(4), 1235–1259.

Mutch, C. (2013). *Doing educational research. A practitioner's guide to getting started.* (2nd ed.). Wellington: NZCER Press.

Mutch, C. & Tatebe, J. (2017). From collusion to collective compassion: Putting heart back into the neoliberal university. *Pastoral Care in Education, 35*(3), 221–234.

Olssen, M., & Peters, M. (2005). Neoliberalism, higher education and the knowledge economy: From the free market to knowledge capitalism. *Journal of Education Policy, 20*(3), 313–345.

Pinnegar, S., & Daynes, J. G. (2007). Locating narrative inquiry historically. In D. J. Clandinin (Ed.), *Handbook of narrative inquiry: Mapping a methodology* (pp. 3–34). Thousand Oaks, CA: Sage.

Roberts, P. (2013). Academic dystopia: Knowledge, performativity and tertiary education. *The Review of Education, Pedagogy, and Cultural Studies, 35*(1), 27–43.

Shore, C. (2007). *'After neoliberalism?' The reform of New Zealand's university system* (Working Papers on University Reform No. 6). Copenhagen/Auckland: Department of Educational Anthropology, Danish University of Education/University of Auckland.

Shore, C. (2010). Beyond the multiversity: Neoliberalism and the rise of the schizophrenic university. *Social Anthropology, 18*(1), 15–29. doi:10.1111/j.1469-8676.2009.00094.x

Shore, C., & Davidson, M. (2014). Beyond collusion and resistance: Academic-management relations within the neoliberal university. *Learning and Teaching, 7*(1), 12–28. doi:10.3167/latiss.2014.070102

Smeltzer, S., & Hearn, A. (2015). Student rights in an age of austerity? Security, freedom of expression and the neoliberal university. *Social Movements Studies, 14*(3), 352–358. doi:10.1080/14742837.2014.945077

Smyth, J. (2017). *The toxic university: Zombie leadership, academic rock stars and neoliberal ideology.* London: Palgrave Macmillan.

Social Sciences Feminist Network Research Interest Group. (2017). The burden of invisible work in academia social inequalities and time use in five university departments. *Humboldt Journal of Social Relations: Diversity & Social Justice in Higher Education, 1*(39), 228–245. Retrieved from https://www.jstor.org/stable/90007882

Vicars, M. (2019). When all hope is gone: Truth, lies and make believe. In D. Bottrell & C. Manathunga (Eds.), *Resisting neoliberalism in higher education. Volume 1. Seeing through the cracks* (pp. 83–96). Cham: Palgrave Macmillan.

Wall, S. (2006). An autoethnography on learning about autoethnography. *International Journal of Qualitative Methods, 5*(2), 146–160.

CHAPTER 8

INFUSING TWENTY-FIRST-CENTURY RESEARCH ACTIVITIES INTO TRADITIONAL CLASSROOMS

Ryan Menath*

ABSTRACT

Modern society searches for information primarily though handheld internet devices. Universities, on the other hand, traditionally rely on printed textbooks. If the main purpose of higher education is to graduate a civically minded and high-functioning member of society, then there is a disconnect between society and the undergraduate when it comes to the ability to research and find information quickly. In other words, the university-societal pact is broken when it comes to digital research. Thankfully, it can be restored. The following chapter highlights the author's technique to eliminate required textbooks and nightly assigned readings. Instead of daily pages for students to read, each assignment is based on the ability to answer historical questions through whatever research methods most interest the student. Using questions, discussion, and debate, the semester revolves around student research throughout the multimedia domain, including social media and online academic databases. In the process, students learn to differentiate between sources, judge online biases, and discover their preferred method of scholarly research. The case studies show that the elimination of assigned textbooks and the re-imagining of research projects that include publicly consumable projects are a unique and engaging way to

---

*The views expressed in this article are those of the author and do not reflect the official policy or position of the United States Air Force, Department of Defense, or the U.S. Government.

integrate twenty-first-century digital research methods into the traditional institution of higher learning. In doing so, college classrooms can once again begin to mend the fractured university-societal pact.

Keywords: Pedagogy; American history; social media; internet sources; scholarly sources; smart devices; research

Imagine the scene: the professor strides confidently into the classroom, nearly oblivious to the students milling around in their seats. As the professor makes her way to the front of the room, she offers the cursory "hello" not bothering to wait for a response. For their part, most students continue staring at whatever device is in their hands. The instructor sets down her briefcase and readies the projector for the slideshow. With few exceptions, the students remain focused on their smartphones or tablets and seem utterly oblivious to the fact that class is about to begin.

The professor dutifully turns on the overhead projectors, logs into the computer, and brings up the PowerPoint slides for the day's lesson. The students remain fixated on their devices; earbuds remain implanted. As the projector comes alive, the professor has three options to open the class. First, she could announce a quiz based on the previous night's homework readings – students will slowly respond, but begrudgingly and perhaps with some under-the-breath cursing. Second, she could forego the quiz and ask what questions students had from the reading – most will remain silent, and after several awkward attempts at class engagement, she will move on. Third and finally, the professor could assume that the students completed their assigned readings per the syllabus and move on with the lesson.

Each of these three conventional options has two commonalities. First, they all required that the students completed some standardized assigned reading as homework. The professor's lesson probably builds off of that reading. Second, the class, almost to a person, stayed fixated on their devices. While stereotypical, the previous scenario is not farfetched – most college professors can relate, or at least sympathize, with the situation. Clearly, smart devices have forced their way into the undergraduate classroom.

To begin, one must understand this work's definition of the "stereotypical" or "traditional" undergraduate course. Every university, every department, and every individual professor brings unique gifts, abilities, biases, and teaching techniques to the classroom. Thus, every classroom varies widely in its methodology and style. This chapter does not wish to undermine the high-quality work most instructors do. There are, however, certain common beliefs or viewpoints that permeate society about the university classroom and its administration derived from cultural misconceptions, previous experiences, the media, social media, or fictionalized accounts. For example, the stereotypical view of the college classroom is one of a lecture hall presided over by an older professor narrating a thesis in front of a slide show or chalkboard filled with formulas. Students seem to hang on the instructor's every word while taking copious notes. In this fictional stereotype, there is rarely, if ever, any student–teacher interaction. If there is, it usually involves an unruly or smart-aleck student. Nonetheless, society understands and accepts these as the "stereotypical" or "traditional" courses.

A quick web search of the phrase "smartphone use in higher education" elicits a plethora of recent scholarship that both praise and decry the use of web-based technology in the classroom (Esmaeili, Eydgahi, & Amanov, 2015). While this chapter does not seek to enter into the fray regarding the pros and cons of classroom smart-device use, it does highlight a modern fact about higher education: internet-based technology is firmly entrenched in student's lives (Pulliam, 2017). Bowen (2012) points out the impact technology has on higher education. He highlights how technology changes

> students and professors, how we access knowledge, the nature of community, the habits of learning, our understanding of patience, and virtually everything about education. It has also created an expanding global market for online learning. (Kindle Loc 172)

Whether professors embrace or ban technology is irrelevant, the fact is that students bring it into the classroom. In a very real sense, technology creates an emotional link in college students to a familiar, extra-collegiate world.

Education is emotional. Learners, especially young undergraduates, enter college and immediately have their long-standing beliefs and worldviews challenged. Student's smartphones are an easy way to stay attached to what is familiar and forgo any negative emotions that come from initial college life. Ella Kahu (2013) speaks of the "culture shock" undergraduates encounter in their college experience. How they handle it becomes a crucial step toward their developing into a complex thinker and a lifelong self-learner. The stereotype of emotionless absolutes, concrete data sets, and scientific principles lend credence to the "facts of the internet." Susan Ambrose (2010) labels this a "quantitative view of knowledge," where the accumulation of the "right facts" constitutes knowledge. Indeed, some of that may be true. The simultaneous rise of smartphone use in society and the continuation of textbooks as the primary source of information in higher education are cause for concern for a straightforward reason, they create a schism between how the university teaches and how society operates. In other words, the university-societal pact established to enable high-functioning citizens in society is broken (Canada, 2013). Discovering information in mainstream society occurs through handheld, internet-based devices, while in higher education it remains primarily textbook-driven (Robinson, 2010).

Mary Huba and Jann Freed (2000) elaborate on the "traditional teaching paradigm" in higher education. They assert that the traditional classroom includes the one-way transmittal of information from the teacher to the students who receive information passively from the professor and his/her chosen instrument, usually a textbook. While their work continues to discuss the role of assessment, their definition of a "traditional" classroom still applies (Huba & Freed, 2000). The professor makes the choices, to include outside reading, and the students must perform. In essence, every aspect of the course rests solely with the professor. Students have little input (Robinson, 2010).

Bloom's taxonomy, and its revision in 2001, discusses the acquisition of factual knowledge and conceptual details like classifications, models, and theories as the lowest level of knowledge (Banta & Palomba, 2015). Some argue that both the acquisition of factual knowledge and conceptual details require academic, scholarly textbooks. According to the commonly held stereotype, only textbooks can quickly and effectively communicate the information necessary for students to progress throughout the semester; without the basic knowledge academic books provide, the course would grind to a halt. Perhaps such a view is correct, but only in individual, specific settings. On the other hand, presenting a question that leads to the required basic knowledge and forcing the student to acquire the information on their own adds the benefit of the search – the ability to seek out the factual knowledge and conceptual details on their own without the aid of a specified textbook. The online quest itself generates the necessary learned action for finding and acquiring detailed information in the internet age. While it is true that the professor must devote class time to helping students identify and separate good sources from bad, the students learn where and how to search for information more effectively (Davis, 2009). Besides, none of this suggests that the professor cannot *recommend* his preferred textbook or research site.

At the heart of the issue is the *assumption* that a specific textbook will produce academic results among the students (Chen, 2018; Echevarria & Bowman, 2018). Within each discipline, there are undoubtedly well-known scholars that upper-division students should recognize and read. Yet not all students learn at the same rate or with the same methodology. With that in mind, a more effective solution would be to assign questions, not textbooks. After all, academic research is about seeking answers. In short, let students search for the information themselves and the disciplinary standard will reveal itself in their research.

To restate: professors require printed texts as the primary source of information while students increasingly prefer to acquire information online. Ultimately, a textbook becomes nothing more than the professor's preferred method for transmitting information. The student has little choice in the reading or research schedule with almost no control of their learning, which leads to a diminishing interest in the subject. Such pedagogy runs counter to a student-centered learning environment, yet the literature continues to assume a textbook-driven academic environment, even if the textbook is delivered online. Altering traditional teaching methodology to reflect societal norms can bridge the gap between academia and modern culture (Brennan & Teichler, 2008; Cantor, 2007). Robert M. Diamond (2008) concedes as much and flatly states:

> Technology, changing demographics, failure to engage students, and new ways of thinking about the nature of knowledge in the Information Age have prompted many instructional changes on college and university campuses. In addition, new opportunities available through the Internet and e-mail, increased use of active learning, as well as internships and extended-classroom activities, have significantly altered how we teach by requiring enhanced interaction among all members of the learning community… The learning-centered syllabus places students at the center of the question, "What do students need to know in order to derive maximum benefit from this educational experience?" (p. 286)

In other words, what does society expect from universities? The author explicitly mentions technology and the internet.

Higher education needs to adapt to the rapidly changing online environment, something that traditionally conservative (meaning reluctant to change) institutions are hesitant to do on a large scale. Institutions of higher learning must embrace internet-based research to remain viable within a social-cultural construct that thrives on Google and Wikipedia.

The university-societal contract is also broken because higher education remains insular, whereas society has embraced public, open communication. This chapter proposes to highlight the author's techniques of adapting higher learning to societal norms through the elimination of assigned textbooks, assigned readings, and research papers in favor of student-driven open research and web-based research projects. Case studies include two semesters of an American history survey course wherein daily assignments were question-based rather than text-based and research projects revolved around creating publicly consumable products, such as websites or podcasts. In the process, the teacher becomes a consultant, concentrating on helping students sift high-quality, academic research sources from untrustworthy blogs, op-ed writings, or "fake news" so that they can create and digitally publish a high academic quality product. Students learn to critique sources and discern between bias, propaganda, and one-sided arguments.

Further, this research-based learning is overwhelmingly digital, using online archives of primary sources across print, audio, and video instead of traditional, text-only based research. It also promotes greater use of online academic journals and databases. As a result, post-course feedback demonstrated that participants gained ownership of their class projects, had increased interest in the subject, persistence in their work, and boosted student–teacher interaction in the classroom.

The following case study, instituted through student research-based projects and activities that improve engagement, has introduced three significant changes to traditional classrooms. Those changes include the elimination of assigned textbooks, the opportunity for students to choose their own research sources, and the requirement that they bring in their citations.

First, professors should eliminate assigned textbooks and allow students to choose their material but establish guidelines as to what constitutes an academic source. During class, require students to bring in their citations for discussion and critique. Next, get rid of assigned reading. Instead, assign questions for each lesson, not pages or books. How much time each student spends answering those questions is entirely up to them, as long as the question is answered in detail. Once a student figures out an acceptable research solution, they gain the ability to save time while developing the skills required for their academic discipline. Finally, reduce research papers. Research papers are inherently a one-way transmittal of information from the student to the teacher, often a regurgitation of what the instructor has already taught during class or what the student read in an assigned textbook.

Research is essential, but the research *paper* is not necessarily the best medium of communication. Instead, when the student is allowed to choose which medium is best to present their research, they gain ownership of their project. Websites, podcasts, video blogs, TEDx-like recorded presentations, magazine-style articles, or academic essays are all innovative methods for students to communicate their research while generating interest and ownership in their project (Hoover, 2006).

Ultimately, when an instructor breaks the traditional rigid course model of assigning a pre-selected textbook with mandatory readings followed by a research paper, they force the student to seek out and critique the reliability of sources. Through the process, the instructor becomes a consultant to help the student enter into an academic dialogue with society. In this scenario, students determine what constitutes an "academic" or "scholarly" source versus any other type of information. There is a lot of discussion in the literature about sources, and some articles offer excellent exercises in helping students determine the difference between scholarly and unscholarly online information (Calkins & Kelley, 2007). Unfortunately, most articles give one or two exercises throughout the *semester* in which the students are asked to determine the academic quality of their online research. Students require *continual* practice before they understand the differences in online scholarly information; only the daily habit of finding, assessing, and critiquing source material as it relates to a specific question will generate student understanding. Most students know how to search for and gain access to information quickly, but few spend the time assessing that information for accuracy. Google and Wikipedia are student favorites that generally make professors cringe due to their stereotypical inaccuracies and user-defined, open-sourced information. By restricting online research, instructors are inadvertently widening the gap between society and academia.

Society uses social media daily; thus, only the daily interaction of online source material is sufficient to prepare undergraduates for cultural norms outside of the university. Overall, this class model restores the university-societal contract by embracing extensive and consistent digital research and communication. Social media is rarely considered a legitimate academic source. As the students bring information to class, professors can highlight the various types of biases and misinformation inherent in social media. When done continually, students learn to assess and critique online information, even from academically non-trustworthy websites. Furthermore, when used effectively, social mediums can provide a valuable academic benefit (Noor Al-Deen & Hendricks, 2012). Encouraging students to bring in social media allows the instructor to engage, highlight, and critique the quality of the source material. Eventually, one can hope that the ability to quickly sift good information from bad on the internet will bridge the university-societal divide and produce a citizenry equipped with a critical eye in an era of fake news and unverified online accounts.

A benefit of assigning questions instead of reading is that when a student attempts to answer an assigned question based off of what they gleaned from social media, the instructor can highlight the unscholarly nature of such sites (Yaros, 2012). At the same time, high-quality and academically sound scholars are using social media to present their research. Not only would those sources be valuable to students, but the students would learn who the "heavy-hitters" are in their discipline and begin to interact with them and their followers in real-time. In some cases, scholars around the world could interact with local students, creating interest in their projects and bridging the university-societal divide.

Major course homework assignments in the following case study follow the same question and answer format. Student research confined or restricted to specific textbooks, or products limited to traditional research papers, hinder student's ability to discover, critique, review, or report on all available material. D. Sandy

Hoover (2006) elucidates as much when she explains that the plethora of audio and video sources available to students, including primary sources as well as podcasts, can significantly increase student engagement and research. Including these unique sources in student projects bring the technological aspect of research full circle.

Unfortunately, when a student's research paper has no other audience than the instructor, the student's only motivation is their grade. Instead, when a course allows for a wide range of assignment mediums, especially those that go beyond the classroom like web pages or podcasts, the students gain a greater sense of project ownership. Podcasts, webpages, and publicly consumable presentations add a degree of attention to the work. Further, the instructor can add the stipulation that his or her academic peers may view the student's online project. Overall, students feel more pressure to perform when their work is online.

The elimination of textbooks, assigned readings, and research papers all work together. Throughout the course, students practice assessing and critiquing sources daily. By the time they begin their final projects, students have evaluated webpages, YouTube channels, social media sites, podcasts, academic journals, magazines, traditional textbooks, and primary sources. They should, by the latter part of the semester (and hopefully much sooner) understand the value of factually supported information, web-based or not, and be able to choose an outlet that allows them to present a coherent research project. While some students still choose to write a traditional research paper, most opt for a website or podcast with the understanding that the information they upload is publicly consumable with their name attached.

There are, as always, drawbacks and pitfalls to eliminating assigned textbooks and readings. One must be careful not to assign nightly written work to the research questions. In other words, do not ask the students to bring any other homework to class. The goal is to allow them to spend as much – or as little – time as they need on the subject while trusting them to arrive prepared. One of the benefits is the fact that if a student is as good at online researching as they believe, then they could save time over the assigned-reading method. Adding written material that students must turn in daily undermines the trust between professor and student, and trust is paramount (Bain, 2004).

CASE STUDY – AMERICAN HISTORY SURVEY

The following section is a case study from two semesters of an American History survey course using the aforementioned techniques. Most of the syllabus is reproduced in this work as figures, albeit without any personal or institutional-identifying information. The specific course number is gone; otherwise, the syllabus displays the general guidance for the course and is a near-exact representation of what students receive before the first day of class.

The student load in the case study varied from 11 to 18 students per class. There were two sections per semester for a total of approximately 50–60 students over the course of the year. While this smaller class size is preferable when using these techniques, larger class sizes can work. The professor may need to adjust the discussion to ensure that all students participate. In huge sections, small groups could substitute for individual students, though the instructor must ensure research continues and hold students accountable.

Research data was collected formally through mid-semester surveys, end-of-course critiques, and informally through post-class discussions with students. More than 80% of students responded to the post-course formal survey, generating a relatively large number of end-of-course comments.

This section also includes an example list of questions covering the first several class sessions. Throughout the semester, the instructor picked a series of three to five questions per lesson and emailed them to the students weekly (usually Friday afternoon). The goal was to allow students to research and get ahead if they so choose, but not to provide a comprehensive list at the beginning of the semester. That way, students had to maintain a constant pace without getting too far ahead. Overall, the intent was to choose a factual-type question, an analysis-type question, and an overarching-type question for each lesson. The factual question should be somewhat easy to research, whereas the other two necessitate a deeper level of insight. As students became more comfortable with their source material, the time dedicated to research decreased.

Expectations for Students upon Arrival

Each student was expected to arrive prepared to answer the daily questions and know the sources that they used (Fig. 1). They did not need to bring anything, nor were they expected to turn in any daily written work. Since the class revolved around discussion, most students were called on at least once to share their thoughts, which worked well in a 16-student class (Davis, 2009). Often, the professor would ask for students to shout out their most interesting source and where they found it. In doing so, the instructor gleaned a quick insight into how the students were researching and what sources were popular. As a generalization, Google Scholar and Wikipedia were early favorites; by the end of the semester, JSTOR was overwhelmingly the students' primary source of information.

Every lesson opened with the professor re-stating the homework questions and waiting for a response. The initial answer provided the direction for the class and allowed the instructor to either facilitate a discussion, provide direction and

---

Textbook(s) and/or Assigned Readings

This course will not use a dedicated textbook. Instead, you will research and respond to certain questions for each lesson; the sources you choose in answering the questions are up to you. I will provide the questions on a weekly basis. I can also suggest some excellent works and websites for your research, but as long as you are comfortable answering the posed question you can use whatever source you want. Be forewarned: Wikipedia will not provide sufficient answers. Ensure you know what authors you are reading and be ready to provide your sources in class.

Fig. 1. Textbook Policy from Syllabus.

> EXAMPLE QUESTIONS AS HOMEWORK:
>
> Lesson 3: Earliest America
> 1. What civilizations existed in America before the arrival of Europeans?
> 2. What was going on in Europe that caused the Spanish to explore west and the Portuguese to explore South?
> 3. What role did religion play in shaping the cross-cultural interactions and experiences of the people in Europe, the Americas, and Africa in the early 17th century?
>
> Lesson 4: Collision of Cultures
> 1. How did a culture that had taken centuries to develop become conquered in only two years?
> 2. Why did the French seem to have a better relationship with Native Americans than the English?
> 3. What was the "Glorious Revolution," and why was it important?
>
> Lesson 5: British Colonies I
> 1. Why were the first colonies established? Business or Religious purposes?
> 2. What was the difference between the Puritans and the Pilgrims?
> 3. What was the Mayflower Compact, and why does it have lasting impact in American history?
> 4. Compare and contrast the colonies of Jamestown and Massachusetts Bay. What was the purpose of each? What made each unique? How did each survive/thrive? Who were their leaders?

Fig. 2. Example Homework Questions for Students to Research.

guidance toward better research material, guide the class to a different topic, or move on to the next question on the list (Fig. 2).

Two notes of caution: first, the instructor must be willing, able, and flexible enough to allow the dialogue to move in any direction necessary so long as it remains centered in the academic discipline – that includes the topic-of-the-day itself, a sub-topic, or the research surrounding the topic. Second, the instructor must spread the conversation to as many students as possible. Class participation is critical in this type of learning environment and reserved students must feel enabled to contribute.

Further, like Social Media, the "social" aspect of the class is vital and all students are expected to contribute their research (Yaros, 2012). All of the students must participate in order for the professor to adequately assess and evaluate student growth and research trends. As they do, one can sense where the discussion needs to go and what guidance the instructor must provide.

Debates and Expectations

In addition to the daily research questions, there were several more significant assignments throughout the semester, the first of which were a series of ten debates (although post-semester feedback determined that ten was too many, five or six would suffice). Students were required to submit two short, research-based, papers that outlined their argument for each side of the debate. Short means short: 250 words maximum defending each position for 500 words total. The goal was to force brevity. Footnotes, however, were not included in the word count. In that regard, students were able to expound on an argument or source at length in the footnotes if they so choose. Between the 250-word argument and the

> **Debate Series**
> Six of you will get chosen at random to participate in the debates - three per side. Arrive ready to present your case with a 250 word summary of your argument per side (so two, 250 word documents). While only your debate papers will officially get graded, your preparation and performance during the debates can/will affect your participation points. Here are the rules for each debate:
> - You will have 5 minutes to prepare the case with your team.
> - Each side will have 5 minutes to present their argument to the group.
> - After both sides have argued their position, the audience will summarize the main points (5 minutes, max).
> - Next, each group will get a 2 minute rebuttal.
> - The floor is then opened to questions.
> - We will debrief strength of arguments, presentation skills, research, etc. after the debate - the goal is to make you better.
>
> DEBATE QUESTIONS:
> #1) Were the Puritans committed to religious freedom?
> #2) Was the British mercantalistic system a help or hindrance to the American Colonies?
> #3) Was the American Revolution truly revolutionary?
> #4) Did the ratification of the Constitution constitute a conservative counter-revolution?
> #5) Did "Republican Motherhood" improve women's position in the early republic?
> #6) Who had a greater impact on American life during the Federalist Era, Hamilton or Jefferson?
> #7) Was Jacksonian democracy democratic?
> #8) Who was more responsible for Emancipation, Northern abolitionists or enslaved African-Americans?
> #9) Was the Civil War a repressible conflict?
> #10) Was the Reconstructive Era constructive or destructive?

Fig. 3. Debate Guidance with Questions from Syllabus.

lengthy footnotes, the instructor gained important insight into the research and main arguments of the students. The professor was also able to grade these short assignments relatively quickly (Fig. 3).

The papers were graded; students' debate performance was not. During class, four students were chosen at random to participate in a live, timed debate. The specific debate rules were in the syllabus, but the purpose was for all students to arrive prepared in case they got picked through a random lottery (this instructor used an online random number generator associated with each student). There was no limit to the number of times a student could get chosen, so one student may debate on multiple occasions. Thus, all students must arrive prepared for each and every debate.

The goal of the in-class debate was not to highlight or embarrass students, but to allow them to practice articulating coherent arguments in real-time. In a debate setting, students must mentally pull from their research and support their position. Further, they need to address the valid points of the opposition using factual information. Hopefully, they will challenge any unsubstantiated material and highlight what other scholars, academics, and researchers have brought to the discipline. Life moves at the speed of thought, and students need to practice analyzing, critiquing, and adapting to a contrary viewpoint in real-time.

The debate was set up for a 53-minute class period and designed to allow time to debrief after the students finished. The professor must highlight the importance of definitions and academic source material as foundational to the discourse. Also, without defining the terms, each side may argue two divergent aspects of the question. Without citing the source material during the debate, the onlookers cannot tell what information was supported versus what was conjecture. The post-debate discussion is just as important as the debate itself.

The debate prompts were chosen based on their provocative nature and ability to use historical research to argue both sides. Each question also fits within the larger course narrative and accentuated the daily lessons and homework questions. The timing was designed so that students either had several lessons to research the material in conjunction with class discussions, or to jump-start the next few lessons and give them a general understanding of upcoming material. In either case, the debates allowed students to view controversial subjects with a critical eye. Critical thinking is still, after all, one of the major tenets of higher education.

The book review was another essential aspect of the course. While the overall methodology depends on not having any professor-assigned reading, the students do need to read and research. In this instance, students were allowed to choose any book (or ebook) so long as it applied to the discipline. At the instructor's discretion, even a novel could be a useful educational tool. While the rest of the pedagogical coursework revolved around open and online research, this assignment reined in the nature of the course to a more traditional assignment, albeit with a lenient slant. The two critical aspects were that the book applied to the discipline and that it was the student's choice. The latter part is critical; the instructor *cannot* impose a specific text.

The book review asks not to solely review the work, though that is a significant part of it, but rather to critique the book's usefulness to society at large. Students must answer why a lay-person would want to read it. In other words, the student should assess its ability to bridge the societal-university divide. In doing so, they continuously engage with the perception of academia versus culture (Fig. 4).

Position Paper/Book Review
As historians, you must be able to interpret the events and clearly argue the importance of those events in modern society. At the same time, you are preparing to enter the work force. You must understand the proper way to effectively convey arguments using appropriate methods. Therefore, for this series, you must properly format your arguments into a short memo. Specifically, you must write a properly formatted paper that argues the importance of your chosen historical monograph to modern society. In other words, why should anyone outside the discipline of history in the 21st-century read the book you read?

- Do not exceed **500 words**. Learn to edit, because no boss wants to read a lengthy argument.
- Ensure you review/critique the work, but do not summarize the book. This is a book review with a specific objective (modern importance), treat it as such.
- Do not use "I think" or "I believe." Argue your position like a courtroom lawyer would argue to a jury.
- You must use **at least three** sources, **including** the specified book for the block. In other words, you must use the specified book plus *at least* two other academic sources.
- Cite your sources using Turabian format.

Fig. 4. Position Paper and Book Review Guidance from Syllabus.

Like the debate papers, the book review assignment requires a small word count: no more than 500 words. Again, the footnotes do not count toward the overall word limit, thus allowing the students to expound on their thoughts without exceeding the parameters of the assignment and still learning the value of footnoting in the process. The case study in this chapter uses two book reviews per semester, but a course may include more or less depending on its scope. Do not forget that one of the pedagogical goals of the course is to allow the students the ability to manage their own time without adding perceived "time killers" like lengthy assigned reading or daily written homework.

There were two final projects in the course, one individual and one group. The final individual project incorporated extensive research and communication skills but did not necessitate extensive writing nor limit research to only texts. It highlighted the ability to research and present openly, online, and with the option to design and create a website, podcast, blog, video blog, YouTube show, TEDx-like talk, Twitter/Facebook feed, magazine article, or anything similar. Students were still required to use a pre-determined number of scholarly sources (10, with two primary sources and one academic journal) as well as a word limit or timed equivalent (2,400–3,000 words). The underlying premise was to keep and enforce traditional scholarly research and communication but present it to a broad audience using twenty-first-century methods. In essence, the assignment attempted to bridge the university-societal gap by combining significant elements of both traditional university and societal-cultural norms (Fig. 5).

In the case study, students could choose any subject as long as it remained relevant to the course. The choices and their presentation methods were as varied as the students themselves; everything from America's early involvement with Pacific Islanders to Pirates and Privateering along the Atlantic seaboard to the more traditional topics like the American Revolution or the Civil War. Also, because the students were aware that their final projects were online and publicly viewable, many decided to add a degree of interaction to their projects. Websites included quizzes and comment blocks; podcasts and blogs asked for online feedback; one student got into a "Twitter war" with an amateur historian pretending to be a historical character. Overall, the project took on a life of its own as students used scholarly research to interact with society online in a way in which they were familiar. They took ownership of their projects, especially knowing that the

---

Research Project

Prepare a Research Project containing **2400-3000 words (8-10 pages or corresponding timing if speaking, ~15 minutes)** on any topic of your choosing as long as it concerns American history up to 1877. The final project should include at least **10 sources, 2** of which must be primary sources, and **1** of which must be an academic journal article. **This does not necessitate a research paper. Your project could be a website, a video, a podcast, or another medium.** It must showcase your research and communication skills. If you choose to write a paper, it must be geared towards a larger audience (i.e., a magazine).

Fig. 5. Research Project Guidance from Syllabus.

instructor would send their project links to other scholars and faculty members. At that point, the professor became a consultant as the students attempted to put forth the correct historical information and present it to a broader audience in an academically non-traditional way.

The final group project differed in that it was incredibly open-ended, so open-ended that it could become a detriment in some classrooms. Admittedly, this is one assignment that requires continual discussion. During each lesson, members of the class would spend a couple of minutes discussing ideas for the final group project or talk about its progress with the instructor. The only direction was to "prepare a project that ties the course together in a continual narrative of American History." Those instructions were broad and ill-defined; yet, two classes came up with exciting and entertaining ways to weave American history into a unique narrative from an interesting perspective.

The first group created a fictional newspaper with reporters who had "witnessed" many of the significant turning points in American history. Going into the project, the students decided that the paper would attempt to maintain journalistic impartiality but would also have an implicit political bent, mirroring both modern and historical journalism. The result was a physically weathered, fictional newspaper covering approximately 20 major events in early American history from colonization to Reconstruction. Students presented it as an actual newspaper with a separate bibliography. One could sense the pride the students had in the project.

The second group traced the genealogy of a fictional family that participated in monumental events since Jamestown in 1607. While the family was fictional, the events were well-researched. In several instances, the students were able to use their characters to plug historical holes (for instance, discovering who fired the Shot Heard 'Round the World'). Like the first group, the students took pride in their group project and had fun weaving a fictional family throughout history.

Admittedly, the final group project may work well with some classes and not as well with others. In most instances, the instructor will need to decide whether or not to include the project after the start of the semester. That way, he/she will have time to assess and evaluate the composition of the class and determine if the assignment would work within the collective grouping of students. In other words, of all the assignments, the final group project is the most expendable but could also be the most pedagogically valuable.

RESULTS

The method of asking broad questions instead of assigning specific reading from textbooks allowed the students to shift the course toward their interests while discovering multiple academic sources. The students enjoyed the autonomy, and the topics of the debate were a great way to frame the larger historical and historiographic issues throughout early America. The end-of-course student surveys indicated that the debates were well received and that the students thoroughly enjoyed them, though 10 were too many.

Assigning short Book Reviews/Position Papers were a great way to highlight student knowledge and allow the instructor to quickly assess their overall comprehension. The individual final projects wrapped up the course extremely well and provided communication experience across several different mediums, including speeches, websites, blogs, video diaries, social media, and podcasts. These assignments were intentionally broad in order to allow students to take them in various directions. They did need guidance early in the semester in order to get focused, but once students decided on a topic and presentation medium, they became excited about their project.

As previously mentioned, there was not any specific textbook or reading. Instead, students were assigned several broad questions per lesson that they were required to research before each class. Throughout the semester, the instructor noticed a considerable increase in the student's ability to quickly find scholarly sources, assess the author, and articulate the major arguments. The students enjoyed not having to buy a dedicated textbook and felt more in control of their learning. The major downfall of this approach is that while students were able to read and digest a plethora of academic sources (JSTOR became a class favorite), the breadth of the course seemed to diminish. In other words, students became experts in certain areas of early American history but lost some of the greater, overall narratives. The Course Narrative group project was a way to remedy the situation, and it appeared to work.

The Final Research Project succeeded in its goal to foster a student's research and writing skills, as well as communicate their research to a broader audience using a different medium than a traditional paper. Students developed interactive websites, engaging podcasts, and videos. Only two students chose to write a paper. Even though the research remained the same as a traditional paper, students became much more engaged in the process and generated incredible results. Many invited their friends and family to view their websites or listen to their podcasts.

Overall, student feedback was positive according to post-course surveys. No student recorded negative comments on the end-of-course critiques, and written comments suggest that students gained a greater appreciation for research. One student exclaimed that this was the first course that did not try to teach him what to think, but rather how to think. Another stated that this course prepared him to research more than any other course. A third claimed that he spent more time working on the homework for this course not because it was overly challenging, but because he wanted to – he kept finding "rabbit trails" or interesting subtopics to follow and lost himself in the research. Together, these post-course comments and others like them highlight the assertion that students are receptive to research using twenty-first-century methods. Further, they learn to converse with their societal peers through modern mediums from a scholarly bent.

Imagine, once again, the college classroom setting. As the professor enters, students are still engrossed in their digital devices, but instead of a sullen silence, a lively discussion is taking place. One student is excited about conversing with a prominent historian on Twitter that responded to their post. Another is anxious to show off a comment on the YouTube channel they created justifying their academic argument. Two others are engaging in a lively debate about the quality of an online journal. Some students are too engrossed to realize when the professor enters the room, yet several are quick to highlight their nightly research before class officially begins. In this classroom setting, students are engaging with both scholarly sources and mainstream societal communication, thus eradicating the university-societal gap.

REFERENCES

Ambrose, S. A. (Ed.). (2010). *How learning works: Seven research-based principles for smart teaching*. San Francisco, CA: Jossey-Bass.

Bain, K. (2004). *What the best college teachers do*. Cambridge, MA: Harvard University Press.

Banta, T. W., & Palomba, C. A. (2015). *Assessment essentials: Planning, implementing, and improving assessment in higher education* (2nd ed.). San Francisco, CA: Jossey-Bass & Pfeiffer Imprints.

Bowen, J. A. (2012). *Teaching naked: How moving technology out of your college classroom will improve student learning*. San Francisco, CA: Jossey-Bass, a Wiley imprint.

Brennan, J., & Teichler, U. (2008). The future of higher education and of higher education research: Higher education looking forward: An introduction. *Higher Education, 56*(3), 259–264.

Calkins, S., & Kelley, M. (2007). Evaluating internet and scholarly sources across the disciplines: Two case studies. *College Teaching, 55*(4), 151–156.

Canada, G. (2013). *Our failing schools. Enough is enough!* [TedTalk]. Retrieved from https://www.ted.com/talks/geoffrey_canada_our_failing_schools_enough_is_enough

Cantor, J. (1997). Experiential learning in higher education: Linking classroom and community. *ERIC Digest*. Retrieved from www.eric.ed.gov

Chen, C. (2018, January 11). Amazon's textbook rental service is perfect for college students looking to save money and time this semester. *Business Insider*. Retrieved from https://www.businessinsider.com/amazon-textbook-rental-service-for-college-students-2018-1

Davis, B. G. (2009). *Tools for teaching* (2nd ed.). San Francisco, CA: Jossey-Bass.

Diamond, R. M. (2008). *Designing and assessing courses and curricula: A practical guide* (3rd ed.). San Francisco, CA: Jossey-Bass.

Echevarria, G., & Bowman, J. (2018, December 4). Almost 80% of the textbook industry is dominated by 5 publishing companies that make books so expensive most students skip buying them. *Business Insider*. Retrieved from https://www.businessinsider.com/why-college-textbooks-expensive-textbook-publishing-2018-12

Esmaeili, M., Eydgahi, A., & Amanov, I. (2015, June 14). *Perceptions of students toward utilizing smartphone in the classroom*. Paper presented at the 122nd ASEE Annual Conference & Exposition, Seattle, WA, June 14–17.

Hoover, D. S. (2006). Popular culture in the classroom: Using audio and video clips to enhance survey classes. *The History Teacher, 39*(4), 467–478.

Huba, M. E., & Freed, J. E. (2000). *Learner-centered assessment on college campuses: Shifting the focus from teaching to learning*. Boston, MA: Allyn and Bacon.

Kahu, E. R. (2013). Framing student engagement in higher education. *Studies in Higher Education, 38*(5), 758–773.

Noor Al-Deen, H. S., & Hendricks, J. A. (2012). *Social media: Usage and impact*. New York, NY: Lexington Books.

Pulliam, D. (2017). *Effect of student classroom cell phone usage on teachers* (Master's thesis & Specialist Project, Western Kentucky University). Retrieved from http://digitalcommons.wku.edu/theses/1915

Robinson, K. (2010). *RSA ANIMATE: Changing education paradigms* [YouTube]. Retrieved from https://youtu.be/zDZFcDGpL4U

Yaros, R. A. (2012). Social media in education: Effects of personalization and interactivity on engagement and collaboration. In H. S. Noor Al-Deen & J. A. Hendricks (Eds.), *Social media: Usage and impact* (pp. 57–74). New York, NY: Lexington Books.

ABOUT THE AUTHORS

Mohamed Alansari is an honorary academic at the University of Auckland's Faculty of Education and Social Work, and a Senior Researcher at the New Zealand Council for Educational Research. His teaching and research areas span across Educational and Social Psychology, with a specific focus on learning environments and classroom practices that impact the social and academic trajectories of student learning outcomes. Link to university profile: https://unidirectory.auckland.ac.nz/profile/m-alansari. Email: m.alansari@auckland.ac.nz

Arlinda Beka, PhD, is an Assistant Professor for Early childhood and Preschool Programs at the Faculty of Education. She has been involved in Early Childhood Curriculum Development, Early Childhood Development Standards, Education Research, and Education Policies related to recent major developments of Education in Kosovo. She is a part of UNESCO network for Education for Sustainable Development. Through her work to embed principles and pedagogies associated with ESD, She has examined the related issues of sustainability of the individual selves of both teachers and learners, collaborating in a qualitative study with partners from Europe, United States, Asia, and Africa. She was a Professional Adviser of the minister of education (2018–2019). She worked at James Madison University, United States, (2019–2020), through the Fulbright program. Her focus during this period was on the creation of instruments to assess the needs, difficulties, and talents of young children from birth through six years of age. She was also a part of Indiana University, United States with the TLP project. She was a part of the Tempus project, the Erasmus Project, the Global plus project, and other international projects. Besides teaching at University, she is an author of books for children, researcher, and publicist.

Patrick Blessinger, Ed.D., is an Adjunct Associate Professor of education at St John's University, a Math and Science Teacher with the New York State Education Department, and the Chief Research Scientist of the International Higher Education Teaching and Learning Association (in consultative status with the United Nations). He is the editor and author of many books and articles. He is an educational policy analyst and contributing writer with UNESCO's Inclusive Policy Lab, University World News, The Hechinger Report, The Guardian, and Higher Education Tomorrow, among others. He teaches courses in education, leadership, and research methods and he serves on doctoral dissertation committees. He founded and leads a global network of educators focused on teaching and learning. He is an expert in inclusion, equity, leadership, policy, democracy, human rights, and sustainable development. He provides professional development workshops to teachers and professors and regularly gives presentations and keynote addresses at academic conferences around the world. He has received several educational awards, including Fulbright Senior Scholar to Denmark (Department of State, United States), Governor's Teaching Fellow (Institute of Higher Education, University of Georgia, United States), and Certified Educator (National Geographic Society, United States).

Russell Carpenter, PhD, is Executive Director of the Noel Studio for Academic Creativity and Professor of English at Eastern Kentucky University. Recent books include *Studio-Based Approaches for Multimodal Projects, Writing Studio Pedagogy*, and *Sustainable Learning Spaces*. Carpenter is an Editor of the *Journal of Faculty Development* and received the 2017 Turner Award from the National Association from Communication Centers.

Ellina Chernobilsky, Ph.D., is an Associate Vice President for Academic Affairs at Caldwell University. She also serves as the Director of Graduate Studies and is the Leader of the Caldwell University Center for Faculty Teaching and Learning. Prior to earning her PhD, she was a classroom teacher and used action research as a means to study and improve her own teaching in order to help herself and her students to become better learners. Her research interests include but are not limited to multilingualism, action research in education, the use of data and data mining in education, and issues of professional development on all levels of education. She teaches research courses and advises students in the doctoral program at the Caldwell University School of Education regularly. She has spent time teaching in Uzbekistan, China, and Russia.

Jorge Enrique Delgado is a Researcher, Educator, and Editor. He has a PhD in Social and Comparative Analysis in Education (Administrative and Policy Studies) and a Certificate in Latin American Social and Public Policy from the University of Pittsburgh. He also holds a Master's in Education and a Bachelor's in Dentistry from Pontificia Universidad Javeriana (PUJ) from Bogotá, Colombia. He was a Professor at PUJ for 15 years, where he was responsible for research management; faculty professional development evaluation and assessment; university accreditation; and teaching research methods, scientific reading/writing, and public health courses. Currently, he is a Program Coordinator at the University of Pittsburgh Institute for International Studies in Education and teaches Social Foundations of Education, Comparative Education, Higher Education, and Latin American and Caribbean studies. He is the Editor-in-Chief of Universitas Odontologica, published by PUJ. He has held leadership positions with the Education and Education Policy Section of the Latin American Studies Association, the Comparative and International Education Society, and the Communication of Research SIG of the American Education Research Association. His research focuses on the development of research and communication of knowledge among Latin American universities. http://orcid.org/0000-0002-1127-9516. Jed41@pitt.edu

About the Authors

Jennifer Fairchild, PhD, is Professor of Communication at Eastern Kentucky University. Her research has been featured in such journals as *PRISM: A Journal of Regional Engagement, Illness, Crisis, and Loss, Journal of the Scholarship of Teaching and Learning, Journal of Effective Teaching*, and *Communication Center Journal*. She also serves as co-coordinator of the Faculty Innovator program.

Jonathan Gore is a Professor in the Psychology Department at Eastern Kentucky University with a research focus on goal motivation, self-concept, and culture. He teaches courses at both the undergraduate and graduate levels in social psychology, cultural psychology, and research methods. He is also the Director of Undergraduate Research and Creative Endeavors for the university.

Joanne Jasmine, Ed.D., is a Professor of Education at Caldwell University. She is a coordinator of the MA program in Curriculum and Instruction and Co-coordinator of the Ed.D./Ph.D. program in Educational Leadership. Her recent work focuses on multiculturalism and social justice through literature, strategies for improving the teaching of language arts, and lessons to be learned from preschool children. She also teaches Action Research classes regularly.

Engin Karadağ received his BA degree from Gazi University in 2004, MA degree from Yeditepe University in 2006, and PhD degree from Marmara University in 2009. His doctoral thesis won the Best Educational Research Award by the Ministry of National Education. He continued his post-doctoral studies at the University of Cambridge in 2013–2014. In 2010, he was granted the title of an Associate Professor in Educational Management and in 2014 in Industrial and Organizational Psychology by the Turkish Interuniversity Council. He was a recipient of the Distinguished Young Scientist Award by Turkey Science Academy in 2017. He was a Research Assistant at Yeditepe University between 2005 and 2009 and was an Assistant, Associate, and Full Professor at Eskişehir Osmangazi University between 2009 and 2017. He works at Akdeniz University currently, and he teaches research methods and statistics and conducts scientific studies in the areas of higher education, educational sciences, organizational behavior, organizational psychology, and leadership. In recent years, in University Studies Laboratory (Üniversite Araştırmaları Laboratuvarı [UNIAR]) – which was co-founded by Dr Karadağ with Dr Cemil Yücel – Dr Karadağ aims to determine the satisfaction levels of students at Turkish universities and rank universities in terms of the satisfaction level of students in a comprehensive study titled Turkish Universities Satisfaction Research (Türkiye Üniversite Memnuniyet Araştırması [TÜMA]). Besides, in University Studies Laboratory, Dr Karadağ provides unique contributions to higher education literature with Public University Rankings (Devlet Üniversiteleri ve Fakülteleri Sıralaması [DÜS]) by ranking public universities and faculties of universities in terms of academic incentive scores.

Ryan Menath, D.A., is a Lieutenant Colonel in the United States Air Force where he serves as an Assistant Professor of History at the US Air Force Academy. .

He had the honor of being voted as the Department of History's Outstanding Academy Educator for 2018–2019. His academic interests include modern pedagogy, military history, and colonial America, specifically the American Revolution. He earned a Bachelor of Science in Management from the Air Force Academy in 2001 and a Master of Arts in Military History from American Military University in 2012. In 2018, he earned a Doctor of Arts in History from the University of North Dakota, where he focused on implementing modern pedagogical techniques in a history course through the combined use of primary sources and gamification within a student-centered classroom. As a military officer, Lt Col Menath has flight time instructing students in multiple jet, trainer, and combat aircraft. He has taught in a wide variety of classroom, ground, and flight training roles across military, professional, and academic settings.

Carol Mutch is a Professor at the University of Auckland, in the School of Critical Studies in Education. She teaches, researches, and writes on different aspects of educational policy and practice but always with a focus on education for social justice. Her current focus is on the role that schools play in responding to disasters and other traumas and she has a strong interest in supporting the development of early career scholars. Website: http://www.education.auckland.ac.nz/people/c-mutch Email: c.mutch@auckland.ac.nz

Shirley O'Brien, PhD, is a University Foundation Professor at Eastern Kentucky University in Occupational Science and Occupational Therapy and recognized as a Fellow of the American Occupational Therapy Association. She has teaching and research expertise in policy development/leadership, sensory modulation and autism, scholarship of teaching and learning (SoTL) research and pedagogy, and student engagement in online learning. She has received numerous service awards for her work in pediatric occupational therapy and currently serves as Faculty Innovator Co-Coordinator at EKU.

Edith Ries, Ed.D., is a Professor of Education at Caldwell University. Her recent presentations focus on the use of young adult literature as a vehicle for teaching social justice and global awareness. She teaches Action Research graduate-level classes at the university and has mentored several award-winning action research projects.

Enakshi Sengupta, PhD, serves as an Associate Director of HETL and is responsible for the advancement of HETL in Asia, Middle East, and Africa. The associate director works closely with the executive director to fulfill the mission of HETL. She is also the Director of the Center for Advanced Research in Education (CARE), Associate Series Editor of the book series, Innovations in Higher Education Teaching and Learning, Emerald Group Publishing. She is the Managing Editor of the *Journal of Applied Research in Higher Education*, Emerald Publishing, and serves as the Vice-Chair of the Editorial Advisory Board of the Innovations in Higher Education Teaching and Learning book series, Emerald Publishing. She is a Senior Manager of the Research, Methodology, and

Statistics in the Social Sciences forums on LinkedIn and Facebook responsible for managing all aspects of those forums. She is a PhD holder from the University of Nottingham in research in higher education, prior to which she completed her MBA with merit from the University of Nottingham and Master's degree in English Literature from the Calcutta University, India. She has previously held leadership positions in higher education institutions.

Ahmet Su received his BA degree from Cukurova University in 2010, MA degree from Afyon Kocatepe University in 2015, and PhD degree from Akdeniz University in 2019. He worked as an EFL Teacher at the Ministry of National Education between 2010 and 2012, a Lecturer at Harran University from 2012 to 2013, and as a Research Assistant at Afyon Kocatepe University between 2013 and 2015 and at Akdeniz University between 2015 and 2019. He taught English at a public school of Ministry of National Education and Harran University and coordinated various programs at Afyon Kocatepe University and Akdeniz University. He delivered lectures and conducted studies in the areas of organizational behavior, educational leadership, education policies, higher education, and innovation in education at Akdeniz University and Afyon Kocatepe University. He currently works as a visiting postdoctoral scholar at International Study of Teacher Leadership Project at Mount Royal University in Canada. He also works as an editorial assistant at *Research in Educational Administration & Leadership* (REAL) journal which is indexed in various prestigious indexes. His research interests include but are not limited to educational leadership, organizational behavior, education policies, higher education, technology integration and practices in education, and scientific studies.

Jennifer Tatebe is a Senior Lecturer at the University of Auckland, in the School of Critical Studies in Education. Her teaching and research explore educational inequities in schools and initial teacher education. Current projects include teachers' professional identity for social justice and rural school governance in regional areas experiencing rapid urbanization. Website: https://unidirectory.auckland.ac.nz/profile/j-tatebe. Email: j.tatebe@auckland.ac.nz

Matthew Winslow, PhD, is a Professor of Psychology at Eastern Kentucky University. He teaches courses in general psychology, research methods, social psychology, and his research touches on prejudice, same-sex marriage, the scholarship of teaching and learning. He is a Faculty Innovator and serves as the Teaching Enhancement Coordinator for the Psychology Department. In 2017, he received the Acorn Award, given by the Council on Postsecondary Education to the Outstanding Faculty in Kentucky.

NAME INDEX

Academic Ranking of World Universities, 53
Açıkgöz-Ersoy, B., 21
Adams, T. E., 10, 40, 101
Adcroft, A., 22
Aguado López, E., 71
Aguirre-Bastos, C., 72, 73
Akbulut, H., 20–21
Allen, K., 88
Allert, H., 18
Alonso Gamboa, J. O., 71, 75
Alpaslan, F., 23
Alperín, J. P., 70–71, 75–76
Altbach, P. C., 5, 52, 70
Amanov, I., 121
Amaro, B., 75
Ambrose, D. P., 14
Ambrose, S. A., 121
Anderson, L., 105–106
Andrew, M., 102–103, 105, 116
Arabacı, İ. B., 21
Archer, L., 36
Arditi, D., 24
Arends, R., 97
Atila, M. E., 20
Ay, Y., 15
Ayfer, R., 24

Bacanli, H., 23
Bain, K., 23
Bakırtaş, T., 25, 27
Balán, J., 73
Ball, S., 102–104, 116
Banta, T. W., 121
Barnes, D., 21
Barron, B., 14
Bartolome, L. I., 88–89
Baskan, G. A., 20
Becerril García, A., 71
Beckman, M., 15

Beddoes, K. D., 23
Beka, A., 8, 33–34
Bergami, R., 102–103
Berk, R., 53
Beycioglu, K., 16
Bilgin, I., 15
Billot, J., 36
BIREME/OPS/OMS, 71, 76
Birgonul, M. T., 24
Birinci, M., 22
Blessinger, P., 3, 37, 51
Blythe, H., 54
Board of Regents, 56
Bochner, A. P., 10, 101, 105
Boekholt, P., 38
Bogner, F. X., 18–19
Bologna Declaration, 8, 33, 39
Bonds, A., 103
Bottrell, D., 102–103
Bowen, J. A., 121
Bowman, J., 122
Brantmeier, E., 54
Brazile, R., 23
Brennan, J., 122
Brew, A., 14–15
Brignall, S., 22
Brunner, J. J., 73
Brunnhofer, M., 8, 33
Bryce, J., 16
Brydon-Miller, M., 9, 87, 89
Brzozowski, J., 27
Bulunuz, M., 19
Byrne, J., 54

Cajander, A., 24
Calkins, S., 124
Campbell, C., 38
Canada, G., 121
Cannon, R., 17
Cansız, A., 26–27

Cantor, J., 122
Carpenter, R., 8, 47, 54
Carvalho, T., 75
Castejon, J., 40
Çekerol, K., 28n1
Çeliköz, N., 23
CESIS, 21
Cetto, A. M., 71
Chang, G.-C., 14
Chen, C., 122
Chen, D., 53
Chidanandan, A., 24
Childress, L. K., 36
Choi, J., 37
CLACSO, 71, 76
Clandinin, D. J., 105
Clandinin, J., 105
Clark, C., 49
Cogan, J.J., 88
Çöğmen, S., 16
Colciencias, 77
Commission, E., 17
CONICYT, 76–77
Connelly, F. M., 105
Cook-Harvey, C., 14
Cozza, B., 37
Craig, D. D., 48
Cramer, S. F., 53
Crespi, G., 73
Cruz, L., 54
Curran, W., 103
Dag, L. R., 24

Dana, N.F., 89
Daniels, M., 24
Darling-Hammond, L., 14, 36
Davidson, M., 102–104, 106, 114–116
Davis, B. G., 122, 126
Daynes, J. G., 105
de Sagastizábal, L., 70
de Wit, H., 36–39
Delgado, J. E., 9, 69–73, 75–81
Delgado-Troncoso, J. E., 71
Demiralp, D., 17
Demirel, M., 16

Departamento de Evaluación, Medición y RegistroEducacional (DEMRE), 73
Diamond, R. M., 122
Didriksson, A., 72
Dikmen, I., 24
Docquier, F., 26
Dodds, F., 38–39
Dombayci, M. A., 23
Duderstadt, J. J., 6
Dutrénit, G., 73

ECA, 35
Echevarria, G., 122
Ekmekci, A., 18–19
Ellern, J., 54
Ellimoottil, C., 55
Ellington, L., 104–105
Ellis, C., 10, 101, 104–105
Elsevier & Ipsos MORI, 61
Eneroth, B., 17
Erasmus, 36, 41
Eren, E., 22
Erişen, Y., 23
Eskandar, M. M., 23
Esmaeili, M., 121
Eydgahi, A., 121

Fallon, D., 5
Fiocco, M., 40
Fischman, G. E., 70–71
Fischman, G., 70, 71, 75, 76
Flook, L., 14
Ford, G., 54
Fortino, A., 48
Fortney, J. A., 26
Foucher, K. C., 54
Freed, J. E., 121
Freeman, S. A., 54
Fry, H., 54

Garduño Oropeza, G., 71
Garousi, V., 23
Gayle, B. M., 54
Geiger, R. L., 5
Gerstner, S., 18–19

Gibbs, A., 55
Gillett, R. A., 37, 40
Gist, C., 88
Godínez-Larios, S., 71
Gökçe, N., 16
Göksu, A., 21
Gossart, C., 25
Grant, B., 102
Gray, T., 54
Greenwood, D., 9, 87
Gruber, H., 23
Gulacar, O., 18–19
Güngör, G., 21
Güngör, N. D., 26–27
Gupta, M. P., 72
Guthrie, K. M., 49
Güzel, S., 21

Hall, J., 38–39, 73
Harteis, C., 23
Hauptman, A. M., 22
Haustein, S., 70
Healey, M., 15–16
Hearn, A., 102–103
Hendricks. J.A., 124
Hensel, N., 15
Herkiloğlu, K., 23
Hertramph, H., 23
Hilliard, A., 37, 39
Hobbs, L., 38
Holm-Nielsen, L. B., 73
Hoover, D., 123, 125
Howell, S. L., 18
Huba, M. E., 121
Hubball, H., 54
Hürsen, Ç., 16
Hyndman, J., 103

Inglis, S., 15
Inhelder, B., 93
Innovative Research Universities, 48, 51
Irati, A., 78
Işık, N., 21

Jackson, I., 88
Jackson, M., 54

Jenkins, A., 15–16
Jesiek, B. K., 23
Jessop, B., 70
Jewell, E., 14–15
Johnson, M. R., 52
Justice, C., 15

Kahn, P., 15
Kahu, E. R., 121
Kaktins, L., 37, 40
Kalish, A., 54
Kandemir, O., 25, 27
Kang, W., 37
Kaplan, R. S., 22–23
Karabulut, B., 21
Karadağ, E., 7, 13, 20, 23
Karakuyu, Y., 15
Katz, J. S., 25
Kazu, H., 17
Kelley, M., 124
Kerppola, M., 49
Kiley, M., 17
Kılınç, E. C., 21
Kireçci, M. A., 23
Klaib, F. J., 52
Kloot, L., 23
Knox, L., 48
Köksal, N., 16
Konan, N., 16
Köser-Akçapar, S., 26
Kuh, G. D., 15, 53–54, 61
Kultur, C., 24
Kurtulmuş, N., 25
Kurul-Tural, N., 20
Kyvik, S., 25, 63

Laird, T. F. N., 53
Lambert, C., 14
Langley, L., 54
Larrivee, B., 89
Latin American and Caribbean
    Center on Health Sciences
    Information (BIREME), 76
Latindex, 9, 69, 71, 75–78, 81
Laxer, C., 24
Lee, Y. S., 63

Lemarchand, G. A., 72–73
Leslie, L. L., 20
Lindsay, N. K., 18
Lloyd, J., 103
Lohest, O., 26
Lombardi, J. V., 48

Madson, L., 54
Maguire, P., 9, 87
Maltais, A., 37
Manathunga, C., 102–103
Mansfield, B., 103
Marão Beraquet, V. S., 78
Marcketti, S. B., 54
Marfouk, A., 26
Marginson, S., 5
Martin, B. R., 25
Martin, J., 23
Mastropieri, M. A., 19
Matos, S., 73
Matthew, P., 8, 47, 114
McCarthy, C. B., 19
MEST, 34–35
Meyer, C., 22
Miller, S., 15
Ministry of Education, 34–35
Modell, S., 22
Molise, M. K., 14
Molloy, C., 54
Monticino, M., 23
Morris, C., 54
Morrison, G.S., 93
Moss, H., 54
Mothibeli, A., 14
Motlomelo, S. T., 14
Mountz, A., 103
Muessig, R.H., 88
Muter-Şengül, C., 21
Myatt, P., 54

Namal, Y., 20
Neapolitan, J.E., 89
Nejdl, W., 18
Nenty, H. J., 14
Neuman, W. L., 73
Nightengale-Lee, B., 88

Noel Studio for Academic Creativity, 50
Noone, D., 49
Noor Al-Deen, H. S., 124
NTU Ranking, 52–53

O'Brien, C., 54
O'Brien, S., 18, 47
O'Rourke, K., 15
Observatorio Nacional de Ciencia, Tecnología e Innovación (Oncti), 79
Ohana, Y., 117
Olmedo, A., 116
Olssen, M., 102–104
Online Education for Lifelong Learning, 18
Onursal-Beşgül, Ö., 16, 28
Organisation for Economic Co-operation and Development (OECD), 72
Ornstein, A., 97
Ornstein, S., 97
OSCE, O. f., 34
Osher, D., 14
Otten, H., 17
Ozeken, O. F., 20
Özman, M., 25
Ozorhon, B., 24
Öztürk, Ö., 28

Packer, A. L., 71, 78
Pajak, E., 97
Palomba, C. A., 121
Parkinson, A., 17
Peters, D., 54
Peters, M., 102–104
Phillips, B., 54
Piaget, J., 93
Pinnegar, S., 105
Pivovarova, M., 70
Pontificia Universidad Católica del Perú, 72
Posselt, T., 37
Power, J. M., 70
Prat, A. M., 78
Preiss, R., 54

Presidencia de la República, 77
Pulliam, D., 121
Putman, S.M., 89

Radnor, Z. J., 21
Rama, C., 70–71
Randall, N., 54
Redacción Vivir, 77
RedALyC., 9, 69–71, 75–76, 78, 80–81
Reisberg, L., 5
Renault, C. S., 61
Reusch, J., 52
Reymert, I., 25, 63
Rhoades, G., 9, 69, 71
Rice, J., 15
Richter, C., 18
Roberts, P., 102
Robinson, K., 121
Rock, T., 89
Rogel Salazar, R., 71
Rouse, W. B., 48
Rumbley, L.E., 5, 38
Russell-Dag, L., 24
Ryan, A., 10, 49–50, 55

Sadlak, J., 4
Sadowski, E., 55
Şahin, M., 23
Salatino, M., 72
Salmi, J., 22
Sammon, S., 15
Schaal, S., 19
Schodt, D., 54
Schrager, S., 55
Scientific Electronic Library Online (SciELO), 71
Scruggs, T. E., 19
Sebatane, E. M., 14
Seçilmiş, N., 21
Selingo, J. J., 49
Shore, C., 102–104, 114–116
Silva, D., 75
Simmons, N., 54
Šiška, J., 38
Skarupski, K., 54
Slaughter, S., 20

Smeltzer, S., 102–103
Smyth, J., 102
Social Sciences Feminist Network Research Interest Group, 114
Sozbilir, M., 20
Speckbacher, G., 22
Spronken-Smith, R., 14–15
Stewart, K. L., 89
Stivers, J., 53
Stockley, D., 54
Su, A., 7, 13, 20
Superintendencia Nacional de Educación Superior Universitaria (SUNEDU), 72
Sweet, C., 54
Swigger, K., 23–24

Takahara, Y., 36
Tansel, A., 26–27
Taylor, P. C., 53
Teichler, U., 4, 6, 122
Texas Woman's University, 51
Thorn, K., 73
Tomlinson, C. A., 93
Tremblay, K., 37–38
Trinca Fighera, D., 79
Turner, R., 53

Ulubey, Ö., 92
Ünal, T., 21, 78–81
UNESCO, 72
UNIBO, U. o., 36
University of Florida Office of Research, 51
University of Prishtina, 8, 33–35
University of Waterloo, 51
Uribe, R., 70
USAID, 35–36
Üstüner, M., 16
UW Medicine, 53
Uzunboylu, H., 16

Vale, C., 72
van der Wende, M., 5

Ved, P., 4
Venkatasubramanian, K., 4
Verhey-Henke, A., 49
Vicars, M., 102

Wächter, B., 16
Wagner, N. J., 52
Walczak, M., 54
Walker, R., 14–15
Wall, S., 105
Walton-Roberts, M., 103
Wang, C. Y., 16
Warry, W., 15

Weaver, D., 54–55
Western Sydney University, 51
White, B. J., 54
Whitney, G., 61
Williams, P. B., 18
Willingham-McLain, L., 54
Willinsky, J., 70–71
Willis, R., 22
Woldegiyorgis, A., 38

Yaros, R. A., 124, 127

Zúñiga, M. F., 71

SUBJECT INDEX

Note: Page numbers followed by "*n*" indicate notes.

Academia, 37
Academic capitalism, 70
Academic databases, 10
Academic journals, 70
   diversity of journal subjects and institutional policy, 79
   groundbreaking journals and beginning of journal support policies, 78–79
   institutional funding for journals, 80–81
   institutional policies to supporting journals published by universities, 77–78
   institutional repositories, 79
   international, regional, and national contexts influencing journal growth, 71–73
   methods, 73–75
   national contexts, 76–77
   policies on publication format, 80
   processes to implementing journal support policies at universities, 80
   regional context, 75–76
Academic Ranking of World Universities (ARWU), 53
Academic research
   implications, 60–61
   literature review, 51–55
   models and practices, 48
   recommendations, 62–64
   research, 61–62
   results, 60
   work groups, 55–59
Academics, 5, 7
Accomplices, 104

Action research, 89–90, 97
   projects, 89
Active engagement, 91
Affective side of learning, 95
Age of knowledge, 6
American history survey, 125
   debates and expectations, 127–131
   expectations for students upon arrival, 126–127
American model, 5
Analytic autoethnography, 105–106
Andes University, 79
Apprehension, 7
Archivos de Medicina Veterinaria, 78
Atenea, 78
Austral University, 79
Autoethnography, 10, 104–105, 116

Bibliographic analysis services, 71
Bifurcations and hierarchies, 102, 106–108
Bilateral partnerships, 35
Bloom's taxonomy, 121
Bologna Declaration, 8, 39
Bologna Magna Charta Universitatum of 1988, 39
Bologna Process, 17, 28*n*1
Brain drain in Turkey and outcomes, 25–27
Brave Open World, 61
Business of Research, 61

Carnegie Academy for the Scholarship of Teaching and Learning (CASTL), 54
Case study, 8, 49–52, 54–55, 98, 123–131

Central University of Venezuela (UCV), 74
Chile, universities, 73–74, 76–77
Ciencia y Enfermería, 78
Coercive complicity, 103, 104, 114, 116
Colciencias, 77
Collaboration, 23, 50
 in research activities, 25
Collaborative functional teams, 63
Collaborative technologies, 24
Colombia, universities, 76–77
Colombia Medica, 78–79
Competition, 7
Competitiveness, 70
Complicity, 114
CONICYT, 76–77
Conscious complicity, 102, 104, 114
Constructivism, 18
Cooperation, 36
Corporate vision, 22
Council of Chilean University Presidents, 73
Council of Higher Education in Turkey [YOK], 20
Creative dramatics, 92–93
Cuadernos de Administración, 78
Culture, 48–49

Diagnostic evaluations, 80
Differentiation, 10, 92
Discovery approach, 19
Diversity, 6, 88
 of journal subjects, 79

Early career academics, 102
 anomalies, 112–114
 findings, 106–114
 literature review, 103–104
 methodology, 104–106
Eastern Ascendance, 61
Eastern Kentucky University (EKU), 55–56
Education[al], 4, 6–7, 14 (*see also* Humanizing education)
 organizations, 22
 reform, 34
 training programs, 89
Educators, 88
Electronic publication, 80
Emerging scholars, 102
Emerging trends, 6–7
Estudios Filológicos, 78
European Union (E. U.), 34
European Union (EU), 16
Evocative autoethnography, 105
Experienced academics, 102

Faculty
 advancement, 52–53
 development, 36, 50, 53–54
 innovation in teaching award, 58
 leadership award, 58
 productivity, 54–55, 62, 75, 77
 promotion, 77
 recognition, 54–55
 salaries, 70, 72, 81
 support programs, 50
Faculty awards, 57
 outcomes of work groups, 59
 recipients, 58
Faculty Scholars Institute (FSI), 50, 56–57
Follow-up, 80
Fulbright Exchange Program of United States, 35
Funding, 72–73
 for project, 60
 of research in Turkey, 19–21

Game of thrones: Tyrants, gatekeepers, and legends, 102, 106, 110–112
Game-like learning, 90–91
Globalization, 6
Glonacal Agency Heuristic, 9, 71
Google, 123–124
Graduate education, 89
Grants, 20–21
Groundbreaking journals, 78–79

Subject Index 149

Hands-on approaches, future of, 18–19
High-impact practice teaching award, 58
Higher education, 34, 49, 103, 122 (*see also* Turkish higher education)
  performance measurement in, 21–23
  research, 4
  systems, 72
  teacher education faculty, 9, 89
Higher education institutions (H. E. I. s), 34, 48, 52, 62
  brief history of, 19–21
Humanistic approach, 89–90
Humanizing education, 88
  action research, 89–90
  method, 90–97
  modeling of best practices, 98
  pre-service teachers, 98–99
  sources of data, 90–97
Humboldt's reformed university, 5
Humboldtian University, 5

Identities: Harmonies and clashes, 102, 106, 108–110
Impact technology, 121
In-service educator, 90
In-service teachers, implications for, 91, 93–94, 97
Inclusive excellence faculty award, 58
Individualized learning, 98–99
Information analysis, 60
Innovation
  and change, 94
  research grants, 50, 55–56
Innovative Research Universities (IRU), 51
Inquiry, 14
  inquiry-based approach, 19
  inquiry-based learning, 15
Insecurity, 7
Institutional arrangements, 71
Institutional funding for journals, 80–81

Institutional policy, 79
  to supporting journals published by universities, 77–78
Institutional repositories, 79
Inter-university cooperation, 39
Inter-university programs, 38
International collaborations and projects, 23–25
International education, 37
International partnership[s], 34–36, 38
  initiatives, 39
International program collaborations, 37
International projects/programs, 40, 43
Internationalization, 23–24
  of education, 6
Internet sources, 121–122
Inventories, 80
IT, 61

Joint projects, 24
Journal[s], 70
  beginning of journal support policies, 78–79
  indexation, 77
  management models, 70
JSTOR, 126, 132

K-12
  classrooms, 9–10, 89
  students, 89
Knowledge, 14
Kosovo, 8, 34
  education, 34
  H. E. I. s, 36
  institutions, 34
Kosovo Education Strategic Plan [2017–2021], 35

Land Grants Act, 5
Latin America, 75–76
Latin American Council for Social Sciences [CLACSO], 71, 76
Latin American Health Science Literature (LiLACS), 71, 76

Latindex, 9, 75
Learned journals, 70
Liberal governmentality, 104
Lifelong learning, 16–18

Matrix, 15–16
Minga Online, 79
Modeling of best practices, 95, 98
Modernizing Teacher Education at University of Prishtina [Med@UP], 36
Multilateral partnerships, 35
Multinational collaborations, 23

Narrative fidelity, 105
Narrative inquiry, 105
National Commission for Scientific and Technological Research [CONICYT], 76
National contexts, 76–77
National journal evaluation systems, 73–77
National Taiwan University, 52
Neoliberal
    governmentality, 104
    ideology, 103
    university, 102
Neoliberalism, 103
NTU Ranking (see Performance Ranking of Scientific Papers for World Universities)

Online research, 124, 129
Open access (OA), 9, 71
    journals, 80
Open Journal System (OJS), 80
Organisation for Economic Co-operation and Development (OECD), 72

Paper sprints, 49–50, 55
Participation in research, 49
Partnerships, 36, 43
Pedagogy, 97, 122

Peer editing, 98
Peer referees, 70
Peer-reviewed journals, 70
Peer-reviewed periodicals, 78
Performance evaluations, 80
Performance measurement in higher education, 21–23
Performance Ranking of Scientific Papers for World Universities, 52
Performativity, 104
Physical movement, 93
Podcast, 123, 125, 130, 132
Policies on publication format, 80
Policymakers, 7, 14
Portal de Portales, 75
Post-course feedback, 123
Post-doctoral research, 112
Post-industrialization countries, 6
Pre-service teachers, 98–99
    implications for pre-service teacher educators, 92–95, 97
Private universities, 77
Problem-based learning, 15
Productive learning, 17
Professional development, 36
Professional learning communities (PLCs), 54
Programa de Promoción al Investigador [PPI], 77
Publindex, 77
Publishers, 70
Pull factors of skilled immigration, 27
Push factors of skilled immigration, 27

RedALyC, 9, 71, 75–76
Reflective inquiry, 89
Regional comprehensive university, 50–54
Regional context, 75–76
Regional Online Information System of Scientific journals, 71
Regional Research Promotion Program-Western Balkans (RRPP), 34

Research, 14–15, 51, 122 (*see also* Academic research)
  agenda, 6
  collaboration, 8, 61
  grants, 8
  initiatives, 52–53
  paper, 123–125
  partnerships, 38
  policies, 81
  productivity policy, 72
  project, 10, 36, 39, 44, 130
  research-based activities, 15
  research-based education, 14–16, 18
  research-based higher education, 4
  research-based learning, 123
  research-based universities, 5
  research-driven institution, 4
  in social science, 6
  support opportunities, 55
Researchers, 61
Resistant complicity, 116
Revista de Salud Pública, 78

Scholarly journals, 70
Scholarly sources, 130, 132
Scholarship, 7
  stages, 59
Scholarship of teaching and learning (SoTL), 54, 58
  awards, 50s
School of Education, 42
SciELO, 9
Science, technology, and innovation system (STI system), 72
Science Citation Index-Expanded (SCIE), 53
Scientific and Technological Research Council of Turkey [TUBITAK], 20
Scientific Electronic Library Online (SciELO), 71, 75, 77–78
Scientific journals, 70, 73
Sector analysis method, 14
Shared culture, 22

Small Business Innovation Research program (SBIR program), 56
Smart devices, 120
Smartphone use in higher education, 121
Social media, 127
Social mediums, 124
Social Science Citation Index (SSCI), 53
Societal roles, 10
Society, 6
Staff exchange, 37
"Stereotypical" undergraduate course, 120
Strategies, 55
Student
  choices, 103
  communication, 97
  discussion, 15
  engagement, 89, 91
  interaction, 90, 92
  needs, 89
  non-return, 25–26
  research, 10, 124
Support systems, 63

Talent repatriation mechanisms, 72
Teacher
  involvement in international projects/programs, 42
  preparation, 88, 90
  teacher-scholar, 53–54
Teacher education, 89, 93
  faculty, 89, 93
  program, 9–10
Teaching methodology, 40–41, 122
Teaching–learning, 6
Tech Titans, 61
TEMPUS project, 41
Tertiary education, 107
Textbooks, 122–123
Traditional classroom, 121
Traditional teacher preparation programs, 88
Traditional teaching paradigm, 121

Traditional universities, 73
"Traditional" undergraduate course, 120
Trainings, 80
Transformation, 20, 41
Transformation Leadership Program (T. L. P.), 36, 41
Transformational research, 53
Transparency, 49
Turkey
 brain drain in Turkey and outcomes, 25–27
 funding of research in, 19–21
Turkish Academy of Sciences [TUBA], 21
Turkish higher education, 14 (*see also* Higher education)
 brain drain in Turkey and outcomes, 25–27
 brief history of higher education institutions, 19–21
 funding of research in Turkey, 19–21
 future of hands-on approaches, 18–19
 international collaborations and projects, 23–25
 lifelong learning, 16–18
 performance measurement in higher education, 21–23
 research-based education, 14–16
Turkish Ministry of National Education, 16

United States of America International Development (USAID), 35
Universitas Psychologica, 78

Universities, 5, 10, 14, 38
University journals, 78
University of Florida Office of Research, 51
University of Hawai'i at Manoa, 53
University of Michigan, 49
University of Prishtina, 8, 34–35, 39
University of Washington, 53
University of Waterloo, 51
University partnerships, 8, 36
 literature review, 36–40
 research methodology, 40
 research questions, 40
 research results, 40–41
 results of survey, 41–43
University research, 79
University-societal contract, 123
University–industry cooperation, 21
Unwitting complicity, 103, 104, 114–115

Venezuela, universities, 76–77
Venezuelan Observatory of Science, Technology, and Innovation, 79

Wikipedia, 123, 124, 126
Work groups, 55
 faculty awards, 57–59
 FSI, 56–57
 innovation research grants, 55–56
Workshops, 80
Writing accountability groups (WAGs), 54

XML-JATS technology, 76

YouTube, 125, 130, 132